Women in Prehistory

REGENDERING THE PAST

Cheryl Claassen, Series Editor

A complete list of books in the series
is available from the publisher.

Women in Prehistory

North America and Mesoamerica

Edited by Cheryl Claassen
and Rosemary A. Joyce

PENN

University of Pennsylvania Press

Philadelphia

10   9   8   7   6   5   4   3   2   1

Published by
University of Pennsylvania Press
Philadelphia, Pennsylvania 19104-6097

Library of Congress Cataloging-in-Publication Data

Claassen, Cheryl, 1953–
    Women in prehistory : North America and Mesoamerica / edited by Cheryl Claassen
and Rosemary A. Joyce
        p. cm.
    Includes bibliographical references and index.
    ISBN 0-8122-3381-6 (cloth : alk. paper).—ISBN 0-8122-1602-4 (paper : alk. paper)
        1. Indian women—North America—Economic conditions.   2. Indian women—
Mexico—Economic conditions.   3. Indian women—North America—Material culture.
4. Indian women—Mexico—Material culture.   5. Economics, Prehistoric—North
America.   6. Economics, Prehistoric—Mexico.   7. Subsistence economy—North
America.   8. Subsistence economy—Mexico.   9. Feminist archaeology—North
America.   10. Feminist archaeology—Mexico.   11. North America—Antiquities.
12. Mexico—Antiquities.   I. Joyce, Rosemary A., 1956–   . II. Title.
E98.W8C53   1996
330.97′0011′082—dc20
                                                                                                        96-34559
                                                                                                        CIP

Contents

Tables

Figures

1. Women in the Ancient Americas: Archaeologists, Gender, and the Making of Prehistory

Rosemary A. Joyce and Cheryl Claassen

Introduction

There have been few areas within archaeology that have developed as explosively as the intimately related topics of women, gender, and feminism. The rapidly emerging canonical account of these foci credits a single article published only a decade ago (Conkey and Spector 1984) for opening respectable debate on these concerns in archaeology. Within a remarkably short span of time, in North America alone, both a small, selective seminar (Conkey and Gero 1991) and several more broadly inclusive conferences (Claassen 1992b, 1994; Walde and Willows 1991) encouraged a wealth of studies that defy easy classification. Today, we can document over 450 contributions by more than 300 authors concerned with women, gender, or feminism. One fact about this corpus of work strikes us as particularly remarkable: fewer than half of those actively writing and presenting papers on these topics already hold the Ph.D. Given this fact, there are undoubtedly many more papers we have not identified that have been presented at regional meetings, written for graduate seminars, or prepared as undergraduate honors theses. We estimate that over 90 percent of the work produced in this explosive interval is "womanist": concerned with the actions, status, or simply presence of women in past societies.

The rapid development of this literature, the relatively junior status of many participants in this process, and the diversity of archaeologies in which these individuals have trained, all have contributed to an accumulation of sometimes discordant, often incompletely theorized, but always stimulating new visions of the past. Far from any characterization of a concern with women in the past as inherently political, there is little evident overlap between developing feminist and womanist literatures. And neither feminist nor womanist writings consistently address what might be taken as central to both, the problematic status of gender as a concept. The often-cited tripartite division by Alison Wylie (1991) of the development of an archaeology of gender into a critique of androcentrism, a search for women in the past, and a fundamental reconceptualization, as Wylie herself predicted, is not unfolding as a series of stages, but rather is developing in parallel through different writings.

The essays in this volume were selected from those presented at the Third Archaeology and Gender Conference, held at Appalachian State University in Boone, North Carolina, in September 1994. The theme of this conference, gender in ancient America, was chosen in the specific hope that contributions would help build up the body of literature address-ing pre-contact societies. Substantive contributions greatly broadened the range of societies in which gender is addressed, as comparison of these essays with lacunae identified by Claassen (this volume) makes clear. The essays spanned all periods of occupation from the Paleo-Indian on, and geographic areas from the Arctic to Central America. Their coherence comes from a shared decision to treat seriously questions about women's participation in different societies known archaeologically. Womanist writ-ing presented here has challenged archaeological methods in fascinating ways. For individual scholars who are primarily interested in the culture history of different regions, there is some very exciting work—hypotheses, explanations—being generated. This body of literature clearly demon-strates that even if we conclude that women cannot be "found" archaeo-logically, there is much of interest to be gained by looking.

The Issue of Gender

Few of the papers presented at the conference treated gender itself as a central problem. In archaeological writing, gender has largely been treated as self-evident, coincident with biological sex or sexual orientation, and women have often been viewed as almost interchangeable, engaged in uni-versally predictable activities. Papers on the archaeological exploration of two-spirits (alternatively gendered individuals) presented at the conference broadened the scope of discussion from two fixed categories to three or four, but like the literature on ethnographic two-spirits, they could not resolve the problematic relationships between biological sex, sexuality, and sexual divisions of labor. During the conference we asked participants what they understood gender to be about. Although this topic was not a major focus of any of the papers, the responses suggested that a great deal of thought is being invested in this question by workers who continue to use the terms "woman" and "man" as convenient interim proxies without formal definition. It is worth taking some time to examine where this discussion suggests archaeology is headed, before introducing the topics that contributors currently feel comfortable in addressing.

Claassen (1992b:147) asked a similar question at the First Conference on Archaeology and Gender at Boone: "What is the social function of gender?" None of the participants confused gender with biological sex, but what exactly gender was about was less obvious. At that time, Joyce (in Claassen 1992b:149) confidently answered that she took gender as a categorization for organizing labor. Considerable sympathy for that proposition seemed to exist, so it is perhaps predictable that Joyce has subsequently been convinced that this argument is inherently flawed. The nature of the flaws may serve to illustrate where inquiry about the nature of gender may profitably lead archaeologists.

Linking gender to labor organization risks having any division of labor create differences in gender, demonstrably untrue and a violation of the sense that however arbitrary the connections, gender has something to do with sexual differences (e.g., Shapiro 1981, Shore 1981). Any variation on the assertion that gender serves to structure labor requires that labor organization precede gender. Any argument of this sort, then, must become an argument about origins. Once originated, gender would cease to be problematic and simply reproduce itself with every new generation, except perhaps when challenged by shifts in labor organization. But considerable evidence exists to the contrary. Not only does gender not replicate itself, but there seems to be considerable social investment in attempting to reproduce specific forms of gender. It is, in fact, the material media that aid in this process—items of costume, human images, and specialized tools associated with gender-stereotyped activities—that Joyce (1992b, 1993) has used to examine the social construction of gender in the Central American societies she studies.

As an alternative, Claassen (1992b:148) suggests that gender may be about sexuality: the marking of individuals in ways that allow for sexual pairing within a society. This suggestion has the advantage of clearly linking sex differences to gender—however the links may be conventionalized in different societies. The projection of divisions of labor on individuals of diverse genders is in no way impeded by the proposition that gender is "about" sexuality. Two further lines of argument may support this direction: first, the effects of introducing age as a variable in analyses of gender; and second, the implications of the instability of gender.

By examining issues concerning women in the past, a number of archaeologists have come to realize that variation in age is crucial to understanding gender. Elderly women may appear to be more like men than young women; children may fit into no adult gender. Claassen (this volume) suggests that if children have a separate gender, child gender may be related to their stage of sexuality and productive activity. When children's labor becomes essential to the work of society, their child-gender stage is foreshortened by adult-gendered expectations. What we treat as normative female gender may actually correspond only to a small segment of biological females, those young women, junior in their households, beginning the sexual liaisons through which aspects of their full life-course may be determined. Paradoxically, the young adult women who are the presumed normative females may be the object of both too much emphasis (overriding larger numbers of women of other ages in any particular society) and too little attention (particularly to the circumstances surrounding their sexual and social maturity).

Inherent in the realization that age makes a difference to gender is acceptance of gender as something that varies not only within society, but on the scale of the individual as well. If gender develops after childhood and changes in later adulthood, then what kind of entity is it, anyway? Here archaeologists can draw on a rich literature on gender in other disciplines, including social anthropology. The ideas that gender is a social category, an aspect of core personal identity, or any other fixed and immutable construct existing before the individual actor have been debated, and for the most part shown lacking, by scholars in other fields. Instead, gender appears better understood as something that develops through particular practices engaged in by individual actors and evaluated differently in different cultures or cultural settings. Or, to put it another way, following Judith Butler (1990), gender is performance, marked by distinctive postures, gestures, and dress. Butler's analysis, as Claassen (1992b:152) noted during the first Boone conference, is one of the few that explicitly assumes gender is "about" sexuality.

If gender is "about" sexuality, then issues must be raised that are different from those implied when gender is taken as a means to organize labor. The way individuals dress and act at different times and in different settings constructs gender-as-performance. The characteristics that build up distinctions in gender are linked to a whole sphere of evaluation of attractiveness that is seldom admitted into analyses of the social functions of gender, perhaps because it is seen as too idiosyncratic. The descriptions of young Aztec women recorded by the sixteenth-century Spanish friar Bernardino de Sahagún do more than simply catalog the appropriate appearance cues and behaviors for females at different ages. They associate the stereotyped manner of dress and proper execution of tasks with attractiveness in young women, and with justifiable pride in older ones. Admitting these evaluative dimensions of gender into discussions, of course, makes its archaeological investigation even more problematic, not less.

Toward a Peopled Archaeology

So what can we do? What most of the deeply committed authors, working largely independently, who have begun writing about women in the past appear to have decided is that they are not willing to ignore the evidence that all observed human cultures are marked by some kind of differences between social men and women. They insist on asking where differences like this might have existed in the past societies studied through archaeology. And because the default gender in much conventional prehistory is not neuter but male, this leads many authors to pose womanist questions about the past.

The chapters in this volume exemplify why this kind of research matters. Fundamental reexaminations of conventional prehistory are not merely way stations on an inexorable movement down the road toward a postmodern realization that all unities are artificial. Nor does a concern with women in the past require development of special methodologies for their detection—although one of the more fascinating points made by such research may be the likelihood that female-specific spatial settings are waiting to be found archaeologically. Bat Cave is being interpreted as a women's camp, the BBB Motor site may be a menstrual seclusion area, and Ramey pottery may be menstrual ware (Claassen, Galloway, this volume).

These essays, and the wider range of literature they represent, are improving archaeological constructions of prehistory by approaching conventional data sets with more complex, and therefore more realistic, models of social differentiation. By assuming diversity among the actors who created the sites we examine, archaeologists concerned with gender have worked through unexamined implications of standard methodologies. Brumbach and Jarvenpa (this volume) demonstrate that typical site catchment circle sizes encompass the terrain of women in hunting-gathering societies and thus are likely to reflect the activities not of a neuter or male gender but, disproportionately, of a female gender. There are now numerous claims that women's gathering activities determined settlement patterns and that groups moved not to capitalize on men's geographical knowledge but to capitalize on women's knowledge. The proposal that maize may have been used in the Mississippi Valley first as an infant formula seriously challenges both models of the introduction of this grain and the validity of the sampling strategies used to explore ancient diet through bone chemistry (Claassen, this volume).

The chapters in this volume represent four distinct strands of womanist writing, each one spanning culture areas and social typologies. Several scholars have taken up the challenge of identifying material evidence for women's actions in the archaeological record (Brumbach and Jarvenpa; Hendon; Galloway). Other analyses assume that as in all ethnographically known societies, women in viable prehistoric groups were social agents. While not necessarily making direct arguments for material evidence of women (but see Claassen and Wilson), these studies all ask how aspects of what are explicitly assumed to be women's activities would have affected women in general (Rautman, Prezzano), specific categories of women (Wilson, Hamann), or their communities (Williams, Rautman, Prezzano).

A third strand represented in this volume moves from concerns with women in prehistory to social women. Two-spirits present one of the clearest challenges to projecting dichotomous male/female gender onto the prehistoric Americas. But despite a wealth of descriptive information, the archaeological identification of two-spirits is as difficult as the identification of women—or, for that matter, of men (Hollimon). Indeed, as ethnographic studies would lead us to expect, the rhetorical uses of symbolism of gender, including the words that might seem the most immutable social markers of these statuses, should be expected to complicate identification of women and men as past social agents (Gillespie and Joyce).

Serious consideration of propositions that gender is a malleable cultural construct requires that scholars interested in prehistory not only identify different genders in the past, but also be aware of how particular archaeologically recoverable material may have served as media for creating genders. The final contributions to this volume add to the burgeoning body of studies of human representation as one of the sites for the production of gender, a site that—unlike fleeting performances that are irre-coverable in most archaeological settings—can endure (Koehler, Lesure).

The authors of these essays draw on a wide range of data for their analyses. Burial assemblages, because they are directly associated with skeletal remains that sometimes can be assigned a sex, have been a favored kind of data for explorations of women in the past. It is widely recognized, of course, that assignment of biological sexual identity to skeletal remains is an interpretive act, and some archaeologists have even taken into account the observations of students of modern biology that contemporary sex as-signment is not simply an observation but a construction of genitally based sexual identity. Representations of gendered individuals, especially in the form of figurines and large-scale carving or painting, have been a second favored body of data to explore past constructions of sex and gender. Both burial assemblages and representations are promising for an exploration of cultural constructions because they are particularly likely to have been strongly structured by social notions of what gender is and how the indi-vidual person is gendered. Both of these kinds of data also reflect cross-cutting dimensions of social reality, especially age and social status.

The prominence of these two kinds of data by no means reflects the entire range of methods used to approach gender in archaeological anal-ysis. Indeed, as the sample of essays in this volume shows, students of gender draw on scientific analyses of bone chemistry, assessment of skele-tal pathologies, micro- and macro-scale distributional studies (including catchment analyses), and analogical arguments from ethnoarchaeology and ethnohistory. The methods employed are in no way different from those typical of traditional, genderless archaeological interpretation. Even the apparently privileged areas of study—mortuary remains and represen-tational imagery—are approached in highly traditional ways and used for analyses that are concerned only incidentally, if at all, with gender.

What seems to distinguish the use of these traditional data and meth-ods in studies that take gender seriously is a commitment to the social im-portance of difference. Difference between individuals is not simply noise to be factored out of general propositions that can hold true for all mem-bers of the past societies that created the sites we attempt to understand. Difference is, instead, at the heart of the creation of distinctive settings for action, and distinctive kinds of action, that we can perceive archaeologi-cally. One of the most profound contributions of authors concerned with gender is a revaluation of the diversity of the archaeological record, which becomes not simply particularistic culture historical detail but the testimony for the past existence of complex human societies. By imagining what such societies might have been like, the authors in this volume clearly make the task of explaining the past much more difficult. But the difficulty was there all the time; it has simply been conveniently ignored by prehistorians who grant to our ancestors less freedom of action and unpredictability than any living human beings demand and take. The questions raised by the contributors to this volume will all, if taken seriously, enrich the interpretation of archaeological remains, even if in the end they come to be seen as untenable in their particulars.

Beginnings: An Overview

This collection, then, contributes to the destabilizing effect of the burgeoning literature on the archaeology of gender and of women. Contributors who ask whether women's activities might be identifiable in the archaeological record pose methodological and interpretive challenges to conventional assumptions. Hetty Jo Brumbach and Robert Jarvenpa, who use women's hunting behavior in modern Chipewyan society as a source of analogy, make several observations relevant to the archaeological record of all hunting societies. They find that sex roles are more flexible than typically assumed. Catchment analyses using rings of 3 to 5 kms, or 5 to 10 kms if water travel is likely, "encompass the food animal resources that are primarily of interest to women." They argue that women's hunting-related activities are more evident, being located in base camp sites, than are men's activities, conducted at some distance from the base in ephemeral camps that would rarely be detected archaeologically. Women hunters working close to the base camps maintained and curated specialized high-investment tools in tool kits. Despite their own success in proposing radically different interpretations of hunting societies, Brumbach and Jarvenpa question the utility of recent ethnographies for understanding women's work, noting that requirements for mandatory child education cause mothers and children to take up more or less permanent residence near a school, and that a marked increase in number of births to individual women can be documented in this century.

Following a similar line of argument for the complex sedentary states of the Classic Maya, Julia Hendon reasons that since women were major participants in household life, their activities must make up a large proportion of the archaeological record in domestic contexts. Hendon demonstrates from the distribution at Copan of artifacts usually considered diagnostic of female action (weaving and spinning) that women's actions pervaded this site. She uses this materialist reexamination of her database to question the way women are left out of models of social action at this site and in the Maya area in general, arguing that the only distinctively gendered individuals discernable here may be those engaged in stereotypically female action. On the basis of the presence of tools of distinctive women's tasks, Hendon suggests that previously identified "young men's houses" at Copan either accommodated groups of mixed gender or were actually young women's houses.

Patricia Galloway reviews the Western history of menstruation and then searches for menstrual huts in the archaeological record of the Southeast. When she finds none, she offers several test implications for their location within villages, and the artifacts that might be expected to accompany seclusion. At any given time, up to one-tenth of the women in a community might be secluded, suggesting that such facilities should be substantial and archaeologically visible. In a striking piece of revision, Galloway suggests that the figurines at the famous BBB Motor site in the American Bottom (see Koehler, this volume), its Ramey pottery, and numerous other aspects mark it as a women's seclusion site.

These three chapters all support the conclusion that archaeological sites do not represent an even or statistically representative sample of the activities of members of every gender status within past societies. They concur in identifying some aspects of women's activities as more likely to be represented or identifiable in the kinds of sites usually encountered in American archaeology. One implication of these essays, explicitly stated by Hendon, is that models of societies generated from these common archaeological contexts need to be explicitly gendered, assuming the presence of diverse genders and, particularly, women as social actors. Cheryl Claassen contributes a review of the previous literature that has gendered North American pre-contact sites and societies, and she identifies some problems that could, and should, be gendered. Claassen makes several original suggestions about women's participation in subsistence activities. She argues that strongly sexed activities developed after the adoption of maize agriculture, which she speculates was employed initially in the Mississippi and Ohio river valleys as supplemental food for infants. Noting multiple studies suggesting that women's gathering activities determined settlement patterns and that there are women's sites for nutting, plant processing, and seclusion/ritual, Claassen proposes that the caves of the Mogollon highlands were women's camps distinguished by gender-specific patterns of involvement in seed processing.

The dimensions of analysis employed by Claassen—concern with spatial segregation, evaluation of possible differential involvement in specific kinds of labor, and attention to those points in time when women's status changed—typify, to a greater or lesser extent, the other contributions concerning women as social agents. Susan Prezzano focuses on the history of explaining the Iroquoian transition from band society to tribal society. Of the two outstanding features of historic Iroquoian groups, male aggression and female status, only the former has been incorporated into models of Iroquoian tribalization. Women's activities in subsistence and household organization should reflect the process of tribalization, yet villages and households have rarely been the fodder for modeling this social change, despite the actual predominance of these contexts in excavated sites. Much gendered literature on sex roles has described complementarity of men's and women's activities as though their activities were sharply circumscribed. Prezzano points out that at least for the Iroquois, there were no arenas in which women did not take an active role, so complementarity is not pertinent here.

Alison Rautman turns to the household to explain what happened during the pithouse-to-pueblo transition in New Mexico. Her particular focus is on pottery production organized at the household level. She proposes that prior to the adoption of pueblos, women controlled both ceramic production and its distribution. The move into pueblos signaled a change in the spatial scale of regional social networks that brought about changes in sex roles. After that transition, Rautman speculates that men, rather than women, controlled the distribution of pottery and that historically observed sex roles of the Southwest were established.

Diane Wilson examines gender, sex roles, and social status of Powers Phase (Missouri-Mississippian) skeletons of the Turner Village site by looking at the spatial distribution of burials, grave goods, mortality curves, and dietary isotopes. She argues that Powers Phase sites had gendered space, and that the village was gendered in the same way that female-sexed individuals were gendered. Within the village, she finds that goods and food resources were distributed preferentially to females. Like Prezzano's study, Wilson's work suggests that archaeological contexts in which women are not categorically subordinate should not be uncommon and may be susceptible to detection.

Mary Beth Williams and Jeffrey Bendremer assert that women's foraging activities determined the timing and frequency of residential moves
as gathered plant and animal resources diminished around camps. They
attribute the increasing sedentism along the New England coast in the
Late Woodland and contact periods to women's increased focus on shellfishing for local consumption, trade of meats, and wampum production,
whereas other authors have given the causal role to the adoption of maize.
As women increasingly spent time shellfishing, their mobility declined
relative to men's. Those gender differences in mobility affected political
organization, territoriality, trade, technology, economic specialization,
and so forth. Women's utilitarian materials and tools diversified and were
elaborated, while projectile points became homogenized. In the early
contact period, women were probably producing many of the goods used
in trade—dried shellfish, shell, wampum, and pottery.

Byron Hamann combines rich texts documenting preferred interpretations of royal genealogies with considerations of women's economic
importance as spinners and weavers in Mexican societies to suggest the
possibility that a particular woman's influence can be perceived today in
such diverse materials as architectural ornamentation, the practice of
specific religious cults attested to in burials, and the adoption of a particular style of writing. Granting such potential importance to individual
women—even if, as in the Classic Maya area, they were not themselves
rulers—requires a much more complex conceptualization of the bonds
and fissures between and among different women and men.

Collectively, the chapters that consider women as social agents and
those that directly address the archaeological identification of women
demonstrate that the unitary category "woman," opposed to an equally
unitary "man," breaks down under archaeological examination. Among
the obvious dimensions of variation cross-cutting these assumed categories, seniority, social dependency, and class stand out as sometimes having
greater weight. The remaining chapters deal not with women but with
gender, delineating two extremes in the consideration of gender and exploring specific instances of social construction of genders. As suggested
earlier, although the chapters in this volume, in general, do not take "gender" as central and problematic, they all contribute to making it harder to
ignore.

Two spirits were a widely distributed phenomenon among Native
American groups in historic times, and probably in pre-contact times
as well. Sandra Hollimon presents rich ethnohistorical detail about the

female-linked burial responsibilities of California two-spirits (*berdache*). Her discussion of the ethnographic and ethnohistoric reports shows how fluid this category of social women was. Despite the association of some specific material practices with the specialized undertaker role of at least some Californian two-spirits, Hollimon suggests that we are unlikely to find easy test implications that can identify the presence of such individuals. What her analysis does suggest, however, is that any archaeologist working with data (such as mortuary assemblages) where gender might be expressed should regard ambiguous segregation of grave goods by biological sex as potential evidence for more fluidity in gender performance, apparently typical of native societies in the Americas.

Susan Gillespie and Rosemary Joyce describe another aspect of social womanhood, when gender is completely divorced from its presumed grounding in the "facts" of biology or sexuality. Like Hollimon, they draw heavily on ethnographic accounts to place their archaeological problem in perspective. Dealing as they do with the literate Classic Maya, they have the advantage of drawing on textual documentation, however debated its precise interpretation. The general issues they raise about gender's potential significance within a society as a symbolic language for representing social interdependence need to be considered in any analysis where the social category of gender is being inferred from symbolic media. But far from concluding that this elusive quality of gender blocks all attempts to understand the status of social men and women, they suggest that symbolic valuation of gender cannot be entirely divorced from practical, lived experience; if being socially female is associated with high status, at least some aspects of performing gender in everyday life must have a positive value as well.

Although Gillespie and Joyce look at ways gender is extended as a rhetoric of social relations to particular symbolic media, the interpenetration of gender and representation is equally evident in media that construct genders. Lyle Koehler examines ceramic imagery, carvings and paintings on rock in southern Illinois and Missouri, and French and Spanish documents to bring the roles of Mississippian women to the forefront. He frequently draws comparisons with Fort Ancient, Hopewell, and Mexican cultures. In art, women were Earth Mothers, household goddesses, reproducers, nurturers, chiefs, war goddesses, warriors, and hunters. Koehler documents material differences in gender, giving us evidence of women's and men's hair styles and clothing styles. The representational media Koehler reviews had more than a passive role as reflections of these material markers of difference. By inscribing them in permanent form, sometimes in large scale or in symbolically important spatial locations, representation converted the ephemera of performative gender into transcendant facts (compare Joyce 1994).

Richard Lesure takes a sophisticated look at the potential for manipulating concepts of persons by manipulating human images, using the Formative societies of Mesoamerica at the beginning of institutionalized social stratification as his case study. His presentation makes clear how crucial good micro-scale distributional data are to this kind of archaeological examination. It is only through the documentation of change through time in features of human representation that the repeated features that characterized a particular moment in time can be isolated. The decision to represent only some members of society, and those members at particular points in their social lives, gave real material existence to abstract identities. Lesure's argument that these identities included gender rests on the association of one stereotypic depiction with particular biological characteristics that significantly include not only markers of biological sex but also of age. His argument implies that these characteristics refer to the sexuality of young women as heterosexually marriageable subjects. To Lesure's analysis we would add the implication that these small-scale human images were themselves handled in face-to-face encounters, making possible a literal materialization of control over people that must have been part of their power as media for constructing social relations.

A Final Note

Although we have emphasized some of the common threads that run through the chapters in this volume, and through the broader literature of which they are representative, we would reiterate in conclusion one of the most striking features of the emerging literature on gender and women in archaeological analysis: the diversity of viewpoints represented by the large number of authors individually engaging in re-peopling, and gendering, the past. Just as concerns about women and gender make it imperative that our models of the past include more dimensions of variation, account for more kinds of data, and adopt multiple methods to interrogate the archaeological record, so a concern with gender has vividly released a wide spectrum of researchers, increasing the diversity of voices engaged in conversations. The regrettable fact that too much of the burgeoning literature has yet to actively engage other contributions is, we hope, an artifact of the explosive development of this field and the still impoverished body of papers published in generally accessible form and fully detailed argument. Our hope is that the references cited by the contributors to this volume will be pursued by others, and that a true dialogue will begin. The nature of the topic and its impact on the archaeological record demand that this happen.

PART I

Women in the Archaeological Record

2. Woman the Hunter: Ethnoarchaeological Lessons from Chipewyan Life-Cycle Dynamics
Hetty Jo Brumbach and Robert Jarvenpa

Introduction

Faithful to its title, the 1968 *Man the Hunter* volume (Lee and DeVore 1968) rather dogmatically portrayed hunting as the exclusive role of males. In this vision of cultural evolution, men were characterized as "cooperative hunters of big game, ranging freely and widely across the landscape" (Washburn and Lancaster 1968). The exclusively male hunter model was constructed, in part, by a questionable manipulation of the original codings for subsistence variables in Murdock's "Ethnographic Atlas" (1967), and by ignoring contradictory evidence presented in the original symposium proceedings by several ethnographers. In essence, by narrowing and redefining the scope of "hunting," the symposium participants obscured women's very real participation in a behaviorally and culturally complex enterprise.

Dahlberg's edited volume *Woman the Gatherer* (1981) served as something of a rejoinder, but it did this by highlighting the role of women as gatherers of plant foods, which often contributed more than half of some foraging people's subsistence. Thus, while one of its essays demonstrated the importance of female hunters among the Agta of the Philippines (Estioko-Griffin and Griffin 1981), the volume at large has come to be best known for its discussion of women as plant gatherers "par excellence." Unfortunately, such extreme views, rendered as mutually exclusive "man the hunter" versus "woman the gatherer" models, have come to sum up the way many archaeologists interpret the economic roles of men and women.

Why women do not hunt or, more accurately, why some anthropologists have difficulty envisioning women as hunters is a complex issue best left for consideration in a separate essay. Despite a growing literature on the topic (Nelson 1980; Estioko-Griffin and Griffin 1981; Watanabe 1968; Turnbull 1981; Leacock 1981), the ethnographic evidence for women as

hunters has had negligible impact upon archaeologists interpreting artifacts, features, and other residues recovered at prehistoric sites. As Conkey
and Spector (1984:8) have pointed out, there is a deep-seated assumption
that women in prehistory were "immobilized" by pregnancy, lactation,
and child care, and therefore needed to be left at a home base while the
males ranged "freely and widely across the landscape."

If these rigid assumptions have merit, then what of the role of women
in circumpolar arctic and subarctic societies where plant foods contribute
very little to the diet in terms of calories? Do women play any role in the
food quest in these environments?

Cultural Context and Research Methods

To address this problem and to shed light on the issue of women's contribution to subsistence, we turned to the methods of ethnoarchaeology,
particularly the archaeological study of ongoing populations. Since the
mid-1970s we have been engaged in carrying out ethnoarchaeological
research among the Chipewyan, Cree, and Metis Cree populations of
northwestern Saskatchewan. Much of this study has focused on the historical and ecological basis of ethnic-cultural adaptation and differentiation, including the roles of native and European groups in the upper
Churchill River fur trade (Brumbach 1985; Brumbach and Jarvenpa 1989,
1990; Brumbach, Jarvenpa, and Buell 1982; Jarvenpa 1987; Jarvenpa and
Brumbach 1983, 1984, 1985, 1988). This work involved survey and mapping
of late eighteenth-, nineteenth-, and early to mid-twentieth-century sites,
including extensive on-site collaboration with native interpreters.

Additional research carried out in 1992 was directed at conducting a
more systematic analysis of male and female interpretations of archaeological remains (Jarvenpa and Brumbach 1993, 1995). For analytical purposes we adapted Spector's (1983:82–83) idea of "task differentiation," a
framework developed explicitly to break the bounds of androcentric bias
in archaeology. Spector used the approach profitably in examining male
and female activity patterns for the Hidatsa of the Great Plains. Ethnographic information on the historical Hidatsa was reanalyzed to identify
tasks performed by males and females, as defined on the basis of four dimensions: (1) social unit (age, gender, and kin relations of personnel co-
operating in economic activity); (2) task setting (locations, locales, or
geographic range of activity); (3) task time (frequency, seasonality, and

other temporal contexts for activity); (4) task materials (implements, technology, and facilities employed in activity). The resultant patterning is suggestive of the ways that women's and men's lives differentially affect the formation of the archaeological record.

In our modification of Spector's approach, we interviewed both Chipewyan women and men, integrating questions concerning the social, spatial, temporal, and material dimensions of specific economic tasks. Additional data were derived from direct observation of such activities in living context. Maps were made of abandoned and still-occupied Chipewyan settlements and individual house sites, emphasizing locations and facilities used in performing relevant activities.

Because time constraints did not permit documentation of all tasks carried out by the Chipewyan, we concentrated on one set of activities: the acquisition and processing of food resources. Nine resources or resource clusters were identified to reflect the mammal, fish, and bird species emphasized by the women and men themselves and also those known to figure prominently in local diet and economy: moose, barren-ground caribou, snowshoe rabbit, beaver, muskrat, whitefish, lake trout, ducks, and various species of plants (Jarvenpa 1979, 1980).

While plant foods do not play a major role in terms of absolute caloric contribution, we included berries in the analysis as the most common plant food resource. Furthermore, to balance the Chipewyans' overwhelming emphasis on animal products, we added a general category of nonedible or nonfood plant resources, including bark (for baskets and other containers), moss (baby diapering material), and medicinal plants, among other such resources.

For each animal or plant resource, we questioned informants about a comprehensive system of tracking, capturing or harvesting, and processing. For example, our informants' ultimate rendering of the "moose system" included detailed knowledge on locating or tracking, killing, field butchering, transport to a residence or settlement, distribution or sharing of meat, final butchering and thin cutting, meat drying and storage, food preparation, hide smoking, and other usage of antlers, bones, fat, and body organs. Other resource "systems" emerged with their own distinctive pathways and thereby provided extensive information on a range of activities through which animal and, to a lesser degree, plant products passed.

Formal questions concerning the four dimensions were posed to each consultant. These included information on the participants in specific tasks and their kin, marriage, or other ties. The seasonality or temporal scheduling of events was also recorded. Locations were determined either by having informants take us to the relevant places in the case of activities carried out at or near settlements, or by marking locations on maps for more distant areas. The material dimension was explored in much the same way. For some activities our informants were able to demonstrate with the actual tools and facilities employed, whereas other, more distant activities were explained verbally. Direct observation of ongoing hunts or other economic enterprise was possible in some instances. Maps were made of selected settlements and camps with their associated work areas and features. The emphasis on the material aspects of task performance was especially productive.

Each narrator recalled in some detail, and often with considerable emotion, his or her efforts in provisioning a family, whether it was snaring rabbits with a grandmother sixty years ago or butchering a moose with a husband that very week. In some instances we were fortunate to be on the scene when hunting or food processing activities were occurring. These observationally enriched sessions lent an immediacy and clarity to some testimony.

By structuring interviews in this fashion and by posing the same range of questions to both women and men, we hoped to avoid or, at least, reduce biasing the results in the direction of our own gender stereotypes. We asked women about hunting and killing animals, and men about cooking meat and processing hides. For this we were rewarded. While some of our assumptions about gender were affirmed, we also learned that actual performance was far more flexible than we had thought.

Chipewyan Women Hunters

Perhaps the most interesting revelations were about women. We recorded, either through interviews or direct observation, considerable information on women's participation in the meat-acquisition process (which includes all animal products hunted, trapped, or netted), their profound interest in tools and tool kits, and their investment in constructing features and facilities. We also added much to our previous knowledge regarding the complex technologies and procedures involved in women's processing and storage of dry meat, animal hides, and bone grease, and their usage of medicinal plants, among other matters.

One conclusion of this project is the simple but undeniable reality that women hunt. Although the women we studied do not dispatch large mammals as frequently as do men, they are inextricably involved in the broader system of provisioning through pursuit, harvesting, and processing of mammals, fish, and birds.

In recent years hunting by both men and women has declined due to population increase, settlement nucleation, and mandatory schooling for youngsters, among other factors, but hunting still remains an important economic activity for most individuals. In June 1992, upon arriving at the small traditional Chipewyan settlement of Knee Lake, we found the community almost deserted. An elderly couple in their eighties and a middle-aged female resident were away moose hunting. A second elderly couple in their seventies and their forty-year-old daughter had recently returned from an extended moose hunting trip. Drying and smoking facilities in the settlement contained evidence of recent success in the capture of moose and fish (Figure 1).

Ethnoarchaeological study of Knee Lake and several other communities provided us with a wealth of information on social units and task set-

Figure 1.   Chipewyan woman with smoke house at the village of Knee Lake.

ting, time, and materials. One relevant observation is that while the tracking and dispatch phase of hunting usually takes place far from encampments and domestic settlements, the processing or the conversion of carcasses into meat, clothing, tools, and other useful items most often takes place at the residential settlements. Thus the materials produced by post-kill processing activities are spatially concentrated, unlike the archaeological residues created by kills, which are rarely recovered.

Another issue, however, will be highlighted here: the impact of life-cycle dynamics on women's hunting activities. While there is considerable individual variation in the intensity with which women participate in hunting, much of this variation is related to life-cycle dynamics. Adolescents and younger women are quite active, often as apprentices or partners to older relatives. It is within these mother-daughter or, more commonly, grandmother-granddaughter partnerships that many Chipewyan women learn necessary hunting and food-processing skills that aid them in adulthood and marriage. Many women in our interview sample remained active as hunters into their twenties, during the early years of marriage, either alone or with their husbands or other relatives. Most women reported a decline in long-distance travel for purposes of pursuing large mammals, when in advanced pregnancy or faced with increased family responsibilities, although some women continued managing snarelines or fish nets closer to home. In their middle and later years, with a decline in child-rearing responsibilities, many of the women significantly increased their participation in a wide range of hunting activities.

Other Chipewyan women continued hunting sporadically throughout their lives. One woman, a middle-aged widow, regularly hunted moose and other game, and she also managed a trapline and fishing operations. Many of these activities she carried out independently, but she has teamed up with male and female partners. Another woman, widowed with three young children in the early 1920s, undertook the full range of hunting, fishing, and trapping tasks to feed her family (Longpre 1977:40). In yet another instance, one of our informants noted that as a girl of fifteen she took on many adult responsibilities for her family when her father was permanently disabled. With some instructions from her father, she cut and transported logs and built her family's winter dwelling. With the help of even younger siblings, she tended the fish nets and rabbit snares that provided the bulk of her family's food supply for several years.

Samples of oral testimony underscore the close link between the intensity of women's hunting activities and their position in the family life cycle:

I always have hunted with my husband since early in our marriage. But I wouldn't go hunting after the third or fourth month of pregnancy. . . . I would help, together with my husband, pulling the moose out of the water and cutting it up in the bush. When I got back to camp, I would be the only one to do further butchering and making all the dry meat, as well as making the moosehide. Sometimes I would get help with hide making, like from my older daughter or another woman. In my early days of marriage, we would not haul the moose to Knee Lake village, but instead do all the butchering and hide making and all that in the bush, because it was hard to carry things a long way. (D. B., 70 years)

My grandparents, Bernard and Mary, would always hunt together in early marriage and also in their late marriage, but not in the middle years with children. . . . In the old days, when my grandmother was young, the women did all the men's jobs. They would shoot a moose, cut it up, bring it back with a dog team, and fish through the ice. And some women would be helpers or partners for making moosehide and fishing and call each other "sitseni." . . . If they bring in too many ducks, we would can duck meat in glass sealers. I did that for my grandma. Also with excess moose meat or any kind of meat we did that. Fall ducks [*dul ingaii*] we would also hunt. Before my first child I would go duck hunting with my husband. My husband did the shooting. We brought the whole ducks back home to clean. (A. M., 44 years)

I used to hunt rabbits with my mom. We had a little trail where we went. From our house we would cross a lake and go into the bush in winter [ca. 2.4 kms], and she would put rabbit snares. She would kill seven or eleven rabbits. I was seventeen years old. We would keep the skins for moccasin warmth. At the end of the trail my mom would kill a rabbit for a meal, make tea from snow, and have some bannock. We used snares. We would bring other rabbits back home whole. She would sometimes gut them and leave the hair on them and keep them frozen in a shed outside. We especially hunted rabbits in winter. But in summer my father and mother would snare rabbits in other places. (D. N., 64 years)

I have gone beaver hunting with my husband. But before marriage I used to paddle with my grandma . . . for one day in a small canoe for beaver and muskrat hunting in the spring time. Sometimes we trapped and shot them. Sometimes my grandma made me shoot them, but often I missed. But I always caught them with traps. . . . Later, I always went with my husband. We would go on the same trail, yet we each individually set our own traps. (D. H., 40 years)

I learned from my mom and grandma how to trap muskrat and how to skin them. In older days both men and women trapped, because money was hard to get. . . . Each woman had her own place for trapping so that it wouldn't overlap with brothers' or sisters' places. I would travel down the Churchill River in a canoe with Grandma to Dreger Lake, past Wagahonanci. I was seven or eight years old. We used an old-style wood-frame canvas canoe. They tear easily on rocks, and if we didn't have glue, we used "bush gum" and applied it with hot steel to seal on the patch. The gum comes from a . . . spruce. (J. D., 40 years)

When I was a young girl snaring rabbits at Dipper Lake, I did the work alone. I was nine years old when I started that. I used to be scared of wolves and things. . . . I would walk a distance away, like from here to the reserve [3.2 kms]. I'd bring back a load of rabbits sometimes, so that I'd leave some under the snow to get later. I'd snare rabbits all year round. . . . My father used to collect old string and soak them in rabbit blood, and we'd put them on a log to form stiff snare circles. (L. P., 73 years)

We used to trap fur, not only muskrats. I used to go with my grandparents to trap muskrats with metal traps, not snares. We would go trapping in Little Flatstone Creek and Mudjatik River. . . . When going out for muskrat we'd go out and camp for a couple days and then move the whole trapline, move it again, all the way down to the mouth of Little Flatstone and then working our way up to Patuanak. The skinning of muskrats, usually that's a man's job, but women would help if there were lots of animals. I am faster than my husband. My grandma used to make large birch-bark baskets, square but tall boxes, taller than wide. She would use these to store the dried muskrat meat. . . . We used to snare lots of rabbits at Little Flatstone, me and my grandmother. (L. N., 52 years)

As noted previously, most Chipewyan women reported a decline in hunting activities during the years when pregnancy and child-rearing responsibilities were greatest. A range of available government services, as well as Western technology, have triggered major changes in demography, with increased family size in recent history perhaps being the most relevant to this study. Although data are incomplete and somewhat difficult to compare, examination of three census lists revealed an increase in the number of reported subadult children over time. Shifts in family demography are central to our argument that changes in women's economic roles, particularly reduced involvement in hunting, occur quite late in history. Contemporary observations of family size and hunting, therefore, cannot be used uncritically to model prehistoric gender dynamics.

Three Chipewyan Censuses

1838 CENSUS

In 1838 the Hudson's Bay Company (HBC) conducted a census of all its fur-trading posts, including the Ile a la Crosse post within the English River District, which served as the major point of trade for the southern Chipewyan or *Kesyehot'ine*, the people considered in this study (HBC Archives 1838). Of the 489 Chipewyan enumerated for the English River District in that year, only 108 were identified by name. These "Hunter's Names" were broad transcriptions of Chipewyan names (e.g., Chee na Gun, Jennay afsee, Houlcho E azze) for adult male family heads and some of their male relatives and comrades.

The remaining 380 Chipewyan in the 1838 census were enumerated anonymously in columns following the roster of male family heads: "Wives" (119 individuals), "Sons" (107), "Daughters" (103), and "Followers and Strangers" (52) (see Table 1). The listings provide a general picture of variation in family size and structure at that time. Since Catholic missionization did not penetrate the region until 1846, polygynous marriage

TABLE 1.   Chipewyan population data from censuses in the English River District, Canada.

Census year	Men	Women	Boys	Girls	Followers and strangers	Total population
1838	108	119	107	103	52	489
1906	25	40	36	42	10[a]	153
1974	112	101	112	112		437

[a] "Other Relatives" in this case included two males and eight females.

was still common. Twenty-six of the named hunters, or nearly 24 percent, had at least two wives and some had three or four. Without information on age, however, one can only assume that "Sons" and "Daughters" represented subadult or dependent offspring who had not yet married or otherwise formed independent families. In the early twentieth century Chipewyan grooms were on average about six years older than their brides, a pattern that may have held for the nineteenth century as well (Brumbach and Jarvenpa 1989:259). If so, young women may have been moving from the "Daughters" to the "Wives" category in their mid-teens, whereas a comparable transition for men may have been delayed until their early twenties.

More problematic for comparative purposes is the "Followers and Strangers" category, suggesting a variety of dependents and hangers-on beyond the nuclear family. Only seventeen of the families, or about 16 percent of all families, accommodated such individuals in 1838. The category was not used by the HBC in all its censuses, creating some ambiguity. Perhaps the most reasonable assumption is that "Followers and Strangers" represented distant kin and/or friends, in some cases deriving from other regional bands, perhaps experiencing misfortune or hardship, and who formed temporary or short-term alliances with Chipewyan families in the English River District.

1906 CENSUS

The year 1906 marked the beginning of Canadian federal involvement in local Indian affairs with the extinction of land title through Treaty No. 10. The subsequent establishment of legally recognized bands and reserves affected the majority of the southern Chipewyan population, for whose attention the HBC and the French Roman Catholic church had contended for decades. The annuity payment list for the English River Band of Chipewyan established in 1906 is simultaneously a census of the community (Canada 1966). The seemingly low count of 153 individuals (Table 1) does not reflect a massive population decline among Chipewyan since the early nineteenth century, however. The English River Band was one of several regional bands of southern Chipewyan in the old English River or Ile a la Crosse trading district. The 1906 population, therefore, is a regional subset of descendants of the 1838 population discussed previously.

The treaty roster listed 41 family units, most of them identified by named male heads (25), but many by named females (16). The latter apparently were widows, about a third of whom had dependent children. Catholic baptism had introduced French first names for most individuals, but older Chipewyan nomenclature was retained in surnames (e.g., Jean Baptiste Estralshenen, Marie Yahwatzare, Norbert Darazele). By this date, all marriages appear to be monogamous, another artifact of Catholic influence.

Although the 1906 census contains no information on age, it provides a tabular listing of "Men" (25 individuals), "Women" (40), "Boys" (36), "Girls" (42), and "Other Relatives" (10) for each of the 41 named family units, paralleling the format used in the HBC's earlier census. In a similar vein, other than the named family heads, all remaining individuals are enumerated anonymously. If we assume that the ages and social positions of "Sons" and "Daughters" were parallel to that of "Boys" and "Girls," and that "Followers and Strangers" were roughly equivalent to "Other Relatives," then the two census documents are comparable.

1974 CENSUS

A list of federally registered Indians in the English River Band for 1974, an annually updated document produced by the Canadian Department of Indian Affairs and Northern Development, represents the direct contemporary descendants of the Chipewyan community identified in the 1906 treaty census (Canada 1974). Barring radical rates of in-migration, therefore, the almost threefold rise in population (from 153 to 437) over seventy years (Table 1) reflects the level of natural increase for this community. Occupying the settlements of Cree Lake, Dipper Lake, Knee Lake, Patuanak, and Primeau Lake, the English River Band has been the focus of our ethnographic and ethnoarchaeological work since the early 1970s.

Unlike the previous census documents, the 1974 registry identifies each individual by name, registration number, and family cluster, arranged in alphabetical order by surname. Some of these names retain the binary character of those in the 1906 treaty list (e.g., Joseph Dawatsare, Vitaline Deneyou), but many others have a more anglicized or Canadianized flavor (e.g., Gregoire Campbell, Mary Djonaire). In addition, a tabular format of codes indicates the marital status, religious affiliation, sex, and birth date of each individual, providing a level of specificity unavailable in the earlier censuses. There is nothing equivalent to the "Followers and Strangers" or "Other Relatives" categories, but for comparative purposes we can draw a distinction between adults and children in the 1974 census by using the age eighteen as a dividing line. The latter is a legal age of majority in the registry, at which time individuals are issued new registration numbers and separated into independent family clusters whether or not they have married.

Demographic Trends and Women's Burden

The general age- and sex-class data for the three time periods summarized in Table 1 are used to generate sex ratios (SR) in Table 2. These ratios generally indicate an excess of females over males in earlier history, with a remarkably unbalanced situation in 1906 (SR = 70). However, the ratio rebounds to a slight excess of males over females (SR = 105.16) by 1974. In such small populations, a combination of hunting accidents, disease, or other chance events could have easily reduced the male population at the turn of the century.

More relevant for the present discussion is the ratio of children to adults through history, expressed as a raw percentage in Table 2. Chipewyan children account for 48.1 percent of the total population in 1838. This

TABLE 2.   Chipewyan sex ratios and subadult children per woman for three census periods.

Census year	Adult sex ratio	Child sex ratio	Total sex ratio	Children as percent of population	Children per woman
1838	90.76	103.88	96.84	48.1%	2.8 (R: 1–5)
1906	62.50	85.71	70.00	51.0%	3.1 (R: 1–8)
1974	110.89	100.00	105.16	51.3%	4.8 (R: 1–12)

increases to 51.0 percent in 1906 and 51.3 percent by 1974. The change is subtle, but it suggests an increasing burden for women who generally were, and are, responsible for the daily care and nurturance of young children and other dependent family members.

The final column in Table 2 ("Children per woman") provides a more revealing means of interpreting women's child-care responsibilities over time. For example, the 1838 census material indicates an average of 2.8 children, with a range of 1–5, for each Chipewyan woman who was listed as having at least one child. The latter distinction is important. We counted only those women with at least one child to generate this statistic. Because the census did not indicate the women's ages, we wanted some means of excluding elderly women with adult children, as well as very young women who had not yet started their own families.

By 1906, the comparable statistic had increased to 3.1 children, with a range of 1–8. More recently, in 1974, the figure had further increased to 4.8, with a range of 1–12. The averages tend to underestimate the total number of children a Chipewyan woman bore in her lifetime, since they represent family size at a single time. Thus, unborn children or adult children who had formed their own households were omitted. Nonetheless, these figures represent the average number of children a woman would have to care for at any time.

Conclusions

The ethnoarchaeology of hunting can be used to identify and reassess women and women's roles in the archaeological record. Several implications have emerged from our work.

1. Based on information concerning the spatial dimension of task performance, Chipewyan women that we studied tend to hunt closer to the home village or base than do men. In part, this range is due to women's greater concentration on smaller mammals, and men's on larger quarry, although the two patterns overlap considerably. When Chipewyan women report hunting activities carried out in the course of a day, they typically report several hours of travel, either by foot and/or canoe, from the home base. One archaeological implication of this is that catchment analysis of food resources located within 3 to 5 kms of a settlement site, or 5 to 10 kms if water travel is likely, will encompass the food-animal resources of primary interest to *women*.

2. Spatial analysis of task performance *within* settlement sites reveals that women's participation in hunting may be more easily identified in the archaeological record than that of men. The carcasses of small game animals are often returned whole to the village site for further processing. In contrast, kills involving one or only a few large animals are likely to take place far removed from the archaeologically more visible settlement sites (Jarvenpa and Brumbach 1983) and hence may be more difficult to recover. Alternately, when large game animals were killed at some distance from the base camp, more common in earlier history, much of the community, including the women, would remove itself to the location of the kill. In such instances the processing of game animals, or the conversion of carcasses to meat, hide, and other usable products, was carried out at the newly established camp, primarily by women. In this case, the archaeological evidence in the form of faunal remains, hearths, and related features would evidence women's activities.

3. Moving from a general regional or inter-site analysis to more specific artifactual analysis, our study has demonstrated that women's activities are directly mirrored in the use of tools. Although the Chipewyan no longer use many stone tools, the women we studied maintained and curated an assemblage of implements used to process moose and caribou hides. Every older woman we interviewed owned a set of these tools, consisting of a selection of bone or metal scrapers, butchering knives, files, hide rougheners, and rope or cord to tie the hide to stretchers (Figure 2). These tools are carefully maintained; wrapped in a cloth or canvas and tied with string, cloth strips, or leather thong; and stored securely away in the house or tent.

These rather elaborate hide-processing kits are not what archaeologists would classify as "casual" or "pick up" tools to be used once and then discarded. If recovered archaeologically, they would no doubt be classified as "high investment" or "curated" tools. Far too often, such "high investment" implements are uncritically perceived as indicators of male activity (e.g., Hayden 1992). Yet it is apparent that women also made investments in the manufacture and curation of tools with which to carry out complex and multifaceted economic and domestic lives. Such behavior was neither idiosyncratic nor casual. A more critical analysis of artifacts recovered archaeologically would undoubtedly reveal other evidence of women's contributions to the food quest in past times and places.

It should be noted that other tool kits or tool-kit-like assemblages are used by both Chipewyan women and men to carry out a variety of hunt-

Figure 2.   Chipewyan woman displays the contents of a tool kit used for processing moose and caribou hides.

ing, fishing, trapping, food-processing, and manufacturing tasks. As in the case of women's hide-making tool kits, and certain men's hunting and butchering kits, some of these other assemblages are spatially condensed both in use and in storage. However, other complexes of implements may have a more involved storage situation as items are frequently moved between various locations and activities. The composition and use of these other kits deserve a fuller discussion than is possible here.

   4. Clearly women participated in a broad range of hunting activities. The level of participation varied from individual to individual, as well as from population to population, and according to life-cycle dynamics discussed previously, but it is apparent that it is not accurate to interpret all archaeological evidence of hunting and processing of animal products as indicators of an exclusively male enterprise.

   A dramatic increase in the childbearing and child-rearing responsibilities of women, especially in the past seventy years, may go a long way toward explaining the decreased participation of some contemporary women in hunting and in other tasks that occur at some distance from home. Such demographic trends also raise questions about models of work and gender based on synchronic ethnographies conducted in recent decades. Archaeologists would be wise to consider issues such as variable family size and the kinds of life-cycle changes in hunting participation reported by the Chipewyan women in this study. There is little reason to assume that women, by nature, were "immobilized" by pregnancy and child care and were therefore unable to take part in a full range of activities. The present study suggests that prior to European contact and even quite late into the historical period, Chipewyan women bore fewer children, reared and cared for smaller families, and were more fully integrated into a comprehensive range of hunting activities.

Acknowledgments

This paper is based on research supported by the Canadian Studies Faculty Research Grant Program, Academic Relations Office, Canadian Embassy, and by a Faculty Research Awards Program grant from the State University of New York at Albany. Alice Kehoe and Janet Spector, among others, provided many helpful comments on our project, for which we are grateful. Our deepest debt is to the Chipewyan people of Patuanak and Knee Lake, Saskatchewan, whose continuing collaboration and friendship over the years made this project viable and rewarding.

3. Women's Work, Women's Space, and Women's Status Among the Classic-Period Maya Elite of the Copan Valley, Honduras

Julia A. Hendon

Wylie (1992) has recently argued the advantage of a gendered approach to the archaeological record (see also Conkey and Gero 1991). I propose to reconsider the rich set of data from recent excavations in the Copan Valley, Honduras, from this perspective. I draw on archaeological remains from a series of sites in the Sepulturas zone to the east of the civic/ceremonial center (the Main Group; see Figure 1). Earlier work on this area demonstrated conclusively that it contains residences of the polity's nonruling or subroyal elite, defined here as people of high status outside the ruler's family (Hendon 1987). Interpretation of the burial contents, artifact distribution, and architectural form has been oriented primarily toward constructing models of social organization (Diamanti 1991; Hendon 1991; Sanders 1989). Of special interest to me has been the interplay between social organization, the use of space, and building construction and decoration, which shows that, while architecture and burials mark differences in social status, the distributional patterns of artifacts indicate that ritual and basic domestic activities took place in each individual residential site (Hendon 1991, 1992a). To date, although burials show that women were clearly a part of the social groups living in these sites (Lee and Storey 1992; Storey 1985, 1986), there has been little discussion of what role gender may have played in this social system (Hendon 1992b). I look at these distributional patterns of activities from an engendered perspective that concentrates on three issues: first, the identification of activities attributable to women; second, the spatial distribution of these activities within Sepulturas's residential patios; and third, what new insights these activities and their locations give to our understanding of women's, and specifically elite women's, economic and social roles in Copan society.

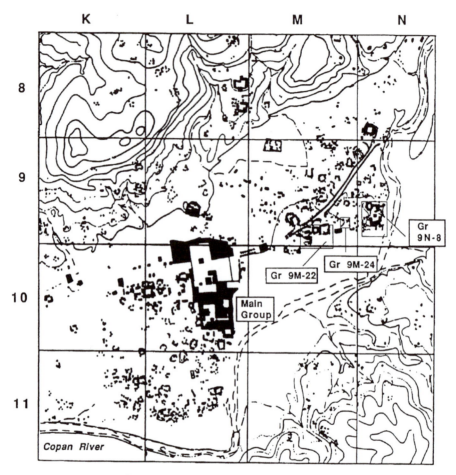

Figure 1.   Map of settlement around the Main Group in the Copan Valley, Honduras, showing the location of the three sites discussed in the text.

The Copan Valley

The Copan Valley is in western Honduras at an elevation of 600 m above sea level. It is watered by the west-southwest-flowing Copan River, which eventually drains into the Motagua River in Guatemala. Prehistoric settlement radiates out from the Main Group to cover most of the fertile valley floor and surrounding foothills. Survey, test-pitting, and excavation programs carried out since 1975 have shown that most sites outside of the

Main Group are residential and date from the Late Classic period, ca. A.D. 600–1000.

The heart of the Classic-period Copan polity is the Main Group, adjacent to the river. Surrounding this collection of public architecture, royal palaces, and monumental art is a dense ring of elite residential compounds. These compounds are made up of large stone and wattle-and-daub residences, outbuildings used for cooking and storage, and a small number of religious buildings (Hendon 1991). Although the size and quality of construction of inner-zone residences vary, they are, on the whole, larger and better built than the majority of the houses and associated structures found in the rest of the valley (see Webster and Gonlin 1988). In both zones, the layout of most compounds conforms to the usual Maya pattern in which the buildings form a rough rectangle around a central courtyard. Again in both zones, although more frequently in the inner one, individual compounds often abut one another to create larger groupings, suggesting the existence of social ties among the compounds (Hendon 1991; Sanders 1989).

This essay draws on data from two multicompound groupings, Groups 9N-8 and 9M-22, and a single, isolated residential compound, Group 9M-24, located in the inner settlement zone and excavated from 1981 to 1984 by the Proyecto Arqueológico Copan Fase II (PAC II) directed by William T. Sanders (Sanders 1986; see Figure 1). Group 9N-8 is one of the largest of such groupings in the valley, with at least fifteen compounds. Group 9M-22 consists of three abutting residential compounds. Architectural, mortuary, and artifact data all combine to indicate the high status of the majority of these compounds' residents compared to those of the outer-zone sites. At the same time, these data reflect the differences in rank among the people living in each compound as well as those between groups in different compounds. The overall impression is of a series of ranked social groups.

The PAC II excavations in Sepulturas were oriented toward a common set of goals and employed a common methodology (see Sanders 1986). Emphasis was placed on complete exposure of the final architectural phase of construction, including all structures and adjacent open spaces, rather than on extensive trenching. This exposure was accomplished by removing all overburden, including collapsed architecture. In order to test for the possibility of the presence of middens and in situ materials, care was taken to separate any material lying below the collapsed walls from the wall fall and overburden. A number of structures had associated material of this sort. The result of this type of excavation is information on a series of architectural units in association with contextually distinct sets of artifacts spanning a relatively short time period over a relatively large physical space.

The artifacts that I draw on here come from two types of deposits. First are those materials found below and unmixed with collapsed construction which were in contact with horizontal construction surfaces (floors). In some cases, these deposits contained intact (whole or reconstructable) artifacts that formed a set of functionally related objects. An example of such a set is the cluster of objects found on the floor of a small room in the northwestern structure of Patio B of Group 9N-8. Three metates, a portable brazier for heating food, several storage jars, and obsidian blades were found on the floor of the room, suggesting its use as a kitchen (Hendon 1987: Table 4.18). These clusters were designated features by the project and considered to be in situ. In other cases the artifacts found below the fallen walls were small and fragmentary, mixed in with the dirt resting on the floor. Here the material is best interpreted as trash that, because of its size, was not entirely removed from the rooms or terraces.

The second type of deposit I draw on is midden. Residential structures and outbuildings where food was prepared usually had trash deposits behind them in the three groups excavated. Middens found by PAC II are characterized by their position underneath the collapse of their associated structures' walls, a lack of constructional debris within the midden itself, a rich and varied inventory of cultural materials and animal bone, and the presence of ash, carbon, or other signs of burning. This midden material did not serve as a source of construction fill as it may have done at other Maya sites.

Women's Work

Analysis of artifact function, the co-occurrence of artifacts in in-situ deposits, and statistical patterns of association among artifacts from middens have allowed me to identify a number of different activities that the residents of Sepulturas engaged in (Hendon 1987, 1988, 1989, 1992b). In this paper I draw on my analyses to summarize the kinds of activities that residents of Groups 9N-8, 9M-22, and 9M-24 habitually engaged in, and I consider the implications of these activities for our understanding of gendered work and space at Copan. Activities identified include cooking, food preparation, food serving, storage, craft production on a small scale, and ritual observances. Artifacts provide direct evidence for the production of shell ornaments, bone objects, obsidian tools, and textiles in a number of patios. More indirectly, use-wear studies of the obsidian blades indicate their use as sewing, scraping, slicing, and planing tools used to work a variety of organic and inorganic materials (Mallory 1984). All these activities take place in a domestic setting and thus represent actions carried out by members of the social groups residing in the compounds. But which members carried out which activities? More precisely, can any of these activities be associated consistently with gendered categories of people?

Economic relations in modern and historic Maya societies are inextricable from notions of gender (Devereaux 1987). All cultures create gender categories by associating sex differences with certain traits, actions, or roles. Such gender categories represent culturally constructed categories rather than expressions of essential and immutable biological differences (MacCormack 1980). Maya concepts of gender rely heavily on action, and especially ritual and productive action, to create distinct but complementary male and female social identities. Ethnographic and ethnohistoric material on Maya and other Mesoamerican societies shows us that from the Postclassic period on, textile and food production are important ingredients in the definition of women's social identity (Brumfiel 1991; Devereaux 1987; McCafferty and McCafferty 1991; Paul 1974). This work-based identity, reinforced by specific rituals, complements that of men, who before the Spanish Conquest were defined as farmers, hunters, and warriors (Farriss 1984; Joyce 1991b).

That these gender categories existed in the Classic period can be deduced from depictions of Maya men and women in figurines, on ceramic vessels, and on monuments. Figurines and scenes on pottery show women engaged in spinning, weaving, maize grinding, and food serving, while men are shown hunting or dressed as warriors (Hendon 1992b, 1994; Joyce 1992b, 1993). Monumental art lacks scenes of overt productive activity but creates the same association through images of women holding or wearing the results of their labors (Joyce 1992a). Large-scale public art, figurines, and scenes on pottery present women as the creators of culturally valued and economically significant products through the transformation of natural resources into the food and textiles necessary for subsistence and ritual (Joyce 1992b).

The Sepulturas data provide evidence for both food preparation, including cooking and maize grinding, and textile production, including weaving and spinning. The rest of the activities identifiable from the archaeological record, however, cannot be assigned exclusively to one sex or the other, nor, with the exception of ritual, can they be shown to carry the same symbolic importance in the cultural definition of gender. Given the domestic nature of the Sepulturas sites, it is not surprising that none of the male-counterpart roles—farmer, hunter, warrior—are evident in the residential groups (Gero 1991). (However, the presence of deer and other animal bone, as well as that of grinding stones, indicates that men were hunting and farming elsewhere.) Even if we could show that men produced objects from shell, bone, or obsidian, we could not consider this production comparable to farming, hunting, and fighting (or food preparation and weaving for women) because, based on the depiction of men and women in various media and modern and historic practice, the Maya did not assign them the same symbolic weight. My discussion of gender in Sepulturas, therefore, focuses on women at the expense of men and draws on two activities: food preparation and textile production.

The evidence for textile production in Sepulturas consists of spindle whorls, centrally perforated clay disks, and bone tools, specifically needles, pins, and weaving picks (Table 1) (Hendon 1992b). Both spindle whorls and centrally perforated clay disks served as weights for spindles used to spin thread. Most Copan spindle whorls are spherical to elliptical or hemispherical in cross-section with incised designs decorating one side. These designs combine curved lines, crosses, triangles, circles, and pentagons with cross-hatched areas and small dots. Birds are the only clearly representational design. (See McMeekin 1992 for a discussion of the meaning of some seemingly geometric or abstract designs on spindle whorls.) The

TABLE 1.   Weaving and spinning tools from Sepulturas.

Tool (suggested use)	Number	Size Range (cm)
Spherical spindle whorl (spindle weight)	11	2.8–3.7 diameter 1.0–2.0 thick
Hemispherical spindle whorl (spindle weight)	14	2.5–3.8 diameter 0.9–2.0 thick
Pottery disk with central perforation (spindle weight)	66	1.8–6.0 diameter 0.1–0.9 thick
Bone needle (sewing and weaving)	41 [a]	4.8–10.8 length
Bone pin (sewing and weaving)	4 [a]	3.6–4.6 length
Bone brocade pick (lifting warp threads)	186	5.1–15.5 length

[a] An additional 78 broken examples are either needles or pins.

other type of spindle weight takes the form of a flat to slightly concave round disk with a single hole drilled in the center. Such disks were carved from the walls of pottery vessels, probably after the vessel had broken. Pottery disks are larger and thinner than the spindle whorls. Such differences in whorl size and weight have been shown to relate to the type of material spun and the fineness of thread desired, with maguey or similar fibers requiring a larger spindle than cotton (Parsons 1972).

Tools made out of bone that relate to sewing or weaving also appear in archaeological contexts from Sepulturas residences. These include needles of various sizes, pins (identical to the needles but lacking an eye), and brocade picks. Bone needles and pins have a circular to oval cross-section. The needle's eye may be either carved or drilled. As Table 1 shows, needles and pins vary considerably in length, suggesting their use on a variety of materials. These implements may be used both for sewing and weaving. Brocade picks (often labeled "awls") are usually made of deer bone. Twice as long as they are wide, they taper to a sharp point and are used to lift warp threads when creating brocade design.

Artifacts indicative of food preparation include grinding stones and several ceramic vessel forms, such as flat griddles (*comals*), large basins (*calderos*), hemispherical bowls, and three-pronged braziers. (Animal bone and plant remains, other possible indicators of food preparation, are not used here because animal bone was not collected consistently over the four years of excavation, and the analysis of the flotation samples has not yet been published.) Most metates and manos from Sepulturas are made either from a local rhyolite or an imported basalt (Spink 1984). The basalt metates generally have three supports, closely resembling metates common in the Ulua River valley to the east (Joyce 1991a). The rhyolite metates lack supports and are roughly basin shaped.

Copan comals are shallow, evenly curved griddles with two horizontal loop handles and a rim diameter of 40–42 cm. Their interiors are slipped and their exteriors often burned, indicating their use over open flames. Calderos are large bowls with out-flaring walls but no handles. The rim diameters of the reconstructable examples found at Sepulturas range from 24 to 54 cm. Reconstructable heights range from 15 to 24 cm. These basins may be unslipped or have an interior slip. Many show signs of burning both inside and out, suggesting their use as both food-preparation and cooking utensils. Hemispherical bowls are smaller than calderos. (I include here only unslipped or monochrome bowls. Polychrome hemispherical bowls were probably used for food serving [Hendon 1987].) Their curving walls may create a slight restriction at the opening, which ranges from 7 to 24 cm in diameter. These vessels have no handles and were used as containers for preparing food. Three-pronged braziers are a composite form consisting of a conical base, some 28 cm high, supporting a shallow plate that has three hollow prongs rising from its rim. Parts of the walls of the base have been cut out in roughly triangular shapes. The inside of the plate is often heavily burned. (See Hendon [1987:335–339] for a fuller description of this form, its possible parallels at other sites, and my reasons for considering it a brazier rather than a censer.) Three-pronged braziers served as portable stoves (Hendon 1987:307–310, 314–353; 1988; see also Longyear 1952).

Women's Space

Gender may also serve to structure spatial relations, but symbolically and on the ground (Spain 1992). By linking direction with gender, the Maya create a spatial dimension to their construction of gender categories. These relationships, like the work-based definition of gender, display a long continuity in Mesoamerica. Joyce has shown how the placement of pairs of stelae depicting male and female actors served to "divide space within Classic Maya centers into two halves, along a variety of axes: front and back, outer and inner, right and left, north and south, and up and down" (Joyce 1992b:65). These sorts of spatial associations are most clearly marked in relation to religious and political action or in the representation of such action (Gossen 1974; Joyce 1991b; Vogt 1976). Within the household, similar structural principles may underlie Maya concepts of domestic space, but they do not segregate men and women nor provide a way to predict their location (cf. Flannery and Winter 1976). Although modern highland Maya women are associated spatially with the hearth area, both men and women spend time near the hearth, and women are not restricted to only certain parts of the domestic space (Earle 1986; Vogt 1969).

The distribution of artifacts indicative of food preparation and textile production creates spatial patterns within and across patios in the three groups (Hendon 1989, 1991). The residents of Groups 9M-22 and 9M-24 used small platforms with perishable superstructures as food-preparation areas (Figures 2 and 3). Some of these ancillary structures are freestanding, and others are attached to residences. Such platforms are less common in Group 9N-8, where food preparation occurred most often on the large terraces or inside small, benchless rooms adjacent to the main sleeping rooms

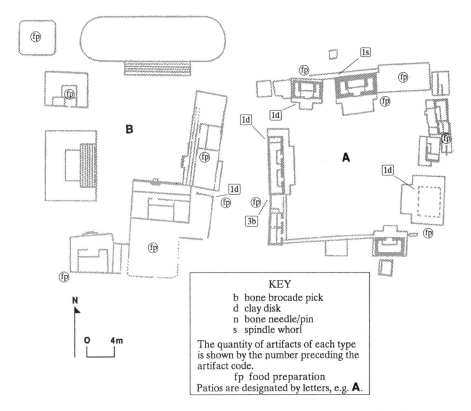

Figure 2.   Map of Group 9M-22 Patios A and B showing the location of artifacts relating to textile production and food preparation.

of the residences (Figure 4). Although architecturally distinct, neither type of space exhibits any consistent location within patios. Some ancillary structures sit behind residences; others are built within the courtyard area. Such variety in location mitigates against any regularity in directional orientation as well. Food preparation areas are found on the northern, southern, eastern, and western sides of patios and of the residences.

Artifacts related to textile production are not distributed evenly throughout the three groups either (Hendon 1992b). Most tools come from Patios B, D, and H of Group 9N-8 (Figure 4), with lesser concentrations in Group 9M-22 (Figure 2) and none in Group 9M-24. They are associated with residences where a number of other domestic activities

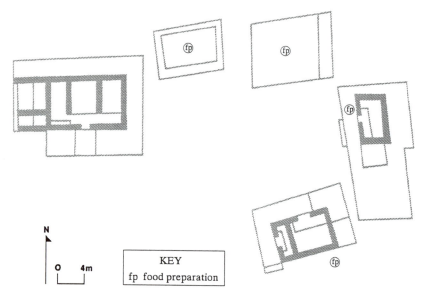

Figure 3.   Map of Group 9M-24 showing the location of artifacts relating to textile production and food preparation.

were carried out, including food preparation and small-scale craft production such as the manufacture of shell ornaments on the west side of Patio H and of bone implements on the north side of Patio H and in Patio D. Spinning and weaving tools were also found in deposits from two residences, one on the west side of Patio A and the other on the south side of Patio B, both identified by Sanders (1989) as young men's houses, partly on the basis of presumed architectural differences and partly on the occurrence of ball-game equipment (a stone yoke and several stone hachas) in the building in Patio A. The presence of tools related to textile production, which are accompanied by food-preparation and food-serving utensils, suggests the presence of both men and women and argues for a more generalized domestic function for these buildings.

Given the identification of food preparation and textile production as gendered female tasks, the Sepulturas data show us where, as well as how, some women spent some of their time in elite residential patios. Women ground maize, cooked, wove, or spun in close proximity to those people, male or female, who manufactured obsidian tools, shell ornaments, or bone items, and carried out rituals. The location and number of food

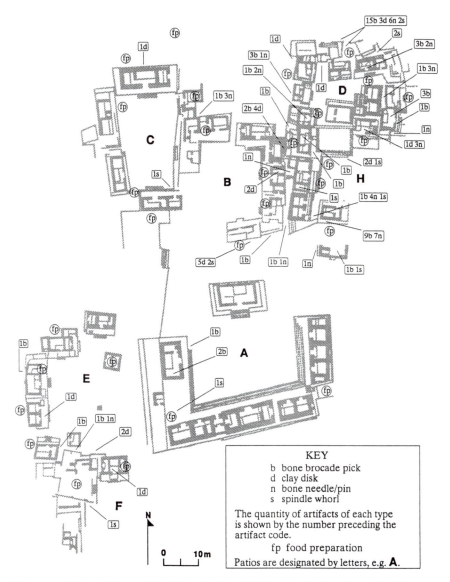

Figure 4.   Map of Group 9N-8 Patios A–F and H showing the location of artifacts relating to textile production and food preparation.

KEY
b bone brocade pick
d clay disk
n bone needle/pin
s spindle whorl

The quantity of artifacts of each type is shown by the number preceding the artifact code.

fp food preparation

Patios are designated by letters, e.g. **A**.

preparation areas may reflect the existence of several families in a single compound, families that were linked by economic and religious ties into a single household. Differences in the distribution of spinning and weaving tools suggest a greater emphasis on textile production in Group 9N-8 than in Groups 9M-22 and 9M-24. Within Group 9N-8, Patios A and E, although not devoid of spinning and weaving tools, show a lower concentration than the patios at the northern end of the group. Artifacts and burials of adults of both sexes as well as children (Lee and Storey 1992; Storey 1992) associated with residences in Patios B, D, and H emphasize, however, that such differences cannot be used to define a symbolically meaningful segregated "women's space" either within an individual compound or for Group 9N-8 as a whole. In other words, the gendering of space achieves cultural significance only in certain contexts. Maya gendering of space relates more to the structuring of cosmological relationships and the expression of political ideology than to the shaping of day-to-day domestic life. During the Classic period, it is public space under the control of the ruler that is most visibly gendered. The placement of monuments and the images they carry create a series of associations between direction, gender, and action designed to reinforce the ruler's centralizing and integrative role (Joyce 1991b, 1992a). Thus gendered spatial relations are an important part of Classic period political ritual. Although a work- or action-based definition of gender played an equally important role in the domestic sphere, the ideological significance of the gendering of space is not replicated here.

Some Thoughts on Women's Status

The prevalence of food preparation and textile production in Sepulturas, especially in one of its highest-ranking groups, Group 9N-8, speaks to the economic and ritual importance of food and textiles. The lack of separation of these activities from other types of economic production, which may have been carried out by men or women, and from other basic household activities suggests to me that women were not confined to specific areas of the living space. Both textiles and food play key roles in religious ceremonies that maintain relations with the supernatural world while cementing social relations. Although in the modern cargo system men hold the major offices, it is widely recognized that successful completion of an office's duties requires an equal contribution from the wife (Devereaux

1987; Mathews 1985). Similarly, although women were limited in their participation in temple ceremonies (although by no means completely excluded) during the Postclassic period, their products were essential elements (Joyce 1992b). It has been suggested (Brown 1983; Clendinnen 1982) that depictions of women in public art indicate that such restrictions did not apply during the Classic period, at least for the elite. Most images of women in Classic monumental art, however, emphasize their productive capabilities by showing them dressed in elaborate textiles and holding bundles of cloth or pottery vessels containing food or ritual paraphernalia (Joyce 1992b). These associations are reinforced by figurines that show high-status women actively engaged in weaving and spinning (Hendon 1992b).

Regardless to what degree women participated in actual rituals during the Classic period, their labor was critical to the success of these ceremonies (see Brumfiel 1991). The ability to carry out these rituals, with their attendant feasts and prestations, was an important element in the constant competition for status among Maya elite. With its emphasis on appropriate kinds of work to define gender roles, leading to a fundamental economic and social complementarity (Devereaux 1987), Maya society creates the possibility of parallel sources of political and social power for men and women (Strathern 1984). As in many other cultures where cloth functions as a material symbol of power and a source of wealth (Weiner 1989), control of textile production and, possibly, of distribution emerges as one arena in which women, especially elite women, may be able to act independently of men (Leacock 1986).

The nonruling elite in the Copan Valley, despite their incorporation into a single, centralized political system, represent a decentralizing force through their ability to control the resources of their households and to manipulate symbols of political power (Hendon 1991, 1992a, 1992c). The gendered perspective used here illuminates how women's labor and its products helped sustain this autonomy.

Acknowledgments

The data analysis on which this chapter is based derives from my dissertation research, which was supported by a National Science Foundation Dissertation Improvement Grant (BNS-8319347), the Owens Fund of the Peabody Museum of Archaeology and Ethnology, Harvard University, and the Proyecto Arqueológico Copan Fase II. Permission to use these data by the director of PAC II, William T. Sanders, and the Instituto Hondureño de Antropología e Historia (Victor Casco López, director) is gratefully acknowledged. I bear sole responsibility for all errors and interpretations presented in the chapter.

4. Where Have All the Menstrual Huts Gone? The Invisibility of Menstrual Seclusion in the Late Prehistoric Southeast
Patricia Galloway

Overture

> . . . she invariably had three things with her on the ledge of her ground-floor box: her opera-glass, a bag of sweets, and a bouquet of camellias. For twenty-five days of the month the camellias were white, and for five they were red; no one ever knew the reason for this change of colour, which I mention though I can not explain it.
> —Alexandre Dumas fils

"She," of course, was Alexandre Dumas fils's Camille, the Lady of the Camellias, a very expensive Parisian courtesan who renounced everything for love. Today the best-selling line of French "sanitary napkins" is brand-named "Camellia," but then that is the kind of mildly smutty public discourse that straitlaced Americans would expect from the French. And it is a far cry, indeed, from a high-flown literary allusion to the grubby term "menstrual hut"—or is it? Both terms were coined by Western cultures, and both share the tendency to hide female practices accommodating the "wound that does not heal." As archaeologists we are deluding ourselves if we think our own professional practice is unaffected by that same tendency. If the most basic move toward engendering archaeology is finding women in the archaeological record, the search for evidence of menstrual practices is about as direct a way to do it as there could be. Yet it is a search that pretty clearly has not been made. This is unfortunate, since anthropological studies suggest that menstrual seclusion may be an important correlate of social organization, and social organization is just what researchers concerned with the late prehistoric Southeast have all been claiming to be interested in.

Literature Review

The term "menstrual hut" is already very evocative; why not "house" or simply "structure"? We know in a general way that in historic period Southeastern nonstate societies women subject to rules of ritual seclusion during menses withdrew to specific structures for the duration of their period of "pollution." But Southeastern archaeologists do not find menstrual huts routinely, even when investigating settlements; they have apparently assumed that the structures reserved for that purpose were too squalid and temporary to leave evidence worth looking for, and the term "hut" is an index of that assumption. But why have such assumptions been made? Is this really the reliable import of the ethnographic literature?

In the first place, "the ethnographic literature" for the early historic period in the Southeast is almost exclusively limited to the work of John R. Swanton. We should remember in dealing with the information he provides that this is the same John Swanton who presented the explicit sexual material in *Myths and Tales of the Southeastern Indians* (1929) in Latin, and his reticence in dealing with reproductive matters with most of his contemporary informants is reflected in the fact that his sources on the topic of menstruation are mostly limited to the fortuitous testimonies of eighteenth-century male European missionaries and colonists and (for the Creeks) other ethnologists of his own time. Neither Swanton nor his colleagues obtained information about menstrual huts from female informants, so all that we have regarding this matter, even now, amounts to external observation at best. A sample of Swanton's evidence for menstrual practices and taboos follows:

1. *Timucua*: fish and venison food restrictions, prohibition of fire kindling; similar food restrictions after childbirth (Swanton 1946:713). Note that Swanton's source for making of "a separate fire" by women during menses is its listing as a superstitious sin in the 1613 *Confessionario of Francisco Pareja* (Milanich et al. 1972:25).

2. *Creek*: menstrual seclusion in house "by herself" for four days (as at childbirth); utensils for food preparation and consumption reserved for use during menses; prohibition on consumption of meat from large animals and on presence in garden; bathing required downstream from men, prohibition on presence upwind of men; required bath and change of clothes for purification at the end of menses. Early-twentieth-century informants and ethnologists re-

ferred to "a house," a "seclusion lodge," "a separate tent or house," and "a small house near some spring or stream" (Swanton 1928a:358–360, 1947:714).

3. *Chickasaw*: menstrual huts, built far from dwellings but near enough to the village to be safe from enemies, used monthly and at child-birth; required bath and change of clothing afterward; food restrictions during pregnancy, also *couvade* practices (abstention from work, avoidance by other men) by the husband after birth. Adair refers to the relevant structures as "small huts" (Swanton 1928a: 358–359, 1946:715–716).

4. *Choctaw*: small cabin "apart" monthly and for childbirth; food restrictions at childbirth; *couvade* practices (food restrictions) (Swanton 1946:716). Note that this comes from only one source, the ca. 1730s French "Anonymous Relation."

5. *Natchez*: A brief remark taken from the descriptions of marriage by the missionary Father Le Petit notes that during menstruation there was a prohibition on marital intercourse; Swanton notes nothing further for the Natchez on this subject (1911:97).

Thus where information is available for Southeastern Indian groups, it all definitely points to ritual seclusion during menses carried out publicly, generally in a structure specifically reserved for the purpose, with accompanying taboos. It is relevant that where such ritual seclusion took place for menstruation, it was also required along with many of the same taboos for childbirth, often apparently in the same structure. Unfortunately the evidence is rather vague on the details of such structures, suggesting that many of those who reported them may not have seen one. The overwhelming evidence for such structures makes it all the more curious that none has been found by archaeologists.

The Anthropology of Menstruation

The topic of menstrual practices has served along with female puberty initiations and childbirth practices as a hobbyhorse for nearly every strain of anthropological thought (see Buckley and Gottlieb 1988b). Lately, as a result of attention from feminists, menstrual practices have come in for a good deal of popularizing "anthropological" and "psychological" treatment, being linked with the old notion of primal matriarchies and the New

Age "goddess" movement in several popular books (cf. Delaney et al. 1976; Shuttle and Redgrove 1978; even Weideger 1976 overgeneralizes from very poor anthropological evidence). However praiseworthy a clear-eyed look at menstruation as experienced by modern women is, these books have not clarified matters by viewing menstrual seclusion as "universal" and a "cruelty" imposed by patriarchal authority jealous of "women's mysteries," and in any case they all virtually ignore prehistoric cultures.

Several relatively recent serious anthropological studies are, I think, much more helpful in thinking about prehistory because they grapple with the problem of how menstrual seclusion works within cultures and its possible correlation with social organization. Paige and Paige (1981) have treated the topic as part of an analysis of the sociopolitical functioning of "fraternal interest groups" under a version of exchange theory; Douglas (1966) and Schlegal (1972) have analyzed menstrual seclusion as part of cross-cultural studies of pollution and male domination, respectively; several of the essays edited by Buckley and Gottlieb (1988a) focus on the experience of the practice itself and on its advantages to women; while Martin's (1992) work on Western female embodiment stresses the usefulness of menstrual taboos to modern women. These rather heterogeneous studies appear to agree that menstrual seclusion and its accompanying practices are advantageous to women and are characteristic of societies where husbands and males in general are not particularly dominant, especially matrilineal societies where residence rules are generally matrilocal. Paige and Paige (1981) go on to generalize that such societies—societies with "weak fraternal internal groups"—are characterized by a subsistence base that is not valuable enough to require defense, such as shifting agriculture with hunting and gathering. This is not inappropriate as a description of the historic tribes of the Southeast, but it is more problematic as a characterization of the rather aggressive chiefdom model now accepted for the late prehistoric societies that preceded them.

Kinship and residence in Mississippian societies have been more assumed about than understood. Knight (1990) has recently discussed the relation of kinship to sociopolitical structure in some detail, foregrounding the problematic nature of ethnohistorically attested kinship forms in the early colonial Southeast, but concludes that archaeological correlates "are yet to be worked out." And although Paige and Paige (1981:121) argue generally that matrilineal, matrilocal societies do not have an abundant and rich resource base, they have discussed one example of an advanced agricultural society, the Nayar of India (which is matrilineal and matrilocal), that practices menstrual seclusion and is even characterized by nonresident husbands.

Clearly much more work remains to be done in understanding whether menstrual seclusion does actually correlate reliably with matrilineality/matrilocality, since the cross-cultural sample used by Paige and Paige (1981) was based on largely androcentrically biased ethnographies and coding practices (cf. Buckley 1988:192–193). It is, for example, quite possible that matrilineality/matrilocality in the Southeast was an artifact of the protohistoric disease holocaust period: Harris (1988:34–37) suggests that warfare or other disruption is a strong pressure for matrilocality, and it stands to reason that since matrilineages would select for female children to expand the lineage and attract bridewealth, they would also favor population increase and prove an ideal vehicle for post-catastrophe population recovery.

Still, it is not beyond the bounds of possibility that the known population expansion of the Mississippian period might also be explained in this manner; that the Natchez model, at least for matrilines, is correct for the Mississippian period; and that Mississippian societies might thus be characterized by the same practices—which should be marked materially by the presence of "menstrual huts." If, on the other hand, Mississippian societies did not practice menstrual seclusion, it is quite possible that their kinship organization was not matrilineal, and their residence practice not matrilocal. If that possibility is admitted, then a thorough reexamination of our dependence on post-contact ethnographies is in order. The point is that the correlation between menstrual seclusion and matrilineal kinship seems to be good enough that it should be possible to test for matrilineal kinship archaeologically if we can just figure out what a "menstrual hut" ought to look like in the ground.

Menstrual Taboos and Modern Archaeology

If the ethnographic evidence and the matrilineal model are correct, there must have been thousands of menstrual huts constructed in the Southeast, just from the colonial period from which they are certainly attested. Yet so far no menstrual hut has been reliably reported from a Southeastern archaeological context. The few identifications from elsewhere are unfortunately problematic. J. Heilman's identification of a "women's house" (House II/77) at the Fort Ancient Sunwatch site is the right period, but it remains unpublished and details are lacking (J. Heilman, personal communication, 1992); furthermore, the structure in question is located within the village, which would contradict the need for spatial separation. Robson Bonnichsen (1973:281) suggested a "menstrual retreat" as one possible explanation for apparently female-occupied tent remains at a contemporary multiple-structure Cree camp, but this and the other two candidate explanations proved false when the camp owner was interviewed. Finally, Lewis Binford's halfhearted identification of a possible menstrual hut in the Hatchery West report (1970:40–41) was based solely on the fact that it was a small and anomalous structure. Why "anomalous"? Perhaps simply because menstruation is marked as "polluting" and "dangerous" in our own society's dominant male discourse, and that prejudice is transferred to other societies, including prehistoric one, without much reflection. I am suggesting, in short, that the influence of modern taboos on ethnocentric archaeologists, whether male or female, should not be ignored; just as women rarely menstruate in Western literature, so menstruation is generally ignored in considering women's lives archaeologically, as though women in all times and places similarly hid the condition of menstruation—indeed hid it so effectively that it became invisible in the archaeological record.

The symptoms of this ethnocentricity are not far to seek. Charles Hudson, in his influential normative summary of Southeastern menstrual seclusion practices in 1976, matter-of-factly drew on uniformitarian generalization when he offered the following assertion, now discounted by cross-cultural studies (Hudson's reference in this passage is to Paige's 1973 popular article, which was actually about how Western women are *socialized* to suffer during menstruation):

> The Southeastern Indians may have recognized at least implicitly some sound social and psychological principles. Psychologists have amply verified what folk knowledge tells us about menstruation, namely that women become depressed, hostile, anxious, and even socially disruptive just before and during menstruation. (Hudson 1976:320)

There is very good reason for anthropologists and archaeologists enculturated in Western societies to believe assertions like Hudson's and to experience "negative affect" associated with the very topic of menstruation, despite mounting evidence for the social origin of most of the negative behavioral correlates observed in Western societies (Martin 1992:92–138). Because Western societies practice the hiding of menstruation (as do many "primitive" societies like the Manus of New Guinea [Mead 1939:157–158]), the topic itself is treated with reticence by females, discomfited derision by males, and with pollution anxieties, in many instances, by both. Being seen in public to bleed from the vagina is still one of the most profound humiliations a Western female can experience, despite the fact that at least a majority of American women value their menstrual periods as a sign of their identity as women and of their continuing fertility (Martin 1992).

Beginning with the commodification of disposable "sanitary" supplies in 1921, advertisements for them have stressed invisibility, security of protection from staining, and suppression of menstrual odor, without once using the word "menstruation." These advertisements have frequently featured women wearing white or light-colored clothing (though white clothing is the very last thing a menstruating Western woman would choose to wear) or especially the expensive formal clothing worn on highly public (and therefore dangerously exposed) occasions. Even in the 1990s, very little has changed in terms of the language used (menstruation and blood are almost never mentioned explicitly), although much more frankness in the portrayal of the product (particularly comparative photographs of sanitary napkins, for example) is evident. The fact remains that despite all the pop-psychology discussion of premenstrual syndrome, or PMS, menstruating Western women are still not supposed to betray the fact in public and may still be subject to specific restrictions in private on grounds of religious or other belief (Martin 1992:97–98). And although most Western males do not go so far as John Milton, whose wife had to sleep on the floor while menstruating rather than pollute the marriage bed, many are reluctant to have sexual intercourse with menstruating women.

This is not a trivial issue. The whole topic of menstruation in modern Western cultures is still so avoided by women through shame, or trivialized by men through PMS jokes (even scientific ones), that our discomfort with it may blind us even to paying attention to its significance in other cultures or in subcultures within our own. Modern Miccosuki women use paper plates and plastic utensils in the tribal cafeteria during their periods, while men and nonmenstruating women use china and stainless steel (Pat Kwachka, personal communication, 1992), and the same practice is followed in conservative Creek households (Bell 1990:334). Orthodox Jewish women around the world are forbidden to prepare food while menstruating and are required to take a ritual bath at the termination of the menstrual cycle. I suggest, therefore, that discomfort with the topic and its resulting erasure from scientific discourse are the simple reasons that no one has proposed a model for the archaeological correlates of menstrual-seclusion practices.

Cultural practices that deal with areas of life that the dominant culture does not mark as shameful (and that are the domain of men and, therefore, "unmarked") can be looked at in public, and this is nowhere more graphically obvious than in the treatment of blood: we have become accustomed to gallons of blood and gore from wounds inflicted by (generally male) violence, whether on the evening news or in our entertainment, and even we as archaeologists have exhibited endless fascination with evidence for wounds on skeletal remains. Yet advertisements depicting the absorptive capabilities of "sanitary" supplies prudishly use a thin *blue* liquid for demonstration. Examples of treatment of blood from the female genital area in current entertainment media include horror films (both *Carrie* and *The Exorcist* treat the alleged enormously magnified telekinetic powers of young girls at menarche) and decidedly unusual European films (in both Ingmar Bergman's *Cries and Whispers* and the soft-porn French film *Going Places*, women mutilate their vaginas, in the first case possibly to simulate menstruation and avoid intercourse, and in the second to recover menstrual function lost during a prison sentence). In none of these films is menstruation treated as something that happens ordinarily to every woman, and in the very few television shows that have treated it so (*All in the Family, Cosby Show, I'll Fly Away*), the theme is taken up only once or twice, and blood has been notable for its invisibility.

Considerations for an Archaeological Model

The same kind of gender discrimination, I suggest, carries over into the treatment of archaeological features. Features created by male-dominated or gender-neutral activities, even if they were designed for purification from ritual pollution, do not suffer from invisibility. Indeed several instances of putative sweat lodges are reported in the Southeastern literature (for example, the Fredericks site sweat lodge reported in Ward and Davis 1988). Yet for at least half of the population, the so-called menstrual huts were equally important for ritual purification, both monthly and after childbirth. This helps make an argument for their being more than flimsy "huts."

To suggest something of the possible existential force of the taboos connected with the menstrual-seclusion practice in the prehistoric Southeast, let me offer a specific example from the early eighteenth century, in which a male adult Creek was observed to vomit the *sagamité* he had eaten before learning that it had been prepared by a menstruating woman; he then claimed to see red specks in the remaining food in the pot (Swanton 1931). His European guest thought he was overreacting, but the nineteenth- and twentieth-century Creek materials that Swanton presented and that Bell has confirmed by recent fieldwork—which indicate persistent beliefs that menstruating women should not touch men or gardens and that it was dangerous for men to smell menstruating women, to bathe downstream of them, or to walk where they had walked—indicate that this was likely normal behavior, however androcentrically interpreted. If people in Southeastern societies indeed believed that menstruating women were capable of introducing disruption and disaster at frequent and regular intervals, it was cost-effective for the societies to be serious about their precautions and to provide substantial structures for containing the danger, as other societies have done.

Because of this fear of pollution, the location where menstruating women should be secluded, according to all the testimony offered, had to be at a distance from where men carried on their ordinary activities, and ought to have been downstream from the primary village or hamlet water source (Swanton 1928a). Restrictions on contact with males and with agricultural fields dictated that historic period menstrual huts were placed on the outskirts of the villages, at what might be seen as the village/fields boundary, and the taboo was observed no matter what. In the 1750s, Chickasaw women who so isolated themselves in the face of attacks by pro-French enemies were recognized as valorous, because their action helped to preserve their husbands' virility (Bossu 1962:171). This locational practice can be compared with an example from the South Seas, the Ulithi, who placed the communal menstrual structure parallel to the shore (Paige and Paige 1981:213), thus also at the village/subsistence-source boundary.

Another issue that needs to be addressed when considering how many menstrual huts there were, and how substantial they were, is the average frequency of menstruation for late prehistoric Southeastern women. There is still great difficulty in addressing the issue of birth regulation archaeologically, but modern studies of women without access to medicalized birth control measures show that women can and do regulate birth frequency by means of extended lactation after a birth and complex socially institutionalized practices of abstention from intercourse. Although it is finally being recognized that the Western frequency of regular menstrual periods is unusual and perhaps unprecedented, it is not true that fertile non-Western women were always pregnant. Thus it is possible that if menstrual seclusion was practiced in the late prehistoric Southeast, at any given time as many as one-eighth to one-tenth of the fertile adult female population might have been so secluded. What the women did during their ritual seclusion from village life should be of interest, both because it would suggest what kind of structure was involved and because it would account for a significant expenditure of time. Pollution restrictions would have meant that there were many things menstruating women could not do (evidence for which would therefore not be found): produce household necessities like pottery or cloth, work at cultivation, perhaps take care of children, or cook for the household. With a wide range of activities barred, most of them the very activities that constituted the enormous visible economic contribution of women to Southeastern societies, what was left?

Although, most frequently, "menstrual huts" were also used for all the other activities related to female biological reproduction—including puberty rituals, childbirth, and the purification rituals following it—details of what went on inside them are noticeably missing for the colonial period Southeast as elsewhere (cf. Buckley and Gottlieb 1988b:12–13). Yet it is unlikely that fertile women spent one-fourth to one-fifth of their time while not pregnant or lactating sleeping or looking at the wall. Part of that notion may arise from the general assumption that women were alone in their huts.

There is another possibility worth considering, which is that more than one woman from the same household might be spending the same time in ritual seclusion. The tendency of women who live together or work together in close proximity to synchronize menses is now widely attested medically as well as anecdotally (see McClintock 1971 for the *locus classicus*; Knight 1988:233 lists references from recent medical literature; Knight 1991 builds an entire theory of the origins of culture on the phenomenon). Menstrual synchrony would surely have been experienced by the menstruating women, all of them related, in the extended matrilineage households postulated as the dominant residential mode in the late prehistoric Southeast. The ethnographic evidence from historic Southeastern tribes is not at all clear on how many of these huts there were at any given time, but the possibility of menstrual synchrony suggests that perhaps each lineage had its own women's house, a structure as substantial as any other.

Much has been made of the hard and unremitting work of women in the aboriginal agricultural Southeast, as opposed to the episodic hunting and defense activities of men. Although that picture is surely skewed, no one who works hard is going to mind getting up to a week off once a month, as Hudson has suggested (1976:320; cf. Martin 1992:98). But it is likely that such time would be spent doing something. Even if societies themselves articulate the male-segregated activities as "sacred" and the female-segregated activities as "polluting" (though this is usually attributable to a Western reading of the evidence), that does not mean that there are no activities at all. Instead, it would seem reasonable to suggest that a similar range of activities might take place in the structures dedicated to both and that archaeological correlates might be suggested for them. Buckley's (1988) work on Yurok menstrual practices suggests that they could be seen as directly parallel to the male purification activities aimed at the accumulation of spiritual power, and that the structures used for menstrual seclusion could be as important as men's houses.

Since male ethnographers have been invited to partake of the activities in "men's houses," we do know something of what goes on in them. Men carry out ritual activities or preparation for ritual activities, tell stories about hunting and women, sleep, and make ceremonial items, weapons or boats, or items of personal adornment. Although not restricted to the interior of the men's house by pollution restrictions, the ceremonial items are frequently restricted to use within the men's house because of secrecy requirements. And because male ethnographers are telling the tale, the talking that goes on is usually dignified as instructive for younger men or as reinforcing societal conventions (or, in case the stories go beyond societal conventions, as encouraging innovation). It is rarely trivialized as gossip.

If activities in the women's house paralleled such men's house activities, certainly women must have spent time resting as men did; certainly they also spent time talking and telling stories that could be similarly dignified as instruments of societal regulation. Other social activities, such as gambling, are documented ethnographically (Underhill 1936). We know they ate, because there is evidence that they had to use special vessels that could not be used elsewhere; indeed the Beng women of the Ivory Coast prepare a particularly prized and delectable dish only when menstruating (Gottlieb 1988:71–72). Because they did bleed, they may have had bloodstained breechcloths or other absorbent materials to dispose of by burning or burial. Is there any reason why it would have been unlikely that they participated in ritual activities? Certainly the sun worship that dominated Southeastern ritual practice is connected with fertility, and women in their period of ritual seclusion would at a minimum be concerned with the continuing fertility that their very seclusion proclaimed.

At this point I take a side trip into Southeastern myth to emphasize the connections between women, blood, and fertility by retelling the common story from the region of the origin of corn, with its overtones of the dominance of hunting-gathering by agriculture. In this tale there is a family consisting of a father, Hunter; a mother, Corn; and two boys, one a son of Hunter and Corn and one an adopted son who had been made from discarded deer's blood. After the boys had in mischief released game animals from the secret place where their father kept them, thereby making them scarce and hard to find, they became interested in how it was that their mother was able to provide corn and beans for them to eat instead. One day they spied on her activities within the storehouse and discovered that the corn and beans came from her body. Thinking her a witch, they decided to kill her. Seeing them refuse the food she offered, which they now considered polluted, she guessed their plan and instructed them on how they should do it: clear a large piece of ground and drag her dead body over it seven times. The boys killed her after having cleared only small patches of ground and then dragged her body over it only twice. As a result, corn sprang up only where her blood touched the cultivated earth, and it would make only two crops per year ever after (paraphrased from the Cherokee version as presented in Lankford 1987:148–151; cf. Bell 1990:335 for the relevance of this myth to Creek social reproduction).

This is as clear a connection as could be desired between female fertility, of which blood is the sign, and agricultural fertility, of which female blood is the cause. I would suggest that it may even include a mythical explanation of the origin of menstrual seclusion in the Southeast. I take the liberty of imagining that this connection would have been celebrated and ritualized somehow and, further, that it must have been part of at least some rites connected with the "women's house." It seems to me that the widespread attestation of the existence of "women's languages" in the Southeast (cf. Bell 1990:341 n. 1), correlated as it is with the practice of menstrual seclusion from the community, may also argue for the existence of a "women's house" institution with ritual characteristics that has simply been missed in the ethnohistorical literature for the reasons suggested above.

What might this possibility of ritual activity mean for archaeological correlates? We have had a hard time trying to decide how to identify other structures connected with Southeastern ritual; temple structures are known not only by their division into multiple rooms and the presence of a hearth, but almost indispensably by location on a mound. Clearly a "women's house" would be distinguished by the locational considerations I have discussed, and structurally it would require a hearth, because women would be staying there for several days, but little else of a structural nature can be suggested.

The story would, however, be different with reference to artifacts. If ritual artifacts such as statuettes or pipes or everyday items like pottery vessels, which might have been specially decorated to ensure their recognition and avoidance by others, were used inside the women's house, pollution restrictions would keep them there, where they would likely be found.

Archaeological Implications

What we have to look for, therefore, would be much like any other Mississippian house of wattle and daub or thatch. It would be spatially distinguished because it would be at whatever distance from living areas and field or forest that ritual purity demanded. The pattern of its location might select for nearness to running water because of its requirement for ritual cleansing. It would be downstream from the village or hamlet. If the disposal of soiled garments or pads had to be provided for by burning or burial—as we know was the case with the placenta—evidence of such disposal would be found within the house or nearby. Furthermore, if we reconceive the "menstrual hut" as a "women's house," then the complex of artifactual evidence would be much expanded to include ritual elements—structures, artifacts—and more of the long-term requirements of daily life. The presence of artifacts symbolically associated with females, fertility, and agriculture would fit this scenario, as would a distinctive ceramic assemblage with limited distribution. Both sorts of evidence are habitually assigned to (male) ritual contexts, as at the BBB Motor site (Emerson 1989; Pauketat and Emerson 1991) and the Sponemann site (Jackson et al. 1992) in the America Bottom, but in light of this discussion it might be worth reevaluating the evidence to see if another explanation might deal equally parsimoniously with the evidence.

I am suggesting, of course, that the red bauxite Birger and Keller figurines at the BBB Motor site, portraying kneeling women occupied in agricultural pursuits, and the similar Sponemann, Willoughby, and West figurines from Sponemann may be a clue that there is another possible in-terpretation not only for the "temple" complexes on both sites but for Ramey ceramics as well. Emerson's (1989:65) interpretation of Ramey mo-tifs as "involving fertility and life forces" could hardly be more apposite to such an interpretation. Pauketat and Emerson interpret the symbolism of the Ramey jar, seen from above, as the cosmos (the decorative field) sur-rounding an orifice symbolizing the Underworld, such that the contents of the jar were seen as "associated with feminine life forces—earth, fertility, Under World—or female activities (e.g., agriculture, food preparation)" (Pauketat and Emerson 1991:933) But why not then see the orifice as the vaginal opening, and the contents of the pots (perhaps that dangerous red-flecked *sagamité?*) as coming from the body of the Corn Mother? Cer-tainly pottery with "broad, simple designs . . . highly visible at a distance" (Pauketat and Emerson 1991:922) would be easily avoidable; designs "meant for a special purpose rather than simply being decorations for the elite" (Emerson 1989:63) could be meant to warn of pollution. The care taken in the execution of Ramey pottery, which Emerson (1989:66–67) argues was by "potters who were associated with each specific lineage/ community ritual group," would be appropriate to a ware made by women not burdened by daily tasks (note that there is enough variation in Ramey ceramics that highly restricted specialist production is not suggested), and its relative scarcity fits well with a ware used for periodic seclusion. Such a "'utilitarian' ritual ware" (Emerson 1989:65) might well be included in mortuary offerings (especially for childbirth deaths), would appear in mid-den and garbage deposits, and would be distributed through all levels of the social hierarchy (since all women menstruate and most give birth).

It is worth noting that the BBB Motor site also exhibited other finds that could be reinterpreted in the direction of women's house practices: systematically reexcavated pit features; red ocher pigment and a large quartz crystal with a dramatic red impurity (which Emerson compares to a Cherokee story of a man who regularly fed such a crystal with blood!); and *Datura stramonium*, which could have been used for abortion or dif-ficult childbirths. Finally, the site was separated from the surrounding land by water and marshes during the period of its use. None of this evidence is conclusive, but I suggest that it is worth a thorough reevaluation, especially the sexing of the burials.

The occurrence of figurines similar to those at BBB Motor made a "ceremonial" interpretation inevitable for the Sponemann "Ceremonial Complex" of architectural and pit remains, which includes a "temple" and an adjoining structure interpreted as the temple-keeper's lodging. Because the figurines were evidently intentionally "killed" by being broken into fragments, and because the spread of those fragments coincides closely with the burned "temple," Fortier argues that the figurines had been broken outside the structure and most of the fragments placed within it before its intentional destruction by fire. This destruction supposedly marked a final "purification" step in an episode of "busk" ceremonialism focused on this "household temple" structure, which Fortier identifies by analogy with temples described by Du Pratz for the Natchez (Jackson et al. 1992: 52–70).

Again, however, it would seem that an alternative interpretation connected with women's house ceremonialism and especially purification practices might be appropriate, at least for the "Ceremonial Complex" portion of the site. Fortier suggests that the destruction of the figurines and the "temple" building was part of a ritual act terminating a "year-end busk celebration" and representing "a symbolic act of regeneration and perhaps purification of the sacred busk complex." Further, he suggests that the "sanctity of this act and the busk ground itself" is signified by the fact that the site was not reoccupied after the destruction episode (Jackson et al. 1992:303). Yet if the "temple" and adjoining "lodging" were interpreted as a women's house complex accommodating menstrual-seclusion facilities and fertility ceremonialism, it would seem that abandonment might be as much the product of notions of pollution as of sacredness, and the apparently inauspicious location of the site in a low clayey swale (Jackson et al. 1992:49) would then suggest that it was chosen because of its proximity to water needed for purification.

In both the "ceremonial" and "residential" precincts of the Sponemann site small quantities of Ramey ceramics were found, although the concentration of small sherds in pits, especially in the "ceremonial" precinct, gave Fortier grounds for the suggestion that they were part of assemblages that represented the sweeping out of structures as another part of a "purification" practice. Certainly this kind of distribution for Ramey ceramics—whether associated with menstrual practices or not—helpfully raises the question of whether a possible distinctive "menstrual ware" might not also appear in an ordinary domestic setting, where vessels might be stored or used to obtain cooked foods destined for women in menstrual seclusion. This last surmise shows that finding evidence of distinctive women's houses will not be uncomplicated, but it will not be done at all unless we ask the questions.

There is no way we are going to understand late prehistoric Southeastern cultures until we come to grips with the basic issues of kinship organization and the role of women. Nor can we completely ignore a substantial portion of Southeastern women's lives, particularly one so strikingly connected with the central arcana of Mississippian ceremonialism. Ethnohistorical evidence can only take us so far back; after that, archaeology must serve as time machine. Here, however, ethnographic analogy gives us an actual structure to look for, and it is time we stopped being too ethnocentric to do so.

Acknowledgments

I am indebted to Cheryl Claassen for inviting me to reprise and polish this essay, which was first presented in a less developed form at the 1990 Southeastern Archaeological Conference meeting in Jackson, Mississippi. Since that presentation, I have received many helpful suggestions from colleagues and friends, including Amy Bushnell, Penelope Drooker, James Heilman, Bonnie McEwan, Charles McNutt, LeAnne Howe, Pat Kwachka, Mary Powell, John Scarry, and Bruce Smith. It is interesting to note that whereas female colleagues took this essay seriously from the outset, some male colleagues initially behaved as though they considered it a joke. I am happy to say that they no longer seem to do so.

PART II

Prehistoric Women as Social Agents

5. Changing Venue: Women's Lives in Prehistoric North America
Cheryl Claassen

The attribution of gender to past site and regional culture histories has been a characteristic of American archaeology since its beginnings over a century ago. Some of the earliest New Archaeologists (Deetz 1965; Hill 1966; Longacre 1964) used sex roles and gender relationships in marriage patterns, residence, and pottery production to showcase their revisionist ideas. This century-long interest in social organization at its simplest level has, however, gone undeveloped until quite recently. Building on a century of consensus about what activities and artifacts were women's, archaeologists since 1980 have found evidence for changes in women's and men's labor and gender organization, as well as evidence for gendered sites and settlement patterns. These archaeologists, who place social relations at the forefront of investigations, identify the relationships between women and men and between women as the ones most likely to reveal new insights into technological and social change and a more people centered reconstruction of the past. I review this literature to see what themes are emerging and what methods and theoretical positions are being favored, and to stimulate yet more such studies. The gendered literature produced since 1987 about pre-contact North American societies has radical implications for methodology and historical reconstruction.

In this chapter I will present much of the gendered literature that has been written in the past decade, adding some observations of my own by culture area. Topics that cross-cut culture areas identified in this review are division of labor, gendered uses of space, productivity, female-directed violence, and health. I know of only one other attempt to review the literature on bioarchaeological issues (Cohen 1987). The repetitive themes of division of labor, sex role formation, and women's agency are further developed in the discussion section. Left to the conclusion are comments on methodological preferences for engendering prehistoric data and potential pitfalls in this work, as well as the strengths evident so far. This review of literature and problems shows how engendering research can revive old problems and direct attention toward new problems. It also evidences, in some cases, radical departures from typical archaeological concerns, regional cultural reconstructions, and perceptions of methodological utility.

Regional Studies of Women's Work: A Research Survey

To present the gendered literature about pre-contact North America and several of my own thoughts, I have applied the culture-area concept. In some cases the authors have situated their studies within a regional framework, while in other cases authors make few connections to regional problems, addressing, instead, stereotyped past behavior or archaeological methodology. Several themes repeat themselves in different regions—division of labor, gendered use of space, productivity, violence, health—further suggesting that culture-area boundaries are an artificial organizing tool. I have persevered in using this presentation method because archaeological training is very much directed at regions. I anticipate that those scholars unfamiliar with the products of a gendered archaeology will turn to the record of work in their own area of regional specialization first. Topical discussions can be found in the discussion and conclusion sections below. This review is by no means exhaustive of all the assumptions and attributions about and to females, women, males, and men made over the past century by archaeologists.

NORTHEAST/MID-ATLANTIC

Not surprisingly, most of the essays addressing prehistoric data in this region have done so with Iroquoian sites, the Iroquois being the quintessential matrilocal society. Susan Prezzano (this volume) argues that women's activities in subsistence and household organization should reflect the process of Iroquoian tribalization, yet villages and households have rarely been the focus for modeling this social change. The activities of Iroquois women and captives were found to center in villages and in a sizable area around the villages (Perrelli 1994).

Several studies of design styles, sherd clustering, and marriage patterns conducted elsewhere in North America (Deetz 1965; Hill 1966; Longacre 1964) attracted the attention of Iroquoian specialists. These studies assumed that once a girl learned the art of pottery from her female kin, she would always duplicate the family style. If pottery styles showed little variation within a site, then women must have spent their entire pottery-producing lives in that community, and husbands must have married in. Mary Ann Niemczycki (1980) says, however, that marriage patterns are too much to expect from Iroquoian ceramics. Martha Latta (1991) considers formation processes operating on pottery and challenges the-strange-pot-equals-a-captured-bride assumption. She argues that pottery specialists emerged in the contact period. Furthermore, the focus of display changed from pottery decoration to personal adornment, argues Aubrey Cannon (1991). Laura Finsten and Peter Ramsden (1989) believe that the meaning incorporated in Iroquoian pottery design was not as simple as "where I learned to make pots" but also reflects women's political lives in Iroquoian society. Kathleen Allen (1990) thinks that both pots and projectile points are encoded with the gender system and may reinforce gender identification and differences.

Exploration of women's productivity and division of labor has been made elsewhere as well. Three females and one child were found buried at the Woodland Island Field cemetery site in Delaware with complete flint knapping kits, cores, and debitage. One male was buried with three flint knapping tools (Custer et al. 1990). The authors interpreted the grave goods to indicate that women did much of the flint knapping in their communities. Three female two-spirits is unlikely in a population of 135 bodies.

Two sites in the eastern United States have been interpreted as women's camps. The Mulcaster Island East site, a middle Point Peninsula to late Owasco age site in the St. Lawrence River, contained many sherds and practically no lithics.

> With the possible association of the ground and rough stone artifacts with a pigment production activity, and . . . pigment generally believed to have been associated with acts of spiritualism and ritualism, could this site have been reserved for such truly female-specific and ceremonially important functions and mysteries as menstruation or birth? (D'Annibale and Ross 1994:15)

Cara Blume (1990) interpreted the Woodland period Acorn site in Delaware as a women's nutting station. Cached pairs of cobbles used in nut processing and the large quantity of pottery overshadowed the paltry amount of chipped stone recovered.

The Atlantic coastal landscape is crowded with "women's" activity loci, evidence of gendered uses of space, in the form of shell matrix sites. Kelli Costa (1994) points out that women in coastal settings contributed large quantities of animal protein, and their potential contribution of protein gave them "a generous hand in the decision making of where groups camped, collected, and returned to" (1994:8). She interprets Sweet Meadow Brook site on Greenwich Bay as having evolved into a women's place. Hearth features decreased over time, and refuse pits increased substantially as the site became a shellfish processing station.

Mary Beth Williams and Jeffrey Bendremer (this volume) also assert that women's foraging activities determined the timing and frequency of residential moves. They attribute the increasing sedentism along the New England coast in the Late Woodland and contact period not to the adoption of maize but to an increased focus by women on shellfishing for food, trade of meats, and wampum production.

The ceramic wares and lithic assemblage of the Wheeler's site, a shell matrix Woodland period site in New Hampshire, suggested to Russel Barber (1982) gendered differences in technological influences, specifically the geographical origin of influences. "The lithic assemblage from the Wheeler's site has strong ties southward, while the ceramic assemblage's strongest ties appear to lie to the north. . . . Was some difference between men's culture and women's culture that affected opportunity to receive or inclination to adopt outside ideas reflected in artifacts?" asks Barber (1982: 48). Do changes in site use from encampments to special activity areas reflect a change in the location of women's productive work, an increase in the proportion of women's contribution to their communities, a new type of contribution, or just a new setting for traditional work? Have all women's work loads increased with the addition of the late prehistoric tasks of shellfishing, ornament manufacture, and trade in meats? What other types of sites are candidates for special activity loci of different genders?

SOUTHEAST

Women's work roles probably intensified with the demise of the Pleistocene megafauna, which probably had been pursued by groups of people who shared equipment. Adaptation to the smaller Holocene game and to more intensive use of flora resulted in fissioning of groups into much smaller units, each needing its own equipment, thus accounting for the striking increase in food-processing equipment in the Archaic. Women's work in producing and maintaining equipment and in collecting and processing more flora and small game increased on an individual basis as well as proportionally within their societies (Claassen 1996).

Archaic shell mound sites such as Indian Knoll, Eva, and Stallings Island were created and abandoned for reasons having to do with symbolism. Burials indicate that some women were probably shamans, and it was they who would have stimulated the change in burial symbolism away from shells and toward the symbolism associated with cultivars (Claassen 1991a). Ken Sassaman (1993) has reasoned that shell ring and shell mound construction on the Savannah River and adjacent coast line "required material provisioning that put demands on individual labor," which stimulated technological change, specifically the adoption of direct-heat cooking in ceramic containers. Assuming that women had leadership roles in the rituals at the rings and mounds and in their communities, "then women would probably be the first to develop new technology (pottery) and to accelerate the adoption of innovations that enhanced their social position" (Sassaman 1993:217).

Sassaman thinks the spread of ceramic technology away from the coast some 2000 years after its adoption there was impeded by gender tensions. In the Stallings Island area upriver on the Savannah, the heart of the soapstone export area, men invested in the soapstone trade, and deriving status from that activity blocked the adoption of a cooking method that circumvented soapstone slab cooking. Only when the soapstone trade dissolved did ceramic vessel direct-heat cooking spread beyond the Savannah River valley (Sassaman 1993).

In the Savannah River and the Mid-South, the female shamans would have been a potent voice not only for technological change but also for subsistence change, specifically the move to cultivation. Patty Jo Watson and Mary Kennedy (1991) assert that women were the ones causing the genetic changes in the target plants, and women were the ones causing the habitat changes. They extend this point to the development of Maíz de Ocho in the Northeast, which was farmed beginning 1,200 years ago. Women must have consciously developed Maíz de Ocho from Chapalote maize, conducting breeding experiments, observing the progeny, selecting seed stock; in short, consciously manipulating the gene pool of Chapalote maize.

Patricia Bridges (1989) examined the Shell Mound Archaic (hunter-gatherers) and Mississippian (agriculturists) populations from the Perry site on the Tennessee River in north Alabama to compare data on habitual activities in the two populations. Mississippian males had greater changes in legs and more asymmetry in their arms; females increased their strength in arms and legs. The use of mortar and pestle is the activity most obviously implicated for Mississippian women, while the use of the bow is evident in Mississippian men, apparently reflecting a sexed division of labor for grinding and shooting activities.

The introduction of maize agriculture seems to have brought little difference to the type of work men did, but as indicated by strength increases in both the arms and legs of females, it seems to have greatly changed the type of work women did (Bridges 1989:392). A study on the Georgia coast revealed decreases in strength for males and females in the agricultural group (Larsen 1984), indicating that gathering activities in a coastal setting may have been more strenuous than agricultural activities. An increase in osteophytosis of the cervical vertebrae in females of the maize-using groups probably indicates another aspect of a sexed or gendered division of labor, the use of the tumpline by females to haul heavy loads. The incidence of osteoarthritis increased in agricultural women but remained unchanged in men, as did the incidence of osteophytosis (Larsen 1984).

Two times more women than men were found in the Mississippian period Power's Phase Turner site cemetery. In the lower Illinois Valley, all Mississippian village cemeteries had more females. Females buried at the edge of the Moundville ceremonial center outnumber males (100 females / 77 males) (Powell 1986). That women were disproportionately buried in villages suggests that men were disproportionately buried in ceremonial centers and in mounds.

It is evident from skeletal information that women's and men's life experiences differed according to social status. In the Turner site population, diets differed significantly along sex lines, with some females actually eating different and high-quality protein foods (Wilson, this volume). The skeletons of elite men and women were larger than those of non-elites at Moundville, as they were at Middle Woodland lower Illinois Valley sites, Dallas Phase sites, and the late Mississippian Chucalissa site (Powell 1986).

More males than females, and more elite males than non-elites at Moundville, had broken bones. Broken ribs were found among 9.4 percent of the males and 1.3 percent of the females, and 4 percent of the males and 2.1 percent of the females have broken hands. Elite females have no broken bones, suggesting they led a very sheltered life (Powell 1986). Evidence for female-directed violence—depression fractures on skulls, broken facial bones, broken arms—is lacking in the Southeast (Smith 1996).

A Caddoan population examined for osteoarthritis evidences more males than females with problems. An exception to this observation is in the back vertebrae and neck, where stress is most evident in females, typical evidence of agricultural activities and carrying loads upon their heads. Stress from paddling is greatest in males but not absent in females, while evidence of wood cutting occurs only in males, and evidence of grinding is frequent in females (Wilson 1994).

Mississippian symbolism and iconography are rich areas for gender work but have only recently been tapped. Penelope Drooker (1994) examined the possible gendered meanings in Ft. Ancient ceramics, and Lyle Koehler (this volume) has found abundant images of women in Mississippian portable art, rock art, and early ethnohistoric accounts. Catherine Brown (1982) was the first to startle archaeologists with the revelation that women "warriors" were depicted on many of the shell gorgets. These women hold symbols of high rank and occasionally trophy heads. A protuberance on the chest of many of the gorget persons has been ignored or explained as "male mammaries." They may be women warriors, goddesses, or mythological characters.

The Middle Archaic to Late Archaic transition saw many groups adopt a logistical residential pattern. What changes did the move from collector to forager generate in women's material culture, landscape knowledge, fertility, birthrate, or activity loci (or in men's)? Was life more strenuous on the coast than it was on the larger rivers in the region? What other technological innovations might women be credited with besides pottery and plant breeds? How were changing work loads accommodated by women and men? What were the social relationships that facilitated the spread of pottery from the Savannah River across the eastern United States? Is burial of women in the village and of men in the ceremonial center to be equated with status differences?

MIDWEST

In the Midwest, bioarchaeological studies have provided greater detail on differences in men's and women's activities and health through time. In Ohio, the Hopewellian Middle Woodland lifestyle was more physically demanding, and sexual dimorphism was the most pronounced of all populations studied. In a review of life during the Late Woodland/Mississippian period in the lower Illinois Valley, Jane Buikstra et al. (1986:531) write, "It is clear that female work-related pathology changed significantly (Pickering 1984) in a way that would be consistent with a model of increased labor for women with the acquisition of maize agriculture," particularly in food preparation and food transport. There is evidence for female-directed aggression in some Michigan skeletons (Smith 1996).

Individual consumption of maize varied widely in the Late Woodland and Emergent Mississippian periods, with sex differences in isotopic values noted in populations in West Virginia, Ohio, and Illinois (van der Merwe and Vogel 1978). Hamilton (cited in Buikstra et al. 1986), looking at the deltoid tuberosity of the humerus, found an increased size of female upper arms relative to Mississippian males, which she suggested was due to a change in food-preparation techniques. Several lines of evidence, including vessel-wall thickness and caries, converge to suggest that the larger population evident in Middle Woodland times and later is due to increased reliance on local seeds for weaning foods, which shortened the nursing period and thus eliminated an effective contraceptive (Buikstra et al. 1986).

Changes in food processing are evident also in pottery construction in the central Mississippi River valley of Illinois and Missouri, 2200 to 1250 ya (Braun 1987). Starchy native seeds of chenopodium, maygrass, and sunflower were consumed raw or parched in the Early Woodland (Braun 1983) and thus would have yielded only part of their nutritional value. Beginning in the Middle Woodland period a reduction of pottery vessel-wall thickness made it possible to boil water rapidly and brought about the use of gruels, mashes, and broths. Increased incidence of caries in infants at this time probably means that women were making use of this soft food for supplementing and weaning infants (Cook and Buikstra 1979). It is also noteworthy that Hopewell funerary-vessel technology, which was quite distinct from that evident in domestic vessels, ceases to be distinctive ca. 1800 ya. This change suggested to Braun (1985) greater interaction and cooperation among groups and a rising importance in domestic orientation. Pottery styles show less variety across space, as if economic and social ties between neighboring communities became increasingly long-term (Braun 1983, 1985, 1987).

The intensified use of domesticates during the latter half of the Woodland period did not put an end to nut harvesting and processing. Several sites suggest activity areas within them where women processed acorns, hickory nuts, and other species. The Locust site (Seeman 1985) in central Ohio and the McLean site (McElrath 1986) in the American Bottom are two such sites with nut-processing areas as well as cached tools and areas indicating men's activities.

Patricia Galloway (this volume) remarks that at any given time, up to

one-tenth of the women in an Indian community might have been se-
cluded in menstrual huts recorded for several historic Indian cultures.
However, no such structures have been identified at archaeological sites.
She suggests that the figurines at the famous BBB Motor site in Illinois, its
Ramey pottery, and numerous other aspects of that site mark it as a seclu-
sion site.

Large numbers of vulva symbols are found as rock art in the St. Louis
area (Diaz-Granados and Duncan 1995). These symbols are often combined with others that strongly suggest the Corn Mother image. At the
very least, this distribution of Corn Mother symbols demarcates a particular spiritual landscape for the prehistoric group that pecked them. Might
they also be initiation sites for girls?

What specific types of interactions between women are envisioned or
implicated by these observations about pottery, production, and community relations? What do the changes in household architecture mean for
space use, demography, and gender relations? What were the diet and activities of Early Woodland peoples?

PLAINS

Philip Duke (1991) points out that gender relationships have been treated
as unimportant in hunter-gatherer societies because it is thought that these
people were constantly coping with environmental challenges. Four pre-
contact period sites and the Pecos River region have been the focus of gendered examinations, and each explores the relationship between gender
and the use of space: Horse Creek, Wyoming, a fifth-millennium site
(Guenther 1991); Mini-Moon, 2,300 to 1,200 years old, in eastern Montana
(Hughes 1991); C. C. DeWitt Lodge and burial mound in Kansas of 700
years ago (O'Brien 1991); and Aschkibokahn, a Late Prehistoric site in
west-central Manitoba (Hanna 1989). The cumulative insights from these
studies, all of which assume that historic sex roles were present in the past,
challenge the notion that gender was unimportant in Plains societies, while
implicitly recognizing the importance of the environment in structuring
daily life. Pre-contact Plains groups were dependent on plant products, and
plant seasonality required that the human predators be in certain places at
specific times. Todd Guenther (1991:18) makes the radical comment that
"both seasonal round and choice of site location . . . must often have resulted from the influence of women and their needs."

Gendered space use within camps is unveiled at Horse Creek and
Mini-Moon sites. At the Mini-Moon site, Susan Hughes (1991) interpreted

piles of fire-cracked rock around a large hearth in association with a pile of highly fragmented burned bone as the locality for grease rendering by women, while another hearth with lithic-tool manufacturing debris, and more specialized tools than flakes, was interpreted as a men's work area. Several hearths at Horse Creek were lacking in number and variety of artifacts, suggesting that they were used exclusively for plant processing (Guenther 1991).

Although the Paleo-Indian Agate Basin site in Wyoming is believed by George Frison (1991:158–159) to be a bison-procurement location, the presence of two probable living structures (one with a well-defined hearth), grinding stones, 20,000 flakes, bone needles, and cut and incised rib sections indicates that this site is better viewed as a base camp with women and children present (Hudecek-Cuffe 1994).

Historically observed gendered space within a Pawnee lodge is shown by Patricia O'Brien (1991) to be at least seven hundred years old. She suggests that at least four women and one man were occupants. Drawing upon historic Skidi Pawnee gendered ritual and symbolism, O'Brien argues for the division of the lodge into north and south sectors, each with its own metate, presided over by one mature woman each. She interprets a cluster of new endscrapers, a woman's tool, found against the west wall, the direction of the feminine aspect of Evening Star, to indicate at least one young woman resident. Three storage pits on the lodge floor in the north, center, and south would be associated with young, old, and mature women, respectively. A pit just inside the door apparently contained a medicine bundle, and arrow-making equipment was found near the east wall, the direction of the male aspect, indicating that a male priest lived in the lodge.

Plant-extraction locales and game-processing locales were identified by intensive surface survey of the Hinds Ranch and Blue Hills areas of the Pecos River valley (Saunders 1986). Joe Saunders found chert cores and many unifacial tools at a large number of uniface lithic clusters, which had little in common with lithic clusters containing projectile points. His interpretation of these Archaic period data is that the uniface clusters were the scene of women's sotal and agave collecting and flake-tool production, while the projectile point lithic clusters, often higher in elevation, were the locales of men's activities. The plant processing locales are closer to the numerous occupied caves and rockshelters along the Pecos River. An increase in unifaces in later levels of Hind's Cave is viewed by Saunders as evidence of women returning plants to the cave for processing rather than doing field processing.

Patricia Bass (1991) has engendered the rock art in the Pecos River valley of Texas. The significance or meaning of rock art images has rarely been situated in a gender system. Finding design elements used by contemporary regional Indians to have female and male specificity, Bass interpreted similar ancient designs in rock art to mean that girls and boys marked rocks with their gender sign as well as with depictions of their visions during vision quests.

The association of Plains activities with men is so strong that evidence of women's activities is often overlooked, as a recent reinterpretation of the Agate Basin site by Caroline Hudecek-Cuffe (1994) has shown. What other site interpretations need revision? Where else is there evidence of gendered use of interior space? Plains communities participated in trade fairs—what items were produced by women for these fairs? Is there evidence for groupings of women in the camps associated with the fairs? Do the osteological data support the extremely heavy work loads for women reported in the historic documents? How have women's work loads changed over time in Plains communities? Does the female-directed violence recorded in historic times (Shermis 1982–1984) extend into the past?

CALIFORNIA AND GREAT BASIN

The Early, Middle, and Late periods of the pre-contact Central Valley archaeological record show decreasing dietary breadth over time, resulting in a late focus on acorns and salmon. The Early period is viewed by some as a period of heavy meat consumption and little ingestion of plants—or extensive provisioning by men, and little by women. Carbohydrate-rich acorns—gathered and processed by women—were adopted during the Middle period. Dickel et al. (1984) found little increase in caries over time, leading them to conclude that carbohydrate sources must have been important during the Early period as well as later. A positive-feedback system was established between acorns and population growth, which began with harvesting, processing, and especially storage of acorns, necessitating increased sedentism. Doran (cited in Dickel et al. 1984) speculated that birth spacing decreased as the population grew, but that mortality of children 0–2 years old increased, probably due to increased maternal deaths.

The transition from portable grinding equipment to fixed bedrock mortars is a major time marker in California prehistory. The adoption of bedrock mortars structured intra- and intersite space use in the upper San Joaquin Valley and resulted in a new kind of female activity area. In large winter villages the bedrock mortars were peripheralized, while in small summer camps the mortars were centralized. Men were largely absent from these small camps, which can be typified as women's sites (Jackson 1991).

On the southern coast of California, Sandra Hollimon (1991) examined Chumash men's and women's skeletons from three different time periods for evidence of nutrition, injury, and disease. Early period (5500 to 3200 ya) men had greater access to protein, but women and men had roughly equal rates of arthritis, infectious disease, and traumatic injuries. Middle period (3200 to 850 ya) women had fewer traumatic injuries than men and had less severe infectious diseases. The situation was quite different for Late period (850 to 200 ya) women. They had slightly higher rates of infectious diseases, more trauma, and more hypoplastic defects in their teeth. Women were nutritionally compromised, based on dental data, apparently beginning in childhood.

A gendered inquiry is long overdue for the weaving technology so richly illustrated in historic California cultures as well as in Great Basin cultures. Why were ceramics adopted so late in the western Great Basin and interior (1000 ya)? What impact on women's lives did the adoption of pottery and agriculture have? Why did the women and families of the Middle period want more children, given that women had techniques for preventing pregnancy, ending pregnancy, and killing infants?

NORTHWEST COAST AND PLATEAU

In her 1993 paper on Tlingit culture Madonna Moss concludes that both in the pre-contact and contact eras, proportionately more women than men consumed shellfish, and more women and men of lower rank consumed shellfish. In this case, shell matrix deposits not only correlate to a specific gender but to a specific class. Slaves, in particular, consumed shellfish. Men occasionally collected shellfish and possessed an intricate knowledge of their ecology. It does seem that shellfish played a greater role in late pre-contact Northwest Coast societies than they did during the historic period. A little-developed idea is that some molluscan species were "semi-cultivated" in one way or another (citations in Moss 1993), indicating that women effectively manipulated animal populations in ways that enhanced desirable characteristics.

The keeping of white dogs by Salish women is yet another instance of women manipulating animal populations. The use of the loom by Salish women is a curiosity to ethnohistorians and was unknown to neighboring groups. These two subjects are ripe for gendered investigation. Why and how did Salish women come to adopt these activities? Why didn't women in neighboring groups also adopt them? The Plateau Windust phase (10,000–8000 ya) is a period of greatly increased riverine shellfishing, characteristically women's work. What impact did the addition of shellfishing have on women's work loads and schedules? Why did they adopt intensive shellfishing at this time, and why did they abandon intensive shellfishing at the close of the phase?

SOUTHWEST

Little gendered work has been undertaken with the Southwestern archaeological record despite the wealth of potential topics. Eight articles have intentionally sought to understand women's contribution to the prehistoric record (Brock 1985; Crown and Wills 1995; Hays-Gilpin 1991, 1994; Martin and Akins 1994; Simon and Ravesloot 1995; Spielmann 1995; Szuter 1989).

Christine Szuter (1989) redefines hunting as pursuit and capture of wild animals regardless of size or capture technique. In her data from south-central Arizona (136 sites) Szuter found a heavy reliance on rabbits, rodents, and small and medium-sized animals and concluded that females and children in these horticultural societies contributed substantial animal and fat protein to the family diet by their hunting and trapping activities.

Violence against women has been documented in the Anasazi of the La Plata River valley in northwestern New Mexico, particularly in the frequencies of head injuries. Furthermore, females were five times more likely to show evidence of infection and had a shorter life expectancy. No female with head injuries had associated grave goods or was found in the usual flexed position. These battered women may have been captives (Martin and Akins 1994).

Designs on portable objects, in rock art, and female figurines in northeastern Arizona are the focus of studies by Kelley Hays-Gilpin. The designs found on the portable household items and in the rock art constitute discrete sets until eight hundred years ago. Within Broken Flute Cave the pithouses are confined to the western half of the cave, the kiva and rock art to the eastern half. Design differences and spatial segregation of activities are probably related to organizational scale and gender differentiation. Gender attribution was becoming important in this Anasazi community during the seventh century, she reasons (Hays-Gilpin 1991, 1994), as was matrilocal residence. Female figurines (denoted by aprons, breasts [neither found in rock art] and sometimes by a cleft crotch) were found in pits in the cave and are representational in style. They have been interpreted as part of a fertility cult or as socialization dolls.

Men in seventh-century Anasazi society "may have devised communal rituals partly as a means to integrate men from different natal communities into the community of their spouses. . . . They may also have asserted their importance against the increasingly formalised economic contributions of women" (Hays-Gilpin 1994:9). Gender conflicts were probably constantly being renegotiated in the past, Hays-Gilpin suggests.

Figurines were common in Tularosa Cave, and in the Fremont, Anasazi, and Hohokam cultures. Hohokam had baked-clay female figurines, vaguely Mexican in their style, which have been referred to as a figurine cult. Ann Guillén makes the point that "the role of women as highly visible actors in the dynamics of social-hierarchy formation and accentuation is also obscured by 'cult' explanations" (1993:215). We need studies of these figurines like that by Richard Lesure (this volume) or Guillén (1993), who thinks she has identified individual real women.

The early agricultural caves—Bat, Cordova, Tularosa—are filled with organic debris. Wirt Wills (1988) thinks these caves were base camps for families and winter corn-storage facilities to provision lone winter-spring hunters. But the contents of the caves are strongly suggestive of women's activities, not men's: grinding stones and manos; abundant unifacial flakes; basketry, cordage, sandals; wooden tools, whole and in large numbers; rabbit snares and artiodactyl bones. Women may have hunted the antelope as men did (Brumbach and Jarvenpa this volume). Nothing here is incompatible with these caves being women's special-activity areas, and with the bulk of the debris and tools being produced by women. Did Wills consider the evidence of women to require the presence of men when he labeled these caves base camps? The male and female artifacts are found together in the archaeological record, but I suspect seasonally sex-segregated activities might have taken place in these caves.

Mangelsdorf (in Wills 1988:126) considered the earliest Southwestern maize to have been part of a casual field-cultivation and evolution of maize, facilitated without any deliberate intervention by humans other than weeding. Such a scenario of unintended consequences calls forth Patty Jo Watson's and Mary Kennedy's (1991) critique of the "natural" development of domestic plants in the eastern United States. Following their lead, one can ask of Southwestern and Fremont agriculture several questions that seek out the intentionality of breeding experiments by the women cultivators such as those that resulted in Chapalote maize.

When, where, and why did women breed Chapalote maize? Jesse Jennings (1989:291) asks how a food-producing culture operates where agriculture is not possible, and answers that it rested on the creation of tiny terraces. Who developed these terraces? Jennings and Wills eschew agency, but Watson and Kennedy would attribute agency and innovation to women.

Wills (1988) thinks that domesticates were adopted in the Southwest to allow male hunters to remain effective foragers. Would a supply of stored food not have benefited both foraging men in winter as well as foraging women seeking spring–early summer foods?

Ceramic figurines were made in the Southwest eight hundred years before ceramic containers were (Crown and Wills 1995). How did Southwestern women learn ceramic arts? What aspects of women's lives worked to delay and accelerate pottery adoption and production (see Crown and Wills 1995)? The first pottery, Alma Plain, was a brown ware of good quality made for eight hundred years. What does this stasis in pottery type mean about the interaction of women of different societies? What happened in women's experience to bring about the changes in pottery that occurred at the end of Alma Plain times? Pottery was increasingly abundant over time. Jennings (1989:310) remarks that "the form and overall inventory of Anasazi tools and implements changed remarkably little through time. The major stylistic changes are found in the pottery. . . . Ceramics have provided the clues to regional boundaries and evidence of interregional communication, and they also form the backbone of the chronological system." Why was a product of women's labor and utilization more diversified than those of men? Were the social boundaries evident through pottery maintained by societal endogamy? Factors to explain pottery boundaries other than marriage patterns are explored by Alison Rautman (this volume), including intensified trading to reduce risks associated with food supplies.

The Mogollon dwelling was the pit house, found in eighteen different designs. In early Mogollon times house size varied greatly but then became more uniform. Pit houses were abandoned as loci for domestic activities in favor of pueblos 900 ya. Patricia Gilman (1987) argues that the need to roof more domestic area and domestic activities led to above-ground dwellings, the masonry pueblo. What might the house-size changes be saying about women's fertility, family makeup, spatial organization of women's activities, and changes in women's activities? What might the cultural elaboration of domestic space be saying about the need to increase labor production, and the control of women by men (Hodder 1984:61)? It is interesting that the old house style becomes the kiva, a male seclusion structure.

ARCTIC

While research into the pre-contact period of the Arctic has not made gender a central theme, the concern with questions about adaptation to this extreme environment has made technological innovation an issue. The ulu (women's knife), the umiak (women's boat), and Norton period ceramics indicate changes in several aspects of women's technology. Did the ulu expand capabilities or merely substitute capabilities? How did women and children travel before the umiak? How did men whale before the umiak? Why did Norton women adopt Siberian ceramics? How did these women learn the craft of ceramics? How were they cooking before Norton pottery and how did they cook with it? Why did subsequent women drop ceramics? What can we say about the production technology, the production quantity and frequency, and the impact on women's work loads of each of these innovations?

Discussion

Division of labor and sex roles are here viewed as separate constructs, division of labor being evident in physical evidence on skeletons, and sex roles being a social construction that ascribes classes of work to individuals based on their gender, regardless of their physical capabilities. Defined in this manner, division-of-labor information is to be gleaned from the osteological data reviewed here. The use of the bow, and the tension held by the draw arm, resulted in asymmetrical upper arm sizes, as observed on male skeletons in the Midwest and Southeast. The processing of grains in a mortar and pestle requires that both arms lift and forcefully lower the pestle, and the strength requirements create equal-sized upper arms. Such symmetry has been noted on female skeletons in the Southeast. The increased strength evident in the legs of females in the Midwest has been related to the new activities of hoeing and transporting heavy loads between field and village. But because the strength evident in males' legs is as great as that in females' legs and does not change over time, it cannot be said that only females were transporting and hoeing crops. From the Georgia coast comes evidence that females were transporting loads on their backs using the tumpline, which apparently men were not (Larsen 1984). These sex-labor correlations do suggest that the activities were part of a socially determined sex role, and probably gender role, in late pre-contact times.

SEX ROLES

The bioarchaeological data, as infrequent as they are, do support the assignment of activities such as seed processing and burden carrying to females of the past 2,000 years or less, and hunting (use of bow) to males. Few scholars have attempted to investigate sex roles earlier than the adoption of maize agriculture, but many papers reviewed here question the immutability of sex roles observed in historic times. Men may have intimate knowledge of shellfishing (Moss 1993), and women of hunting (Brumbach and Jarvenpa, this volume), which they can use when they wish.

All studies of North American social organization have assumed the existence of sexed work roles since the hemisphere was first inhabited. Rarely has the generation of these roles been theorized. The development of sexed work roles within preagricultural societies appears to have at least one cause in mother's work loads and expectations of children's labor. Hunting-gathering children may gather food (Hadza children gather up to 50 percent of their food needs), or they may do little to nothing related to the food quest (!Kung). It has been argued that the !Kung children are not productive because the population density of the Kalahari is so low, the plants and animals so well known, and water too heavy for children to carry (Draper 1975). They do not participate in child care because there are enough adults in camp. Although the Hadza camps rarely have adults in them, parents leave children nonetheless, but take infants. Child caretakers are not used in either situation. With the adoption of agriculture or other labor-intensive activities that subtract the mother regularly from camp, however, even infants are left behind. High absenteeism among mothers means that infants' diets are supplemented, infants are weaned earlier, and they are cared for by children.

Draper (1975) could find no work expectations of !Kung girls or boys, no "cultural pressures" in the bush that determined the sex roles or personality traits so commonly associated with men and women in other societies. Yet girls stayed closer to or in camp, had more interaction with adults (particularly women), and had less interaction with girl peers than did boys. Draper speaks in terms of proclivities on the part of girls to stay close to adults, and suggests that this proclivity came to be exploited by sedentary !Kung.

The new types of work for sedentary !Kung women and children are food storage, more-involved processing of new foods (corn and sorghum), and keeping domesticated animals out of harm or from harming. Greatly busied mothers in sedentary villages call upon girl children to run errands and tend children because, as Draper saw, girls are more often at hand.

While the appropriateness of !Kung subsistence practices for understanding preagricultural practices has been challenged numerous times, there is no apparent reason to reject the information on the transformation of !Kung childhood. If !Kung women actually gather and contribute inordinate amounts of foodstuffs in this century because of devastated range and wildlife populations, it would mean that their work load was even less and their presence in camp even greater in earlier centuries, so that child caretakers would still have been unnecessary. Even Hadza children who gather half of their own food are not expected to tend children or undertake other responsibilities.

When production is centered in the household, when women's work takes them away from home several hours daily, or when women's subsistence work is physically demanding, children are expected to be responsible and obedient (Draper and Cashdan 1988:341). Responsibility involves child care, field labor, water fetching, food processing, cooking, storing, animal tending, and errand running. Sexed roles are formed in children in these situations. Numerous authors have observed that responsibility and obedience are stressed less by adults among foragers, simple horticulturists, and in industrialized cultures, and they are coveted most in children of agriculturalists (Gardner 1991; see references in Draper and Cashdan 1988).

The implication of these observations for sex-role development in the social history of pre-Columbian peoples is profound: strongly sexed role formation, the essence of gender to most archaeologists, occurs in specific situations, most notably with the transition to agriculture or when the adoption of subsistence or production regimes took mothers away from the home several hours daily, were centered in the household, or were physically taxing to mothers. It is most likely that such conditions obtained with the development of more-productive maize strains in Mexico ca. 4,500 years ago and in the Southwest some 2,000 years ago, and possibly with the production demands of Adena-Hopewell exchange or of local domesticates and cultigens of the Mississippi-Ohio river drainages some 2,000 years ago (more fully discussed in Claassen 1995), and probably with the move to acorn dependence in California. The adoption of maize agriculture in the eastern United States nine hundred years ago, with its specialized technology, exacerbated sex-role differentiation in adults and instruction in Mississippian period children. Strongly sexed roles may not have developed prior to European influence in the Great Basin, the Intermontane, and sub-Arctic regions. They would have been longer lived in the Hohokam culture area and shorter lived in the Fremont area. Different classes of Aleut, Kodiak, and Northwest Coast peoples likely had differing work requirements of women and thus differing demands on their children.

Agency

The evidence for women's active manipulation of their life circumstances appears again and again in the review of the literature. Women's agency is evident in innovation, in feeding, in birthrates, in production, in status, in ritual. Women are now viewed as having had active roles in the shell-ring and mound rituals of the Southeast as shamans, as laborers in their construction, as provisioners of laborers. Female shamans may have led the way away from shell-ring and mound symbolism into the rituals associated with dirt mounds of the Adena and Hopewell. A woman's vision brought about the Ground Breaking ceremony of the Pawnee (O'Brien 1991) and the peyote ritual, which has culminated in the pan-Indian Native American Church. Girls sought spirit guardians and when successful recorded not only their spirit guardians but also themselves in rock art in the Pecos region. Women had ritual locations such as the BBB Motor site and the Mulcaster Island East site, and they generated statuary and possibly even a unique pottery ware (Ramey) for ritual use. Female "warriors" may have had a place in the pantheon, and a female aspect was recognized by many groups, including the Pawnee (O'Brien 1991). Corn Mother rock art sites of the Mississippi Valley were important nodes in a ritual landscape.

Women adopted and adapted pottery to both hot-rock steaming and direct-heat cooking (Crown and Wills 1995; Sassaman 1993) and were responsible for their diffusion across North America. Women bred new varieties of maize, enhanced the food value of many native crops, developed horticultural and storage techniques, and manipulated the physics of pottery form to enhance food-processing capabilities (Braun 1985). Their work loads were constantly being negotiated as innovations were adopted.

Population growth and population stability should be viewed as inextricably interwoven with women's agency. If population grew by an increased birthrate, as it did in the Midwest (Buikstra et al. 1986), it was because women allowed it to do so.

Production of durables and consumables also attests to women's active roles in their societies. Weaving and basketry production in the Northwest supported family status. The production of dried shellfish meat and shell beads (wampum) linked communities from the coast into the interior of New England. Endeavors in pottery production linked Southwestern Anasazi communities into a mutual-welfare system in times of crop failure (Rautman, this volume). They produced abundant rabbit meat and skin clothing in the Mogollon highlands. They hunted meat throughout the Southwest. They provided abundant protein to societies along the coast of North America. That women provide substantial quantities of fat and protein seriously challenges the foundation of the arguments for why men hunt, as provided by Hawkes (1993) and Friedl (1975).

In procuring food for their families, women determined when and where the community moved in New England, in central California, in the Plains. While foraging they provisioned themselves and men with stored grains in caves in the Mogollon mountains, in the hill country of the Ozarks, and in the Ohio and Tennessee river valleys. Group movement pivoting on women's subsistence activities challenges the notion that women can move and be moved around the landscape with no consequence, while men hunters must stay in an area known to them (Hanna 1989; Hudecek-Cuffe 1994). It could be that men and women had separate seasonal activities, even separate settlement patterns over a year or two-year period in some societies, as do the Tarahumara.

There is evidence of women's appropriation of space for their activities in Plains societies. The spatial requirements of their activities conditioned the internal arrangement of sites in central California and the northern Plains. Maize grinding moved from inside to public locations, while men's activities became increasingly private in the Southwest (Spielmann 1995). The large scale of women's activities led to dramatic changes in architecture in the Southwest (Gilman 1987) and among the Iroquois. Their activities created special use sites for nut processing in California, Delaware, Illinois, Ohio, Alabama, and Georgia.

Women negotiated their status with pottery, with religious roles, with production of consumables and durables. Women achieved and acquired status in Mississippian times and in Northwest Coast societies, and undoubtedly elsewhere as well. They also suffered the consequences of violence.

Conclusions

In the world of feminist scholarship, stereotyped behavior for women has been challenged as limiting women's potential and has been under attack since the 1960s. It is most interesting to me that very little of the gendered prehistoric literature has chosen to challenge U.S. and Western stereotypes of roles and behaviors for women. It should be evident from the preceding review and discussion that stereotyped notions about the division of labor and sex roles are not stumbling blocks for archaeologists interested in social organization of pre-contact peoples. These studies have collectively produced a wealth of information, hypotheses, and perspectives on the lives of women and men in pre-contact America. Some authors have stated an explicit feminist motivation for their work, some have denied being feminist or having an interest in gender, and several authors have incorporated sex as one of several axes of investigation suggested by the data. Methods and theories that dominate these studies reflect those that dominate American archaeology at large. All of these authors indicate a belief in the value of the scientific method as used in the processual paradigm.

Janet Spector's (1983) task-differentiation approach and the direct historical approach are the two most common methodological tools employed by these authors. Spector (1993) now finds the task-differentiation approach too sterile for her own use. The direct historical approach is heavily used by the Plains authors and others working with late-pre-contact data. It has received much critical attention in the past two decades, some from feminist archaeologists (e.g., Brumfiel 1991; Fratt 1991; Latta 1991).

Few of the authors reviewed here make any suggestions for alterations in chronological ordering, field strategies, or laboratory analyses to accommodate their investigations. Methods and techniques currently available and taught in standard curricula are sufficient for addressing sex, gender, division of labor, sex roles, and gender hierarchies. The one methodological modification offered is that site catchments of 10 km or less circumscribe the range of women's hunting and miss that of men's (Brumbach and Jarvenpa, this volume). (A thesis by Douglas Perrelli [1994] strongly implies that typical site catchments, if placed around Iroquois agricultural villages, would exclude the activities of most men and encompass the activities of most women and captives.) The one chronological critique argues that the fixation on lithics during the Paleo-Indian and Archaic periods, and on ceramics in later prehistory, sets up incomparable temporal divisions for studying gender (Sassaman 1992).

The literature not only indicates the richness that is added to archaeological inquiries by focusing on social organization, but also suggests several problem areas of which archaeologists need to be aware. These are the use of !Kung foraging analogy, the association of burial goods with life activities of the deceased, the impact of formation processes, and the complicating nature of class and status affiliations.

Often referencing the modern !Kung ethnographic work, authors appear to be unaware that there is theoretical and factual trouble in the gathering image given us by the !Kung. Many anthropologists view the !Kung as living in an environment denuded of game and, therefore, as unusually reliant on floral foods and unusually sustained by women's gathering. If there were a depletion of game over the millennia in the Americas (a controversial issue), then gathering and plant foods generally, as well as the importance of women's foraging activities, would be increasing as time approaches the present. Women's influence in settlement systems would increase, as would the labor-intensive work of cultivation and, therefore, sex-role training of children. However, the large contribution of women and plants to the !Kung diet probably is not an appropriate analog for Archaic and Paleo-Indian cultures (Cohen 1987).

Numerous authors have exposed the dangers of equating burial goods with the activities and status of the living individual. Grave preparation and inclusions may reflect the mourning party, the ritual, the surviving kin, or something else unrelated to the deceased. There may have been three female flint knappers interred at Island Field, or those tool kits may not signify the dead females' occupation. Unusual burial associations may have to remain just that. The same caveat can be offered for sexual use of space and for assumed women's activities (Bruhns 1991).

I would warn those seeking to gender archaeological data not to lose sight of formation processes. Failure to cope with formation processes was an early critique of gendered studies by Longacre, Hill, and Deetz, and is a major pitfall for authors attempting to gender specific sites. It is an issue raised only by Martha Latta (1991) in this set of papers.

Finally, several studies encapsulated here indicate that women of different status varied in important indicators of life experience, such as trace elements, isotopic ratios, and grave goods. Status differences in past societies tend to override sex-role differences, as they do in today's industrialized societies. While the tendency may be to equate female-directed violence with wife abuse, the study of Anasazi females who had been victims of violence suggests that these women were not integrated into the community and might have been captives (Martin and Akins 1994).

It should be clear that there is much work still to do. Symposia about gendered archaeology at regional conferences should be organized annually until women's sites become as commonplace as men's sites, until gatherer-driven settlement patterns are as common as hunter-driven ones, until women's seclusion sites and activity areas are as common as men's houses, kivas, and hunting camps. The authors reviewed in this survey have used a remarkable variety of methods, data, and knowledge claims to make their cases. In so doing, they have made the social life of pre-contact native peoples, and the endeavor of archaeology, far richer.

Acknowledgments

The major influence on this essay as it entered its final form was Marilyn Smith, women's studies and mass communication scholar at Appalachian State. Rosemary Joyce greatly aided in the presentation of this material, helping me to clarify my thoughts on several issues. Other readers whose comments are reflected in this version of the essay are anthropologist Patricia Beaver, historian Maggie McFadden, and archaeologists Patty Jo Watson, Jane Buikstra, and Stuart Fiedel.

6. Warfare, Women, and Households: The Development of Iroquois Culture

Susan C. Prezzano

For more than forty years anthropologists and historians have marveled at the wealth of scholarly research centered on the Five-Nations Iroquois who, in historic times, resided between the Mohawk and Genesee rivers in New York State. This abiding interest has caused more than one researcher to observe that the Five-Nations Iroquois, which include the Mohawk, Oneida, Onondaga, Cayuga, and Seneca tribes, are among the most studied of all Native American cultures (Fenton 1940:160; Richter 1992:1). The primary explanation given for this academic popularity is an abundance of extant accounts that begin with the encounters between French and Dutch explorers and Iroquoian speakers in the sixteenth and seventeenth centuries. Other significant reasons include the important historic role the Iroquois played in commercial and diplomatic concerns during the colonial era, and their ability to withstand for many decades white encroachment in the form of disease and colonial territorial expansion (Fenton 1940:159; Richter 1992; Tooker 1978:418).

Several recurring themes have persisted in Iroquois studies throughout the centuries. In this chapter, I focus on two of these: namely, male aggression and the status of women in Iroquois society. My goal is to illuminate the influence of these two themes on archaeological investigations, particularly in relation to explanations of the development of Iroquois tribalization: that is, the transformation of Iroquois culture from one based on small bands of mobile hunters and gatherers to one based on agricultural villages and organized into tribes. I begin with the concept of Iroquois aggression.

Warfare

Early accounts of the Iroquois are replete with descriptions of war, capture, torture, and death (Richter 1992:31, 65). Several reasons can be cited for this preoccupation with Iroquois aggression. First, narratives, especially by the Jesuits, provide detailed descriptions of the capture and sometimes ritualistic torture of prisoners at the hands of the Iroquois (see, for example, Biggar 1929:2:65–107; Coyne 1903:31–55; Thwaites 22:251–267, 24:271–297, 33:81–89, 34:87–99, 38:181, 39:55–77, 47:139–153, 50; 59–63, 54:23–35; Scull 1885:28–60). Although these accounts record a long-standing cultural practice, it should be remembered that these narratives reflect considerable observer bias. Pain and suffering in the "wilderness" not only elevated religious stature but increased support of the missions (Tooker 1991:4).

Second, during the mid-seventeenth century the Iroquois launched a series of increasingly distant military campaigns known collectively as the Beaver Wars (Hunt 1940; Richter 1992:50–74). These campaigns successfully dispersed many Eastern Woodlands tribes located as far south as Virginia and as far west as the upper Mississippi Valley. The primary causal factors of these wars were the attempt by the Iroquois to maintain access to furs used in exchange for increasingly vital European trade goods, and to replace (or avenge) family members lost by raids and disease (Morgan 1901:1).

Finally, casting Native Americans as evil aggressors bent on annihilation of Europeans served as a means of fostering in-group cohesiveness by articulating boundaries through the creation of a common enemy (Given 1994:115). The Iroquois tribes, because they retained their homeland and political autonomy until the Revolutionary War, provided a convenient scapegoat for any European settlement that had not managed to sequester their allegiance in the various conflicts between the colonies.

Modern-day historians, through a more sophisticated reading of the documents, have concentrated on relating Iroquois aggression to the broader arena of colonial and native politics and economy (Jennings 1984; Richter 1992). They have also explored the effect that the infusion of European arms and trade goods made on the nature of Iroquois warfare (Given 1994; Richter 1992). In addition, several studies have endeavored to view aggression in light of Iroquois cultural values (for example, Richter 1992).

Powerful Women

The second major theme in Iroquois studies discussed in this chapter concerns the political, social, and economic status of women. Similar to studies of Iroquois warfare and aggression, inquiries into the power and prestige of women are abundant (Beauchamp 1900; Bonvillain 1980; Brown 1970; Carr 1883; Clark 1987; Hewitt 1932; Randle 1951; Richards 1957; Rothenberg 1978, 1980; Tooker 1984; Trigger 1978). One eighteenth-century observer noted that "nothing is more real, however, than the women's superiority. It is they who really maintain the tribe. . . . In them resides all the real authority: the lands, fields and all their harvest belong to them; they are the soul of the councils, the arbiter of peace and war . . . they arrange the marriages; the children are under their authority; and the order of succession is founded on their blood" (Lafitau 1974 [1724]:69).

Researchers cite various reasons for the high status of women in Iroquois society. As the chief growers of corn, beans, and squash they provided the basis of subsistence. These crops were called the Three Sisters because, like women, they sustained the community (Fenton 1978:300). Women distributed and prepared all food, including the game caught by men (Brown 1970).

The Iroquois practiced matrilocal residency and traced descent through women. They organized their communal longhouses around extended families related through women, generally through an elderly matron and her daughters. These houses were filled with the products of women's activities, including food stored in the rafters and the cooking pots at the hearths. In fact, much of the village and the agricultural fields were organized around women's work and women's lives (Richter 1992: 22–23; Tooker 1984; Trigger 1978).

Finally, women wielded political power. Senior women selected and removed the hereditary peace chiefs of their lineage (Hewitt 1932; Lafitau 1974 [1724]:69–71; Richter 1992:42–43; Tooker 1978:424–426). Women, although they did not speak at councils, could select an orator to speak on their behalf. They urged or prohibited raids by providing or withholding supplies, or by controlling the actions of the young warriors of their lineage. They often controlled the fate of captives. Murdock (1934:302) voiced the most extreme view of women's power in his often quoted statement claiming "that native [Iroquois] women enjoy a status at least equal, if not superior to that of men. Indeed, of all the peoples of the earth, the Iroquois approach most closely to that hypothetical form of society known as the 'matriarchate.'"

Several authors have suggested that female political power and prestige have been overstated, perhaps because of a lack of understanding of the concept of gender reciprocity in Iroquois society (Fenton 1978; Tooker

1984). These authors argue that men and women gained prestige not through authority over people, or control over property and economic resources, as is common in Western societies, but through the practice of fulfilling reciprocal obligations. Women did not speak at council meetings, hold power in the public sphere, or travel extensively outside the village—all activities associated with men. Women gained prestige in the domestic sphere; their position complemented that of men.

Much of the discussion over the power and prestige of Iroquois women resolves into the classic debate over women's status in non-Western societies. Can women who lack access to public power, but who wield important influence in the domestic sphere, be thought of as having high status (Clark 1987)? In the case of Iroquois women, however, access to public power and prestige are clearly evident in their role of selecting chiefs.

In sum, many anthropologists and historians have combined concepts of warfare and women's roles in a comprehensive theory based on the reciprocal obligations of the sexes (Bonvillain 1980; Fenton 1978; Richter 1992:22, 42–43; Tooker 1984:118–121; Trigger 1978:63). A woman's world revolved around the village and agricultural fields where she spent much of her year. Her concerns centered on the welfare of the extended family, household, and clan (Fenton 1978:309). Men, in contrast, were frequently absent. Their pursuits of hunting, trade, and warfare took them beyond the "woodsedge": the physical and metaphorical boundary separating the village from the wilderness (Fenton 1978:316; Richter 1992:18). Their concerns focused on extra-village relations.

Archaeological Studies of Iroquois Development

Although male aggression and the power of women are both meaningful subjects in historical studies, they have not had an equal impact on Iroquois archaeological pursuits. From the first systematic archaeological investigations, the theme of warfare and aggression, that is, the presumed pursuits of men, have taken precedence over the roles of women in shaping Iroquois culture. A brief discussion of the role of warfare in theories of Iroquois development will illustrate this point.

In the early twentieth century, Arthur Parker (1916), the first modern Iroquoian archaeologist, advanced a theory of Iroquois development based on a migration hypothesis proposed by Lloyd (Morgan 1901). He contended that the Iroquois originally resided at the mouth of the Ohio

River. For reasons left unexplained, they abandoned this region and migrated through the territory of the Mound Builders, whom they fought and partially absorbed, before arriving in their historic homeland several hundred miles to the north and east. There they displaced culturally inferior indigenous Algonquian speakers. Prior to this migration, the Iroquois already practiced maize agriculture and lived in fortified villages.

During the next thirty years, archaeologists in New York worked under this model; they set about documenting the arrival of the Iroquois into New York and uncovering "pre-Iroquoian" cultures. At the Castle Creek site, for example, Ritchie (1934) identified what he believed was a contact occupation between Algonquian- and Iroquoian-speaking groups. The Iroquois eventually absorbed the Algonquian-speaking groups at this locale, assumedly because of their superior lifestyle.

During the 1950s, the in situ theory of Iroquois development supplanted migration as the chief explanatory model of Iroquois cultural evolution. This theory, developed most extensively by MacNeish (1952), became the leading paradigm in Iroquois archaeological research for the next forty years. In situ theorists argued that Iroquois culture developed in place from earlier indigenous cultures. Changes in subsistence, community patterns, and inferred transformation of social and political organization were assumed to have occurred gradually starting at about A.D. 1000. Linguistic evidence supported a long occupation of central New York by Iroquoian speakers (Lounsbury 1961, 1978:336). Warfare, population, village size, and agricultural subsistence increased throughout Iroquoia during the Late Woodland (A.D. 1000–1550), leading to tribalization and, ultimately, to the formation of the pan-tribal political institution known as the League of the Iroquois.

These trends are assumed to have occurred spontaneously as the result of the introduction of maize agriculture. The majority of Iroquois studies of this period focused on documenting indigenous Iroquois development from its Middle Woodland stage (200 B.C.–A.D. 1000) and Owasco period (A.D. 1000–1300) roots by using numerical and stylistic seriation of artifacts, especially pottery, without the support of contextual data (Lenig 1965; Ritchie 1980). Except for synopses of excavations (Ritchie 1980; Ritchie and Funk 1973; Tuck 1971), based in many instances on the work of avocational archaeologists, little research focused on community patterns and the excavation of houses.

Whitthoft (1959) was one of the few in situ archaeologists to propose a more detailed causal explanation of Iroquois developments. He contends that during the Late Woodland, cultural growth led to stable agricultural villages of a "strong matriarchal cast" (1959:33), with women providing the bulk of the economic mainstay of the community. Hunting, he asserts, became obsolescent, causing men to have minimal contribution to village economy, a view shared by Randle (1951) and later Brown (1970). Warfare increased because "man, as a hunter, was the tool of vengeance; in times when his primary economic significance was fading, he made too good a hunter of men in his attempts to affirm his manly roles in society" (Whitthoft 1959:33). Tribalization and the development of the League was the result of escalating hostilities caused by marginalized men.

Except for Whallon (1968), who was working during the rise of processual archaeology, few researchers targeted transformations at the village level or focused on women's actions. Whallon traced the development of tribalization by linking ceramic variation with degree of social interaction. Because women were assumed to make the cooking vessels, and to have learned these motor skills from their mothers, cultures where women were less mobile should have more homogeneous ceramic styles. Thus, with the evolution of tribes and matrilocality, Iroquois pottery became more homogeneous because of tribal endogamy and the decrease in women's mobility. This study is strictly a methodological exercise, and except for speculation on the association of the rise of matrilocality with the establishment of councils that dealt with the threat of warfare, Whallon does not offer explanations of how or why tribalization occurred.

The frustration with the lack of explanatory rigor of the in situ hypothesis has led to the development of several new theories within the last five years. These theories de-emphasize the role of the introduction of agriculture as the root of Iroquois development, and attempt to place Iroquois cultural trends in a regional perspective. But, similar to older models, emphasis on community patterns and contextual data is minimal.

The core-periphery model proposed by Dincauze and Hasenstab (1989) and refined by Hasenstab (1990) suggests that along the western periphery of Iroquoia, marginal groups encroached into Iroquois territory to extract game resources that were depleted in their own territory by larger polities, such as Cahokia, to their west: "It is proposed that the contact between the indigenous New York Iroquois groups and the intruding populations led to hostility, which promoted the formation of tribal social organization" (Hasenstab 1990:172). Additional booty sought by these encroaching groups included women captured for use in agricultural labor.

Within the past few years, Snow (1994a, 1994b, 1995) has put forth a new migration hypothesis which proposes that Iroquois development was caused by their migration into New York. He argues that the late Middle Woodland Clemson's Island site of central Pennsylvania was inhabited by Iroquoian speakers. By A.D. 900 they expanded to the north into territory occupied by Algonquian-speaking cultures in the upper Susquehanna drainage and later dispersed throughout the historic Iroquois heartland. Iroquois culture predominated because of the early adoption of maize agriculture and matrilocality: "Tight matrilocal communities of Iroquoians quickly overwhelmed the thinner populations previously resident in the region, displacing them, absorbing them, or both. This scenario is consistent with what is known of tribal population expansion and warfare" (Snow 1994a:290).

Snow believes sites of the Hunters Home phase (A.D. 800–1000), which in the in situ hypothesis are conjectured to be transitional between Iroquois and earlier Middle Woodland cultures, represent the first Iroquois occupations in New York. He interprets the presence at the sites of ceramics with styles intermediate between those of the Middle Woodland and Owasco periods as the result of the absorption of indigenous women, probably through capture, into the intrusive Iroquois communities (Snow 1995:73). Abrupt change in "basic motor habits" in ceramic manufacture are unlikely to occur even in rapidly changing cultures or within a "slowly evolving technology" (71). Population intrusion is the more likely cause of mixed ceramic styles. According to Snow (1995:71), archaeologists have tended to ignore migration and warfare as causal factors in the development of Iroquois society because they have overemphasized the effects of the increased role of women as producers.

Discussion

This brief history of archaeological explanatory models concerning Iroquois development elucidates several important points about the themes of warfare and women's status. First, warfare and aggression, especially on a regional scale, are perceived as major components in Iroquois tribalization. In the migration models of Parker and Snow, the dominant Iroquois overpowered their Algonquian-speaking neighbors and expanded into their territory. This viewpoint is directly influenced by perceptions of historic events surrounding the Beaver Wars. Whereas in the colonial era the Iroquois expanded their territory and sphere of influence outward from New York to include large areas of the Eastern Woodlands through the conquering of subordinate groups, in pre-contact times the Iroquois moved into New York replacing indigenous groups. The Iroquois, as aggressors, spawn both historical events and prehistorical cultural developments at a regional scale.

On the surface these theories appear to acknowledge women's role in tribal developments: the Iroquois are deemed superior because of their agricultural subsistence base and/or matrilocality. Yet the consequences of women's actions are never developed, but are presented as a cultural given. What women do forms the background for the actions of men.

Hasenstab's (1990) model is a subtle variation of the same theme. Iroquois culture developed as the result of hostile encroachment into their territory by outsiders who came in search of hunting resources and captives. The resultant village consolidation and organization began the trajectory towards the formation of tribes. Thus hunting and hostile actions, not agriculture, were the primary factors in Iroquois development. The contributions of women enter into this model only in the agricultural services they performed as captives.

A further demonstration of the persistence of the theme of warfare as prime mover is demonstrated by the in situ theory. As described previously, this theory had a negative effect on the formation of models explaining Iroquois development. Except for Whitthoft's (1959) description of tribalization as the result of increased warfare due to the removal of men as the economic providers of the community, few theories based on the in situ hypothesis explore actual mechanisms of change. After the introduction of maize agriculture, Iroquois culture gradually, but automatically, changed toward settlement in larger, more populous villages and, finally, toward the development of tribes and the pan-tribal League organization. Tribalization is the natural consequence of the evolutionary trajectory begun by the adoption of agriculture.

This dearth of explanatory rigor in the in situ theory is a by-product of attempting to track change at a regional scale when investigation of changes at the household and community level would be far more productive. The consequences of subsistence shifts, for example, must be related to the organization of the household and community, to strategies that increased crop yields and storage capacity, and to other "mundane" events that took place in the household and community.

To date, few theories of tribalization are based on women, what they did, or on the assumed domain of women, that is, on the household and community. Ironically, it is women in their roles as potters and as captives, not as economic providers or maintainers of the lineage, who are most visible to Iroquois archaeologists. In Whallon's processual approach to the in situ hypothesis, women are passive recipients of ceramic styles learned in childhood from their female kin. Subsequent events in their lives or their pursuit of active strategies of accommodation and resistance are not considered as affecting how they made pots. Ethnoarchaeologists have noted that although stylistic traditions are clearly evident in ceramics, women potters are not mere "mechanical copycats but active and creative producers" (DeBoer 1990:104).

Snow makes similar assumptions as Whallon about ceramic variation in his contention that captive women made pots exhibiting a mixture of the styles of kin and captors, presumably as the motor skills passed down from mother to daughter were diluted and old styles melded with new patterns. Engelbrecht (1974) and Latta (1991) have called this interpretation of passive ceramic variation "the captive bride syndrome." This characterization differs markedly from observations obtained from ethnoarchaeological studies of women potters. In several documented cases, women entering new households quickly began making pots similar in style to those of their new families as a means of conforming or gaining prestige (Miller 1985). This is similar to tactics practiced by captives among the historic Iroquois who "made every effort to assimilate" (Richter 1992: 68) to assure their continued survival.

While the above statements can be construed as the standard post-processual critique that is applied to many regional processual studies, it has special relevance to Iroquois archaeology. Few analyses have been performed that specifically target community patterns. Although this trend is related to the early destruction by relic seekers of Iroquois sites due to their romantic popularity, it is, at least, based partially on the trend of searching for the causal factors of change at the regional level, and of de-emphasizing contextual components of occupations such as structures and middens. Because contextual data and structural evidence are "most pertinent to the study of households and the products of domestic labor" (Tringham 1991: 100), their absence facilitates the de-emphasis of women and the domestic sphere.

The absence of women and households in theories of Iroquois development is rooted not only in problems of scale, but also in the perception of complementarity between the sexes that is based on historical studies of Iroquois culture. As outlined above, this theory assumes that household and community comprised the domain of women, while the world of men occurred outside the village and included the search for trade goods and war captives and the building of alliances. But those historians adhering to concepts of reciprocity of gender roles often confuse the metaphorical gender principle that ordered the Iroquois world with the actions of women and men. Descriptions of reciprocity show strong underlying assumptions not only of gender roles but also of the positions of households in social and political organizational change. Women and the households they represent are merely passive reflectors of change occurring at a regional scale. Further evidence on women and households will illustrate my point.

The acknowledged women's arena of hearth, house, village, and fields was not characterized by stasis but, as recent studies of material culture, community patterns, and crop production in the Northeast attest, was the center of fundamental transformations. Chronological trends in ceramic variation have been linked to the manipulation by potters of attributes of temper and shape that affect physical properties; this endeavor created utensils better suited for cooking maize (Prezzano 1986). Iroquoian houses changed from single-family dwellings to multifamily longhouses as early as A.D. 1000. Kapches (1990) has traced the reorganization of interior space in longhouses as a by-product and active instrument in the development of more-integrated social groups among Iroquoian cultures. Ethnobotanists have traced the developments in maize that produced the Northern Flint variety and permitted this cultigen to be grown in areas with a shortened growing season. Detailed studies of ethnohistoric records for the Northeast demonstrate experimentation with crop varieties, field preparation, crop production, and storage techniques (Bendremer et al. 1991; Dimmick 1994).

Although women were active in the village and agricultural fields, they were neither conservative nor passive in the presumed arenas of men's activities. Nor did their concerns rest solely on economic and domestic pursuits. Historians have argued that women rarely participated in council meetings or other aspects of the public domain. Richter (1992:43), however, has pointed to documentary evidence that indicates women of the seventeenth and eighteenth century held their own councils; these were virtually ignored by European chroniclers, who were mostly men (Lafitau 1974:1:295; Thwaites 54:281–283). Unfortunately, we will never know the influence of these women's councils on extra-village affairs, but their existence certainly indicates that women took more than a passive role in tribal affairs.

Rothenberg (1978, 1980) has demonstrated that the characterization of Iroquois women as conservative, and their actions as centered only on domestic issues, is a misleading reading of the data. She cites as an example the nineteenth-century Seneca women who were active participants in their own fate and resisted relinquishing their control, as the chief providers of food, of the economic base of their communities in the face of pressure from Quakers in western New York who attempted to make men farmers.

Finally, although the concept of reciprocity in gender roles places warfare squarely in the domain of men, accounts written prior to the Beaver Wars demonstrate that warfare was instigated frequently by women who demanded captives to replace or revenge the death of lineage members: "Traditionally war had been the business of women and young men" (Richter 1992:56). The influx of disease and trade goods significantly altered the political base of extra-village activities in the colonial period and are thus poor indicators of the traditional place of household politics in fueling change in sociopolitical organization. Warfare and aggression originated in the dynamics of the household.

Any model of Iroquois development must include an analysis of what transpired at the household and community level. Households comprise the basic social unit of human society and are the essential scale where human interaction takes place (Ashmore and Wilk 1988:1; Tringham 1991: 102). Production, reproduction, consumption, and the transmission of wealth and social position across generations occur at the household level (Ashmore and Wilk 1988:4). Archaeologically, it is the most visible social unit as represented by domestic architecture. Houses were not simply passive reflectors of change at a larger scale but must be viewed as active components in that change (Tringham 1991:98). Late Woodland occupations uncovered in New York that have the very first evidence of maize agriculture already contain longhouses, suggesting an early association of household organization with social patterns, particularly matrilocality, long identified as Iroquoian (Prezzano 1993). Finally, it must be remembered that the Iroquois called their League the "People of the Longhouse" (Fenton 1978:320). They metaphorically linked the geographic location of their tribes to the longhouse, with each tribe performing duties associated with a specific household function: the Mohawk, for example, were "the Keepers of the Eastern Door" (Tooker 1978:418). Thus Iroquois intertribal politics were perceived of at the household level.

Conclusions

Traditionally archaeologists have focused on broad-scale regional phenomena to interpret developments in Iroquois sociopolitical organization. Warfare, in particular, has been used to explain processes of tribalization. Households, villages, and other components of the domestic sphere, which by convention are believed to be the domain of women, are characterized as static features of the Iroquois landscape. But history and anthropology have demonstrated not only that women were active participants in politics that affected events both within and beyond the village limits, but also that households, generally relegated to the background in explanations of tribalization, are an integral part of sociopolitical change. Thus many of the categories of material culture studied by archaeologists—such as ceramics, many stone tools, structures, and the spatial distribution of artifacts and features—can be seen as the correlates of women's household activities. Recognized transformations of these archaeological materials, such as the improvement of the thermal strength of ceramics, represent the cumulative product of many household decisions. Although, as Snow (1994b: 213) claims, archaeological problems must be conceived of at the regional scale, we must, in addition, develop theories that incorporate processes of the household, because it is at this scale that women and men lived.

Acknowledgments

Elizabeth Chilton provided lively discussions and sources on the captive bride syndrome in Iroquois archaeology. Cheryl Claassen made valuable suggestions concerning the active strategies of women.

7. Changes in Regional Exchange Relationships During the Pithouse-to-Pueblo Transition in the American Southwest: Implications for Gender Roles

Alison E. Rautman

In the American Southwest, the occurrence and spatial distribution of durable goods such as ceramics have been used as indications of inter-village exchange of a variety of items including food, information, and condiments such as salt, as well as perishables such as feathers, basketry, or hides, which are unlikely to be preserved except under unusual circumstances.

One goal of a spatial analysis of artifacts such as ceramics is to discern whether their spatial distribution is patterned, and whether we can determine the causes of this patterning. According to this view, exchanges take place within a social context that can be affected by several variables, including social relationships within and between households and villages. The concept of social distance between groups, for example, emphasizes the importance of social ties, rather than just geographic distance, in structuring interaction.

Another variable that may affect social context can be the gender of the actors, although this variable may not be of particular significance in any given interaction. The study of prehistoric pottery in the American Southwest—the technology of its manufacture, the style of the decorations, and the patterns of pottery distribution within a site and across the landscape—is inherently, however, a gender-laden study, because prehistoric ceramic manufacture among Puebloan groups in the Southwest is commonly assumed to have been dominated by women, as is observed among the surviving pueblos. There has been little discussion, however, regarding the factors affecting the distribution of women's pottery, the possible role of women in this distribution, and possible temporal changes in the organization of household labor that might be involved in pottery manufacture and distribution.

Exchange networks among historic pueblos are compared with characteristics of regional and intra-community social relationships that might be expected during the Pithouse period (ca. A.D. 980–1250) and the succeeding Pueblo period (ca. A.D. 1200–1500) in central New Mexico. I suggest that the myriad socioeconomic changes during the pithouse-to-pueblo transition represent a change in the scale of society—a change that can be expressed as a change in the spatial scale of regional social networks. Exchange relationships between villages are addressed in particular here, since they have been viewed as an important causal variable in the Southwest (e.g., Lightfoot 1984 and also Neitzel 1989), related to many other issues of political organization and social interactions both between and within Puebloan groups (e.g., Spielmann 1994; Wilcox 1984). However, changes in structural scale are also expected to affect the organization and use of space within a community as well as the organization of labor within households. Social and economic changes during the pithouse-to-pueblo transition thus may also help us understand the temporal depth of gender roles that are recorded among historic pueblos in the American Southwest, in particular, the definition of men's and women's work.

Household-Labor Organization and Exchange in the Historic Southwest

Historic Puebloan society can be considered basically egalitarian because theoretically all men and women have equal access to whatever they need in life: food and housing, of course, as well as access to the "means of production," such as seed corn, land, and ritual knowledge. In daily life, however, the actual distribution of wealth and power may not always resemble this ideal. In many villages there were, and still are, important social, ritual, and political positions that tend to be (or are in practice) hereditary or otherwise not strictly "egalitarian" in nature. Unequal access to some of these statuses would result in unequal access to resources, or the power to allocate resources (e.g., Brandt 1994).

In fact, some people (e.g., Gutierrez 1991) view relationships within historic Puebloan societies as fundamentally unequal, with older individuals appropriating labor from the young, and men and women both appropriating the results of each other's labor—women appropriating, processing, and distributing the maize that men grow, and men appropriating the rights of distribution of women's labor in exchanges of women's pottery with other men.

In historic Puebloan society, this division of labor not only specified the tasks that were to be performed by only men or only women, but also spatially separated such activities and roles. According to Hopi women, for example, "a man's place is outside the home" (cited in Gutierrez 1991:20). Women commonly owned much personal property, including the house itself, and controlled most of the activities in and around the home, including food processing, storage of food and seed, and also the manufacture of many goods, including items made of leather and feathers and, of course, pottery. The proper sphere for men's activities was outside the house itself; they commonly worked in the fields, hunted, and participated in warfare. They also made some manufactured items, such as cloth. Women thus traditionally controlled the production of most finished products (such as ground maize) and durable goods (such as pottery); the trading of such products between villages, however, was an activity apparently dominated by men.

A wide range of trading relationships is recorded among the historic Pueblos (Ford 1972). Trade between pueblos might be quite informal and include both men and women, who combined visits to relatives in different pueblos with exchanges of goods and services. More formally defined occasions such as fiestas and trade fairs would also be attended by both men and women. In general, however, trade with other societies was apparently associated with male activities such as hunting and warfare. Trade expeditions among the Tewa, for example, were commonly made up of about six to twenty men who combined trading with the fall buffalo hunt (Ortiz 1969). Some of these men carried trade goods for others of their pueblo, and traders from different pueblos might travel together (Ford 1972). Long-distance trading involved the Tewa (men) in exchanges with a variety of non-Puebloan groups, including the Comanche, Ute, and Apache.

Ford (1972) also describes trade partnerships between ethnic groups. For example, whole family groups of Tewa apparently traveled to the Jicarilla Apache, and were housed by an Apache family with whom they had long-established ties. These associations between families could even be inherited from one generation to another.

All of these exchanges might involve food, ceremonial goods and services, and durable goods and finished products such as processed hides and pottery. Some pueblos apparently were particularly known for their production of certain items or the possession of certain skills (such as midwifery). Pueblos also varied in size, in "wealth," and in their participation in exchanges between pueblos and with non-Puebloan groups.

Within all these contexts, the social relationships between individuals were of primary importance in structuring the nature of their interactions. Exchanges within and between pueblos were generally determined by kin relationships. Trade with other societies could be dangerous without such a predictable social context (hence the association between trading and warfare), unless some sort of quasi-kin relationship, such as the trade partnership, could cement relationships between individuals in different societies. What is not clear from descriptions of these types of exchanges, however, is the temporal depth of these activities and of the gender roles expressed in the sexual division of labor between the production of goods and their distribution. It is tempting to think of historic Puebloan society as highly traditional, and archaeologists often use the direct historical approach to link observed behavior and social organization to that of the past. Social changes associated with Spanish conquest and the imposition of Spanish customs, norms, and laws, however, may have simplified some aspects of Puebloan society (Upham 1982). It is also possible that historic ethnographers did not (or could not) fully appreciate the complexity of Puebloan society (e.g., Brandt 1994). Thus the temporal depth of forms of organization and social institutions that are recorded in historic ethnographies is not known.

In the context of state organization, Hastorf (1991) has shown that Andean household structure and gender roles may have changed through time, particularly as a result of imposition of Inka rule. Brumfiel (1991) also has related changes in gender roles to an overall reorganization within households and villages during Aztec domination. Such organizational changes at the level of the household, and possibly in gender roles, also are expected to be associated with overall economic and political reorganization, even among basically egalitarian societies where there are no such well-defined hierarchical relationships among villages as may occur within a state political structure.

Patterns of household labor and exchange in Puebloan society are therefore seen as potentially variable; they cannot simply be assumed to extend indefinitely into the past. In particular, Hastorf (1991) shows that household organization, including gender roles, can be affected by certain variables such as intensification of production and economic specialization. Change in just these variables is expected to be particularly important during the pithouse-to-pueblo transition in the American Southwest.

Economy, Exchange, and Gender Roles During the Pithouse Period in Central New Mexico

The Pithouse period is distant enough in time, and the archaeological sites "different" enough, so that many of the characteristics observed among historic and modern pueblos cannot necessarily be assumed to apply to the earlier time period. Archaeologists have thus sought information regarding population density, economy, and exchange relationships from other ethnographic sources to develop models of how this kind of society may have been organized (e.g., Gilman 1987; Plog and Powell 1984).

Sites such as the Kite site Pithouse village in central New Mexico (Figure 1) show evidence of a relatively generalized economy, with use of domesticated plants such as maize, squash, and beans, as well as wild plants such as *Portulaca* sp., chenopodium, and cactus. Deer and antelope were hunted, but most of the faunal remains at this site derive from small animals such as rabbits and pocket gophers. In general, one can envision Pithouse period sites in this area as loci where people were based for some portion of the year while planting and harvesting some crops, gathering wild plants, trapping small animals for immediate consumption, and possibly leaving the site periodically during hunting or foraging (or trading) expeditions. During some parts of the year the site may have been abandoned; during some years the occupants may have dwelt elsewhere entirely (Rautman 1993). The pithouse occupants apparently cultivated maize in cleared areas near the site, but wild plants also formed a substantial portion of their diet (Cummings 1990); during years of poor harvest, then, they may have acted more like hunter-gatherers with little disruption of the social and economic institutions that would have defined everyday life.

Exchange between local areas is an expected feature of life in the Southwest, where climatic conditions are patchy, and different microenvironments are created by both climatic patterns and topography. A model of the spatial and temporal patterning in modern climatic conditions in this particular area predicts that "stress years" during which local conditions would be relatively poor would occur relatively frequently, and that these stress years could, in fact, be buffered by obtaining resources from areas approximately 50 km away and located east and southeast of the site (Rautman 1993).

During some time periods, this region might be quite sparsely populated, and groups might be able to travel freely to obtain needed resources from diverse areas. During the Pithouse period, however, the region was populated by other similar communities (Kelley 1984). Under such conditions, social ties between communities would facilitate travel and use of resources throughout the region. These ties could facilitate the exchange of information regarding conditions in distant areas, the mobility of personnel between local areas, and also the exchange of food.

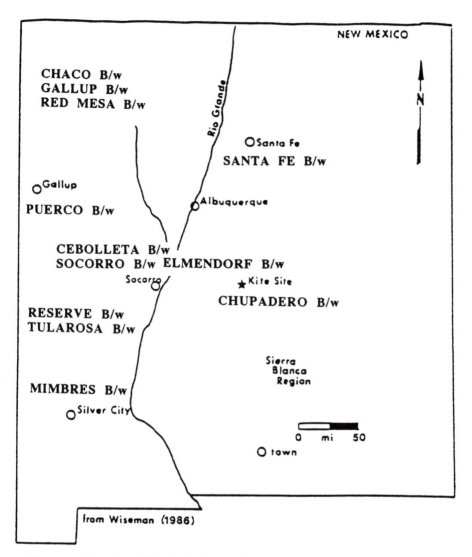

Figure 1. Location of Kite site Pithouse village (LA-38448) in central New Mexico. Social interactions during the Pithouse period are predicted to emphasize interactions with groups in the Sierra Blanca region. Chupadero black-on-white is the "local" pottery type in this area. The source areas for non-local black-on-white ceramic types at this site are also noted.

Ethnographic descriptions of exchange networks in other societies provide some way of envisioning how these networks might actually operate. One of the best-known examples of how social networks can buffer environmental variation is the exchange system called *hxaro* among the !Kung of Botswana (Wiessner 1986). In this society, social relationships of reciprocity are created and sustained among individuals by continued exchanges of nonequivalent items. The social ties that make up these networks of reciprocity are sustained by repeated personal contact: individuals visit their partners and present small gifts to them. These gifts are not immediately reciprocated, but at some later time the partner will similarly present a return gift of more-or-less equal value. The social ties thus created reduce subsistence risk among hunter-gathers by providing alternative residences during times of local resource scarcity. These social relationships involve people who are unrelated, as well as kin (Wiessner 1986).

A system of broadly similar scale and organization to the modern !Kung may have been used by pithouse dwellers such as those at the Kite site. The presence of non-local ceramics at the site shows that social ties with groups located at least 50 km away seems to have been common. Resources in this alternative-resource area could have been obtained by individuals or groups moving into the area, or by exchanges of foodstuffs among communities. Social ties that would maintain access to resources in this area could buffer the most frequently occurring types of expected environmental variation. Interactions with more-distant groups (living more than 100 km away) are also indicated by a small number of non-local ceramics from distant sources (Rautman 1993). This spatial scale of social interactions seems well within the parameters characterizing most *hxaro* relationships. A relatively low level of interaction with a number of areas, or more-distant areas, may represent continuing but low-level interactions in areas that are evaluated by participants to be less "functional" for reducing the risk of local resource variability (Table 1; the proposed ceramic source areas are shown in Figure 1).

The degree of individual mobility inherent in such a model of reciprocal exchanges is also within the range expected for part-agricultural groups at the Kite site. Pithouse sites are not expected to be permanent settlements, and "visiting" might easily be incorporated into hunting and/or gathering expeditions throughout the year. A range of individual mobility is also expected; it is not necessary that every member of society be an equal participant in such a system.

Some types of exchanges described among historic Pueblos include in-

TABLE 1. Local and non-local black-on-white ceramic types from Kite site Pithouse village.

Ceramic Type[a]	Number of Sherds	% of Total
Local Type		
Chupadero	1147	
Non-local Types		
Mancos	2	0.8
McElmo	2	0.8
Red Mesa	22	9.2
Escavada	3	1.3
Chaco-McElmo	3	1.3
Puerco	7	2.9
Snowflake	5	2.1
Klageto	1	0.4
Las Tusas	1	0.4
San Jose	1	0.4
Prewitt	1	0.4
Cebolleta	35	14.6
Socorro	53	22.1
San Marcial	1	0.4
Chaco II	28	11.7
Santa Fe (?)	3	1.3
Galisteo	6	2.5
Reserve	12	5.0
Tularosa	22	9.2
Mimbres	4	1.7
Elmendorf	4	1.7
"Western"	24	10.0
Total Non-local Sherds	*240*	*100.2*

Source: Data from Rautman (1990: Table 5.24) and Wiseman (1986).
[a] Ceramic types are grouped by the geographic region where they were produced.

teractions that resemble this model as well. Between-village visiting among relatives and the institution of trade partnerships obviously share some characteristics of the *hxaro* system, including, for example, widespread participation by both men and women and a high degree of personal mobility. It is also apparent that some types of exchanges among the historic Pueblo differ from this model. Some trading was considered to be a relatively specialized activity, set apart by the timing of its occurrence, the personnel involved, and the volume and nature of the goods exchanged. At some point during the prehistoric past, then, some aspects of trade became more specialized and segregated from the normal everyday life of most people in the community.

The Pithouse-to-Pueblo Transition: A Change in Scale

The transition from pithouse to puebloan architecture apparently represents a period of change in many aspects of society, including differences in individual mobility and economic organization. This period of time thus seems a likely place to look for possible changes in exchange relationships as well.

Gilman (1987) suggests that the transition between architectural forms may be prompted by increasing population and accompanying intensification of subsistence activities. In her model, subsistence intensification alters food-information networks within the village and increases the amount of time and space needed to store, process, and cook food. These kinds of changes are expected to affect a household's use of space because greater interior area, such as that possible in above-ground rooms in a pueblo, would be needed to provide space for activities such as food preparation and storage. In addition, the privacy afforded by use of interior space for these activities allows households to restrict the sharing of food and information about food to smaller social groups (Gilman 1987:556). The changes in architecture during the pithouse-to-pueblo transition thus represent a material response to these changing social and economic needs (Gilman 1987:560). In this model, changes in activities that are considered "women's work" in historic Puebloan society affect the organization of space within the household and also within the village.

I suggest that these and other changes associated with a change in architecture from pithouse to pueblo in the Southwest can be interpreted as a change in the scale of society. The concept of scale is often used to refer to spatial area, but it can also be used to refer to the social context of events (Barth 1978). Scale is a property of systems, both their spatial extent and their organization, and social interactions between individuals can be properly understood only in their proper scalar context. One meeting between lovers, for example, represents a very small-scale event, while another meeting of two individuals, for example between diplomats, is the result of large-scale processes (this example is drawn from Barth 1978). Seemingly identical social events and interactions can thus vary in their social context and hence also in their scale. Large-scale events do not necessarily differ in their location or personnel, but rather in their organization and in the social relationships between participants (Colson 1978).

A change in structural scale may involve a change in the geographic scale of a society, but it need not. Change in structural scale can be expressed in several other ways. Greater structural scale can also be expressed in an increase in (1) the number of roles available for people to assume, (2) the number of differentiated roles organized around the performance of one function, (3) the number of "echelons" or levels in a hierarchical organization, and (4) the number of different "event-types," each with its own associated group of roles (Schwartz 1978:225). A Type 3 change is probably not relevant to the basically egalitarian societies that we envision in the Southwest.

Many of the changes that Gilman (1987) describes for the pithouse-to-pueblo transition are consistent with a change in structural scale. There is "economic intensification" that involves greater specialization on one major cultivated crop (maize); subsistence tasks become more specialized as they are increasingly directed to cope with the needs for processing and storing maize; and household space itself becomes more specialized as certain areas become increasingly differentiated and dedicated to specific tasks. It is also apparent that specialization in subsistence tasks will probably not occur in isolation from the organization of other household tasks: in particular, economic intensification may affect the production of durable goods and craft items such as pottery as well as other tasks such as procurement of wild plant and animal foods.

It is likely that changes toward greater economic specialization during the pithouse-to-pueblo transition could also have profound impact on the definition and organization of gender roles, with gender roles diverging from those we envision for the Pithouse period and possibly resembling more those roles observed in historic Pueblo society. At the level of the individual, such specialization may represent a simplification of actions, with greater efforts devoted to fewer tasks. At the level of society, however, such specialization in tasks and roles represents increasing complexity and increasing scale.

Some of these changes are obviously expressed in the organization of labor within each household, possibly involving increasing differentiation of men's and women's work in the growing, processing, and storing of maize. Other aspects of specialization, however, may affect labor organization between households within a village, and also the organization of interaction and exchange networks between villages. For example, ethnoarchaeological study of ceramic production and exchange among egalitarian societies in the Philippines has shown that changes in household ceramic production can be associated with changes in the organization of pottery distribution and also in the size of the exchange system (Stark 1992). In particular, expansion of the scale of this ceramic-exchange system has resulted in a greater geographic range of exchanges, so that even distant villages inhabited by different ethnic groups are incorporated into the exchange network.

Other changes in different aspects of scale are also apparent. Ceramic production (traditionally women's activity) has been intensified, with some women becoming increasingly specialized producers, and others abandoning production to concentrate on trading. The number of roles available for women has thereby increased. Villages have also assumed different "roles" in this system, as villages themselves have become differentiated and their roles in the exchange system increasingly specialized. In some villages, ceramic production has increased relative to other villages, and some villages have become net exporters of ceramics to others. Accompanying these changes are also changes in the context of inter-village exchange, including development of a new social relationship and role, that of the trade partner (Stark 1992:139). Changes in social scale are thus expressed in geography and also in organizational changes that affect the number and differentiation of roles available to individuals and villages.

In this example, it is evident that changes in household labor organization can affect the relationship between villages as well as the organization and operation of extra-village exchange networks. It is also evident that a change in a society's structural scale could be expressed in activities that take place within households and villages. During the pithouse-to-pueblo transition in the Southwest, a change toward greater economic intensification has been associated with economic specialization at the level of the household. It is likely that exchange relationships among villages would also be affected by these structural changes. Exchanges may differ, for example, in geographic extent, the types of products moved, and/or the social relationships involved in production and in trade.

An Early Puebloan Site in Central New Mexico

If we view the pithouse-to-pueblo transition in a more general sense as a time of change in the scale of society, we can develop certain expectations about how such a change might be expressed in an individual case. Here I concentrate on identifying possible changes in the organization of previously established exchange networks during this period of transition.

Archaeological data from Pueblo de la Mesa, an early Pueblo site in Cibola National Forest about 25 km east of the Pithouse site, provide evidence of architectural form, subsistence, and regional ceramic exchange. Radiocarbon dates from this site range from about A.D. 1160 to 1500 (Table 2). Here, a change in the subsistence economy is suggested by ethnobotanical remains. Maize cob fragments, cupules, and kernels are present in high quantities in all contexts, including room fill, extramural midden, and hearth features. Only twelve taxa of wild plants are represented.

TABLE 2.   Radiocarbon dates from Pueblo de la Mesa (LA-2091).

Context	Lot number	Beta number	Radiocarbon age (±1 sigma)	Calibrated age (±2 sigma)
Kiva 1 above floor	496	72964	515 ± 55 B.P.	A.D. 1310–1350 and A.D. 1380–1460
Rm 5 below floor	569	72965	650 ± 55 B.P.	A.D. 1270–1410
Rm 3 above floor	583	72966	480 ± 55 B.P.	A.D. 1400–1500
Rm 4 above floor	584	72967	790 ± 60 B.P.	A.D. 1160–1300
Kiva 2 base of excavation	604	72968	720 ± 60 B.P.	A.D. 1220–1400

In contrast, nearly all samples at the Pithouse site revealed a number of different taxa of weedy plants. At the Pueblo site, most wild taxa are represented by only one seed; typical numbers of recovered seeds are less than half a dozen. In only one context (a hearth) was there a significant number of carbonized seeds (chenopodium). At the Pithouse site, many more carbonized seeds were recovered; in some samples, hundreds or even a thousand seeds were counted (Table 3). These values seem to indicate real differences in subsistence rather than differences in preservation or recovery of seeds (Trigg 1994). Additional analysis of total diet using human

TABLE 3.   Carbonized seeds and plant parts from the Pithouse and the Pueblo site.

Taxon	Pithouse Site LA-38448 (N)	Pueblo Site LA-2091 (N)
Maize cob fragments	present	3
Maize cupule fragments	356	3458
Maize germ	0	2
Maize kernel (or fragment)	present	194
Chenopodium	301	55
Chenopodium/Amaran	351	0
Amaranth	2	0
Kochia	0	3
Atriplex	0	1
Portulaca	1929	1
Cyperaceae	0	1
Juniper seed	0	1
Grass seed	0	3
Dropseed	0	1
Opuntia	2	4
Echinocactus	0	5
Spharalcea	0	2
Cruciferae	0	1
Unidentified seed	0	3
Juniper needle	0	100
Yucca leaf	0	1
Sueda	2	0
Compositae	6	0
Oryzopsis	3	0
Helianthus	24	0

Sources: Pithouse data from Moore (1990) (42 flotation samples); Pueblo data from Trigg (1994) (25 flotation samples).

bone chemistry is still underway. From the information available, however, it seems that maize was in fact of greater importance for inhabitants of the later site, and that there is reduced use of wild species.

If these changes toward economic specialization represent one aspect of an overall change in structural scale, this change may also be recorded in the participation of Pueblo de la Mesa in regional exchange, which may be indicated by changes in the ceramic assemblage at the Pueblo site (e.g., Pool 1992). Regional social interactions may differ in spatial scale and/or in their structure. The size of the ceramic-exchange network may become larger and more types of ceramic wares may be represented at the site if social relationships expand to include previously neglected groups.

Analysis of the Pueblo de la Mesa ceramics is still in progress. It does seem clear, however, that the Pueblo-period ceramic assemblage is distinctly different from that of the Pithouse period (Table 4). One obvious difference is in the diversity of ceramic types represented. At the Pithouse site, some 17 percent of typed black-on-white sherds were identified as non-local; these derived from 21 different named black-on-white types (Wiseman 1986). At the Pueblo site, no non-local black-on-white types have yet been identified, even though several of those types continue to be produced (data from Wiseman 1986: Table 1). There is a decrease in the proportion of utilitarian local brownwares at the Pueblo site; this change is accompanied, however, by an increased proportion of other "local" deco-

TABLE 4.   Comparison between ceramic assemblages at the Pithouse and the Pueblo site.

Ware Category	Pithouse-period Kite Site (LA-38448)	Pueblo-period Pueblo de la Mesa Site (LA-2091)
Brownwares	89.2%	43.2%
Black-on-white wares, undecorated whitewares	10.0%	26.5%
Redwares (black-on-red, undecorated redwares)	0.6%	17.9%
Polychromes	0.1%	0.9%
Glazed sherds	0	7.0%
Other/too fragmentary	0.1%	4.5%
Total	*100%*	*100%*

rated wares—Chupadero black-on-white and also Lincoln black-on-red (Lincoln black-on-red [Kelley 1984:125–126] is considered to be "local" in this study). The one non-local ware that is abundant at the Pueblo site is a glazeware (Glaze A), presumably produced along the northern reaches of the Rio Grande, about 100–150 km northwest of the site.

The ceramic assemblage from the Pueblo site thus indicates some temporal continuity in network membership, shown by the continued importance of some "local" pottery types such as the brownwares and Chupadero black-on-white. Change in other aspects of regional social interactions is also apparent, however, involving an increase in the spatial size of the exchange network to include the production areas of Rio Grande glazewares, and also an apparent change in the organization (and possible functioning) of regional ties.

The diverse array of non-local pottery types at Kite site Pithouse village (Figure 1) is not observed at the later site, a change that may be structured by a possibly decreased role of risk buffering in structuring social interactions during the later time period. Interactions with groups near the Rio Grande are not predicted to be of importance in buffering local environmental variability near the Pueblo site (Rautman 1993); exchange with groups in this area, represented by the volume of glazed sherds at the Pueblo site, are therefore apparently structured by factors that are not included in the climatic model.

Implications for Gender Roles

These data point to possible internal reorganization of regional interactions and exchange relationships as well as changes in local economy and in architectural form during the pithouse-to-pueblo transition. I suggest that these seemingly disparate changes can be best understood as different aspects of an overall scalar change in society. These scalar changes may also be expressed in the reorganization of household labor, specifically in a reorganization of gender roles during this time, including an increasing differentiation of men's and women's work that may have affected ceramic production and distribution as well as other economic activities.

It is apparent that most Southwestern archaeologists do make clear (although often unstated) assumptions regarding men's and women's roles in economic tasks such as processing food and pottery making, relying on direct historical analogy with the gendered organization of household tasks among the historic Pueblo (e.g., Longacre 1970 and many others). However, there is no a priori reason why greater economic specialization need be expressed in the production of durable items such as pottery, or why a change in structural scale toward an increasing number of roles should result in the differentiation of those roles by gender. In the Philippine example above, for instance, women are the pottery producers, and the new and specialized role of the pottery trader is also filled by women, some of whom used to be potters.

Among Puebloan groups, however, economic specialization apparently did affect the structure of gender roles at some point in the past. Hence archaeologists commonly imagine women laboring to process maize on prehistoric metates, and may envision males negotiating the trade of female-made pottery while on hunting trips. It is more difficult to make such facile assumptions when we are faced with time periods in the past in which the archaeological remains "look" much different from the historic pueblos; for example, when people are inhabiting pit structures and potentially abandoning their villages for much of the year. In these cases we may not find ready analogs among the known ethnographic groups in that particular region.

What we do have, however, are structural similarities between observed groups and groups in the prehistoric past. We can see how exchange networks that are characterized by reciprocity are sustained by individual mobility and strategic maintenance of ambiguous relationships. We can see the ways in which increased geographic scale of exchange networks is associated with a reorganization of household labor and the development of specialized roles. And we can see that a change in society's structural scale can be expressed in diverse ways, which may or may not include the differentiation of certain activities by gender.

Therefore, when archaeologists make assumptions regarding the prehistoric depth of observed social relationships and gender roles, we should do so not because of any necessary connection between the past and present in a given society, but because of a presumed similarity in social organization and in scale. I have suggested that a change in the structural scale of society during the pithouse-to-pueblo transition involves change in the organization of inter-village ties as well as in the organization of household labor, including greater specialization and differentiation of gender roles. I might then expect gender roles among early Puebloan people (such as the inhabitants of Pueblo de la Mesa) to resemble those observed among modern pueblos, rather than those observed among the !Kung, but not because the prehistoric pueblos simply "look like pueblos." Rather, I have these expectations because I see certain structural similarities between these societies in their economic organization, specialized labor requirements, and definition of space.

Inferences based on analogy, such as those discussed above, are often used in archaeology, and their use and verification have long been a subject of debate. A focus on the structural scale of society, and on temporal changes in that scale, is one way of linking specific functions, activities, and roles in living societies with the observed artifacts, and spatial patterning in those artifacts, that characterize a past society. Such a perspective focuses also on the conceptual "locations" of independent supporting evidence. Thus, having postulated a connection between changes in the structural scale of society, intensification in production, and specialization of activities, including those involved in gender roles, we might find further evidence of such specialization in other contexts in production and consumption. This evidence might be shown, for example, in human bone chemistry, in the morphology of processing tools such as grinding stones, or possibly in greater standardization of pottery production (Arnold and Nieves 1992).

In addition, the concept of scale as described here unifies many of the disparate changes that archaeologists observe at the time of this transition. Noting the existence of a relationship between aspects of society such as economic intensification and role specialization does not attempt to explain the cause of these changes, but highlights their mutual interconnections. With this information we can better distinguish the social context within which change is expected to occur, and investigate the conditions under which societies may adopt one or another "solution" when faced with similar structural situations—that is, we can use this information in developing real "explanation" of such changes in general and also in particular cases.

Gender During the Pithouse-to-Pueblo Transition

The Southwestern pithouse-to-pueblo transition may provide clues to the beginnings of a process of gender differentiation and role ascription that in historic Puebloan society results in the classification of certain activities as "men's work" and "women's work," and the spatial segregation of these activities. Part of this gendered division of labor involves a general separation between production of many craft items, such as ceramics, and the distribution of these same items in inter-village trade.

At the level of the individual site or village, and households within a village, a change in structural scale is manifested in changes in architecture and spatial organization of activity areas both within households and within the village (Gilman 1987). Within a region, this same change in scale may affect economic organization and also exchange between communities. The ceramic remains from a Pithouse site and an early Pueblo site in central New Mexico suggest that this change may have affected several aspects of regional-exchange relationships, including the spatial extent of social and exchange networks, the number of exchange relationships that were maintained by any one village, and possibly the role of such relationships in coping with local resource variability.

At the level of the individual, a change in the scale of society can involve increasing task differentiation and specialization, with a greater number of social roles becoming available for individuals. Such a change in scale need not be associated with a change to hierarchical status differentiation and hierarchical control (e.g., Stark 1992), and increased differentiation and specialization of gender roles similarly need not, by definition, imply exploitation of one gender by another (cf. Gutierrez 1991).

Stark's (1992) description of ceramic production and exchange in the Philippines shows that task differentiation does not necessarily involve differentiating these tasks into separate gender categories. In this example, ceramic production has become differentiated from distribution, but both tasks are typically performed by women. The number of economic roles available for women has therefore increased. At some point in Southwestern prehistory, however, this same sort of economic specialization and task differentiation apparently became a strongly gendered one, such that trade in general became associated with farming, hunting, and warfare, other "outside" activities that are generally thought to be "men's work" (even though women participated in many trade expeditions), while "women's work" became associated with the production of ceramics and most other craft items.

It may be that times of change in structural scale, such as that represented by the pithouse-to-pueblo transition, would be times when economic differentiation and specialization could affect a society's definition of gender roles. An understanding of how different aspects of society might be affected by a change in structural scale could therefore help us identify the temporal depth of observed cultural distinctions such as gender differences, and also the way in which such changes might appear in different societies. Gender-role differences such as those observed in the context of ceramic manufacture and distribution among the historic Pueblo may thus represent one way in which a structural change involving differentiation of economic tasks and greater role specialization can be expressed at the level of the individual.

Acknowledgments

Funding for the excavation of Pueblo de la Mesa was provided by grants from the National Forest Service and from the National Geographic Society. A postdoctoral fellowship from the American Association of University Women allowed me the time to develop these ideas and to write this chapter. I appreciate Kate Spielmann's guiding me to Miriam Stark's study and encouraging me to think about how I might use my data on regional exchange to address the issue of gender roles. Discussions with Miriam Stark, Patricia Gilman, and Helen Pollard helped clarify my thinking, although of course they cannot be held accountable for my use of their ideas and observations. The chapter was also improved by thoughtful comments from Cheryl Claassen.

8. Gender, Diet, Health, and Social Status in the Mississippian Powers Phase Turner Cemetery Population

Diane Wilson

The Powers Phase (ca. A.D. 1325–1365) is a Mississippian manifestation that stretches some 250 square kilometers in the middle portion of the Mississippi River valley from the Cairo lowlands of southeastern Missouri into the St. Francis River region of northeastern Arkansas (Figure 1). The ceremonial center, Powers Fort (23BU10), contained four platform mounds; the smaller sites had none. At least seven small towns of 1.5 to 4 acres in size were located within a 6-kilometer arc to the south and east of Powers Fort. Most of these village sites were paired with an adjacent settlement. About seventy smaller hamlets and farmsteads also were located in the Powers Phase area.

Powers Phase archaeology began in the late 1800s with excavation at the Powers Fort site by Cyrus Thomas (1894). Nearly seventy-five years later the Powers Phase project was begun by James Price with a survey of an area along the Little Black River in 1965. In 1966 test excavations were carried out at the Turner site (Price 1969). In the four field seasons that followed, two villages were completely excavated and a thorough survey of the area was made. With the discoveries that all structures were consumed by fire and that all villages contained little refuse, short occupations for the Turner (23BU21A) and Snodgrass (23BU21B) sites were suggested.

The only cemetery that was located and completely excavated was at the Turner site (Figure 2). There were few infants, elderly, and males in the burial population (61 females, 28 males, and 29 individuals for which sex could not be determined). Thomas Black (1979) described the sixty burials that contained 118 individuals. Individuals were sexed on the basis of pelvic, cranial, and femoral structure, and aged on the basis of tooth wear. The incidence of pathology and trauma was also examined, although preservation was very poor at the Turner site. The completeness of the Powers

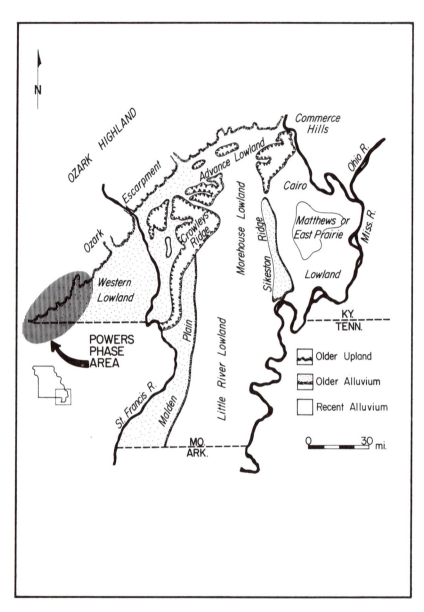

Figure 1. Location of the Powers Phase on the Arkansas-Missouri border (after Price and Griffin 1979:4).

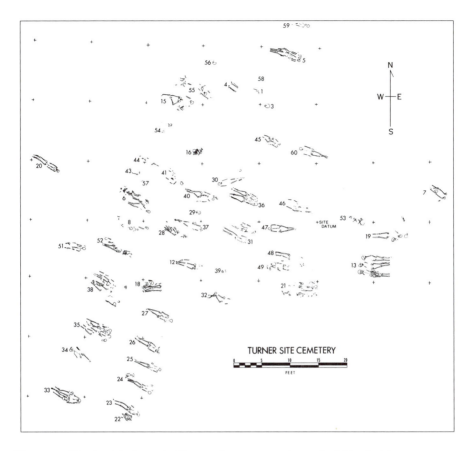

Figure 2.   The burials from the Turner site cemetery, located within the Turner village (after Black 1979).

Phase excavation strategy, apparent brevity of occupation, and, more importantly, the sex ratio of those interred in the Turner village cemetery make the study of this population particularly intriguing.

The research presented here on the Turner burials and on the Powers Phase was undertaken with the following goals in mind: to examine gender, sex roles, and status within this population by examining spatial segregation of burials, grave-good associations, mortality curves, and food distribution; and to test hypotheses previously offered, but not investigated, to explain the spatial segregation of burials in the Powers Phase.

Social-Spatial and Artifact Patterning within the Turner Cemetery

There were very few grave goods in relation to the number of individuals present in the cemetery (103 grave goods for 118 individuals). Ceramic vessels occurred more often than any other grave good, with whole vessels occurring in thirteen burials. Projectile points, the second most prevalent artifact, were found in only six burials.

This type of artifact distribution made it infeasible to infer anything about task orientation for anyone other than the adult females. It seems likely that females made the pottery because ceramics were primarily associated with them. Only one vessel was included with a male burial. Burial 60 was an elderly male with his head oriented to the west (Black 1979:38). Interred with him was an "inferior quality" bowl (Black 1979:38). Two children were also interred with vessels. It is plausible that individuals associated with a feminine gender performed ceramic manufacture and/or primary use of these vessels. If this was the case, the Powers Phase social structure may have assigned them a feminine gender status, or may not have recognize these three individuals as strictly gendered due to their age. Most of the associations observed on artifacts were found with females. In fact, no artifact type could be confidently associated exclusively with males or children. This artifact distribution was probably the result of higher mean numbers of artifacts per female than per male. Comparing females to males throughout the Turner cemetery, females averaged more than twice the artifacts associated with males, at 1.4 and 0.6, respectively.

Males contradicted this pattern, however, with a greater mean number of artifacts in single burials; they average 1.5 items, while female single interments average 1.4. It was in multiple burials where the largest difference between the sexes was seen. Grave goods in multiple burials were concentrated around females. In multiple burials, which averaged more artifacts than single burials, females averaged 1.4 inclusions per person in a given multiple burial, while males averaged only 0.2. If the number of grave inclusions is correlated with social status and/or identity, then it appears that female status and/or identity was fixed but that male status varied within the Turner burial population.

Spatial patterning within the Turner cemetery suggests that females played a central role in the social identity of others. Children seemed to cluster in the westernmost row near the center of the cemetery. Females were found throughout the cemetery but appeared clustered in the center of the cemetery. The female burials in this central grouping included Burials 6, 8, 12, 16, 18, 21, 27, 28, 30, 31, 32, 36, 37, 38, 40, 41, 47, 48, 49, and 52. The only burials in the center of the cemetery that did not contain females were single-child interments. Males were dispersed throughout the cemetery with no visible clustering.

Females were also found to occupy a central place within multiple burials, a position I suggest may be symbolic of their central role in social identity. Only two children and no males occupied the central positions within graves. Females occupying this central position (N = 22) averaged two grave goods, higher than any other category of persons interred at Turner.

Females were the least likely to be interred individually. Children were more likely than any other category of individuals to be interred singly. Thirty percent of children were buried alone, whereas only 24 percent of males and 21 percent of females were buried singly (X = 0.05). The other pattern that was statistically significant regarded with whom individuals were interred. Individuals were more likely to be buried with females than with any other individual or by themselves. Fourteen children were interred with females; thirty-one females were interred with other females; and fifteen males were buried with females. I believe that this interment pattern may symbolize recognition of matrilineal descent.

This pattern alone might also be used to suggest that females may have been included in multiple burials as retainers; however, females averaged considerably more artifacts than other individuals within multiple burials and were located in the central position within the grave. To the contrary, artifact distributions and spatial patterning within multiple burials suggest that the high number of females found in multiple burials may be indicative of female status, emphasized by relationships with other individuals.

Multiple burials were examined for position within the graves and grave goods. In the northernmost position, females averaged 1.4 items, yet males only averaged 0.4 artifacts. Only females and children occupied the central burial position. Children who held the middle position did not have associated artifacts, while females averaged two artifacts apiece. Likewise, in the southernmost position, females averaged 0.9 items, while the two males occupying this position within the burial had none. Although the types of artifacts included in the Turner burials are primarily utilitarian, their very existence suggests that females in multiple burials were not simply retainers.

Average Age of Death and Control over Reproduction, Contraception, and Childbearing

As individuals pass through different life stages, they are exposed to differential risks associated with the aging process, cultural practices, and the natural environment. Examples of variables influencing mortality include nutrition, climate, pathogens, population density, warfare, infanticide, birthing, contraception, abortion, sexual taboos, and migration. Life tables were constructed to help determine whether hunting and/or warfare, as well as maternal mortality, were significant factors affecting the mortality profile of this Powers Phase population.

The sex ratio at the Turner site was unequaled in any other Mississippian cemetery of its size. More than twice as many females as males were buried at the Turner site. Barring catastrophic health conditions, the burial representation by sex suggests a seasonally or socially defined subset of the larger population. Although Buikstra and Mielke (1985) state that Mississippian village cemeteries had a predominance of females and a general lack of males, none has a sex ratio comparable to that of Turner (Wilson 1993). Powell (1992) found an abundance of males interred in Mississippian elite contexts, but it should be noted that this does not mean that more males than females were interred at mound centers, because this has not been found to be the case (Wilson 1993). Unfortunately, the sex ratio at the Powers Fort mound center remains unknown.

To examine specific ecological and cultural influences on mortality patterns within the Turner population, I constructed Table 1. Since Black (1979) could not give a specific age to many individuals analyzed, broader categories (adult, old adult, juvenile, etc.) were used. These age categories were subdivided into years based on general patterns of morphological changes associated with the aging process.

To include everyone in the life table, individuals were assigned probabilities of belonging to a specific 5-year interval. For example, B1 was specified as adult and was therefore included as a 0.2 probability in each of the 5-year intervals from 25 to 49 years. This was done rather than assigning individuals to a median age of 37 years, or excluding these individuals from the life-table statistics.

Since mean age at death is an approximation of life expectancy, and archaeologists do not have access to real life-expectancy observations, the two terms are often used synonymously for archaeological populations. To minimize the effect of subadult underenumeration, life expectancies at various ages were compared. Usually mean age of death at 15 or 20 is examined. Besides reducing bias from low representation of subadults, examining average age at death from older ages allows the sexes to be examined separately. This provides a wealth of information about cultural practices and treatment of individuals based on sex and age categories. For example, patterns of higher female life expectancy are found with low widespread mortality and high levels of social and economic development (Fix 1991).

The Turner population life expectancy at age 15 was 24.2 years, and at 20 it was 20.6 years. Life expectancies for females and males were very similar throughout the adult and older-adult life cycle at the Turner site (Figure 3). Differences were never greater than 2 years in life expectancy at all ages. This similarity is unusual compared to other Mississippian sites,

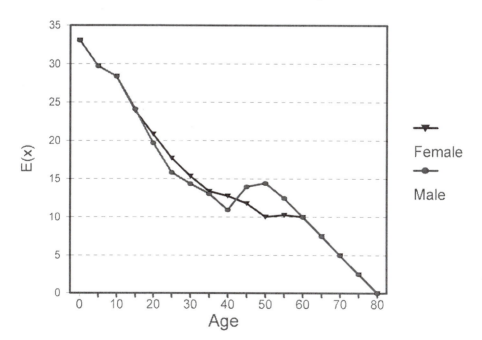

Figure 3.   Average age of death for the Turner females and males.

which exhibit considerably higher male life expectancy. This pattern of male longevity is accepted as the norm throughout prehistory, with females living an average of 4 years less than males (Hassan 1981:128). At the Turner site the pattern of life expectancy was indicative of relatively equal health conditions for females and males. Relatively equal health status may suggest relatively equal social status.

For females at the Turner site, mean age of death at age 15 was insignificantly less than for males (23.9 and 24.1 years, respectively) and at age 20 was higher for females than males (20.9 and 19.7 years, respectively). Females were expected to have lower life expectancy in this age range due to the risks associated with early pregnancy. However, the life expectancies showed that males were equally at risk during this life stage, suggesting that females within the Powers Phase may have had considerable control over reproduction through abortion, contraception, and/or cultural prescriptions such as sexual taboos. It logically follows that females probably controlled the size of their families according to cultural and personal ideals. After age 20, life expectancies for males were consistently lower than for females until ages 45–59, presumably after childbearing years.

A mortality curve for the Turner cemetery population is presented in Figure 4. This curve displays two important features of the Turner mortality profile: first, male mortality is consistently higher than female mortality, and second, all age segments of the population are present. High-mortality populations (low mean age at death) are typically characterized by high female mortality (Fix 1991:211). Higher female mortality (than male) in all ages over 15 years is not uncommon in populations lacking modern medical care, resulting in a progressive increase in the sex ratio of the living population. In such populations, maternal mortality is the primary cause of death. However, higher male mortality among the Powers Phase population may indicate that maternal mortality was not the leading cause of death.

Although male death was more erratic than female death, it was not unstable enough to suggest a catastrophic curve as is seen in populations experiencing excessive mortality over a brief time period. Causes of such curves include warfare, epidemic disease, and famine. If a catastrophic event occurred, certain age segments of the Turner population would be underrepresented. I therefore believe that catastrophic events did not selectively remove males from the Turner population. Black (1979) suggests, with the implicit assumption that only males would have participated, that warfare may have been responsible for the lack of males interred at Turner;

Mortality Curve

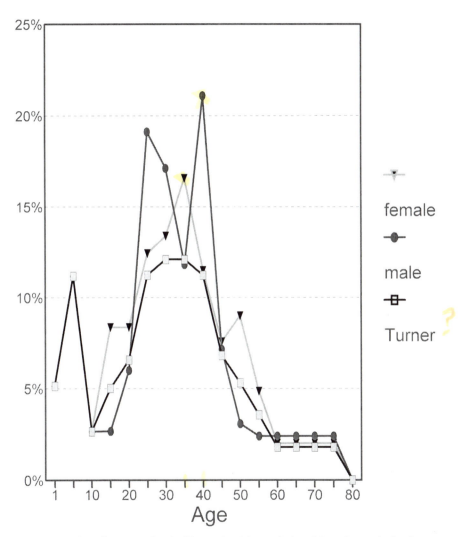

Figure 4. Mortality curve for the Turner burial population. Note that male death is higher than female death at nearly all ages.

however, warfare extreme enough to have removed half of the expected male population would have presented itself in the form of a catastrophic curve. Ceremonial activities, selective raiding of males, gathering food in a dangerous way, rough gaming, and small-scale warfare could all explain the higher male mortality experienced by the Turner population, but these events appear to have occurred on a somewhat regular basis. It is interesting to note that peak death occurs for females and males during the same ages, just to a greater extent among males. It is possible that the same activities were undertaken by members of both sexes, with greater risk incurred by males.

Violent Injury

For females and males the incidence of violent injury was apparently low within the Powers Phase, and particularly within the Turner burial population. Poor preservation may have biased this interpretation. Only 3 of the 155 individuals analyzed by Black (1979) from the entire Powers Phase showed evidence of violent injury, and only one of those individuals was interred at the Turner site. This suggests that the incidence of warfare and/ or violent raiding or other interaction may not have been high during the Powers Phase.

Of the traumatic injuries recorded by Black (1979), two were projectile point wounds in males. The tip of a Scallorn point (Black 1979: 29) was found embedded in the left innominate from B-31C, an adult male. Another point wound was found in the left femur of an adult male buried at the Powers Fort site. The other violent injury was found in B-6 from the Powers Fort site and represented the possible scalping of an adult female.

Stable Isotopes and Dietary Reconstruction

A stable-isotope analysis on bone collagen and apatite was undertaken for a sample of the Powers Phase burial population in order to investigate nutritional-resource distribution. This analysis included thirteen individuals from the Turner site, two individuals from the Snodgrass site, and two individuals from the Powers Fort site. From the Turner sample, two individuals of indeterminant sex (B22 and B65), six females (B17, B25B, B27, B30, B35A, and B35B), and five males (B20, B23, B33A, B55D, and B60) were used. From the other sites, one female and one male were sampled (Snodgrass B3 and B4, and Powers Fort B3 and B6).

All samples were analyzed for delta ^{13}C apatite and gelatin, and delta ^{15}N gelatin to explore photosynthetic and nitrogen pathways represented in the food webs on which the Powers Phase subsisted. Due to poor preservation, delta ^{15}N was not detectable for all samples. All samples fell within the appropriate carbon/nitrogen ratio for collagen (2.9–3.6) (DeNiro 1985). However, because some samples gave low nitrogen yields, they still may be suspect samples that may have given low delta ^{13}C gelatin values (Harold Krueger, personal communication, 1993). These samples are Powers Fort 6 and Turner 20, B25B, and B30.

This analysis was undertaken because food distribution is considered central to social organization. Beyond nutrition, the manipulation and circulation of food can express economic, political, and social relationships, thus expressing gender relationships of the past (Hastorf 1991:132). Food systems are believed to be one of the bases of social systems. Consequently, many ethnographies are centered around the social importance of food (for a review of the literature see Speth 1990 and Hastorf 1991). Food and eating are central to conceptions of social relationships, power, status, reproduction, economy, ideology, and sex, all of which are fundamental in constructions of gender. Dietary intake of females and males can therefore be understood in terms of differential access to food stuffs that necessarily represent differential societal positions in relation to the distribution of nutritional resources (Claassen 1991a, b; Hastorf 1991:133).

Prior to this analysis Boutton et al. (1984) analyzed three samples from the Turner site for delta ^{13}C gelatin in a regional study on the introduction of maize into southeastern Missouri and northeastern Arkansas. The three samples from B21A, B28, and B36B fell within a continuum suggesting increased maize consumption through time in this region. Their results suggested that female and male diets may have differed, since the one male sampled (B21A) had a delta ^{13}C value of − 15.8, considerably lower than the female values of − 13.2 from B28 and − 14.1 from B36B (Boutton et al. 1984:201). When possible, those samples have been compared with the samples presented here (Table 1).

Clearly the Powers Phase inhabitants participated in maize agriculture as indicated by delta ^{13}C values; however, there was considerable variability

TABLE 1.   Stable isotope values in parts per thousand (ppt).

Sample	^{13}C apatite	^{13}C gelatin	^{15}N gelatin	Sex
Powers Fort B3	−8.9	−14.0	+8.4	M
Powers Fort B6	−8.2	−21.7	+4.3	F
Snodgrass B4A	−7.8	−15.4	+8.1	M
Snodgrass B3	−10.2	−13.5	+7.5	F
Turner B17	−9.8	−15.6	+3.8	F
Turner B20	−9.5	−18.5	too small	M
Turner B22	−5.3	−13.5	+8.2	I
Turner B23	−6.0	−14.2	+10.3	M
Turner B25B	−8.4	−17.4	too small	F
Turner B27	−12.4	−19.1	too small	F
Turner B30	−8.9	−17.5	+9.6	F
Turner B33A	−6.5	−15.5	too small	M
Turner B35A	−11.0	−13.1	+6.7	F
Turner B35B	−9.6	−13.4	+7.7	F
Turner B55D	−7.5	−13.6	+7.4	M
Turner B60	−8.0	−14.1	+8.2	M
Turner B65	−5.3	−12.3	+8.2	I
*Turner B21A	–	−15.8	–	M
*Turner B28	–	−13.2	–	F
*Turner B36B	–	−14.1	–	F

* Boutton et al. 1984:201.
δ R Sample ppt = [Rsample/Rstandard] × 1000 (13C/12C standard is PDB 15N/14N standard is Atmospheric Nitrogen).

of diet among individuals. DeNiro and Schoeninger (1983) found variation of 1 and less for delta ^{15}N and delta ^{13}C for animals fed identical diets. They also cited archaeological instances of individuals from the same geographical location and social status having equivalent delta ^{15}N and delta ^{13}C values (1983:202).

Delta ^{13}C values were compared first since they were available in the greatest quantity (including Boutton et al. 1984 data, N = 20). When delta ^{13}C values were compared, considerable variability was noted, although there were only three outliers from the standard deviation (Powers Fort B6 and Turner B20 and B27). The mean delta ^{13}C value was −15.3 (s = 2.4). Until recently, delta ^{13}C values were interpreted as representing calories, but now it is believed that the picture is slightly more complex. Assuming a fractionation factor of 5, the traditional approach would have suggested that maize contributed approximately 42 percent to 58 percent, averaging

49 percent, of the calories in the diet. In low protein diets such as in eastern North American maize agriculturists, delta ^{13}C gelatin values are believed to reflect the protein dietary source (Ambrose 1993). It therefore seems more reasonable to assume that a majority of the protein in the Powers Phase diet came from C4 plant sources.

When both delta ^{15}N and delta ^{13}C values for gelatin were compared from the Powers Phase material (Figure 5), seven of the thirteen individ-

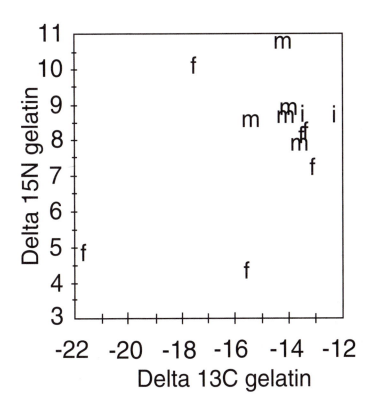

Figure 5.   Gelatin δ 13C‰ and δ 15N‰. Stable isotope values in ‰, where: δR_{sample}‰ = [R_{sample} / $R_{standard}$] × 1000   13C/12C standard is PDB 15N/14N standard is Atmospheric Nitrogen.

uals analyzed had diets that were within 1 percent of each other. These individuals included women and men (Powers Fort B3, Snodgrass B3, and Turner B4A, B22, B35A, B36B, and B55). These individuals had diets that fell just below the means -15.3 dietary value and surrounded the delta ^{15}N mean (7.6), although all values fell within the standard deviation (delta ^{15}N, s = 1.7).

Their delta ^{15}N values suggest considerable reliance on terrestrial herbivores such as white-tailed deer. If the fractionation factor for nitrogen of $3-4$ (DeNiro and Epstein 1981) is considered, then the delta ^{15}N mean value of 7.6 represents an ecosystem value of 4.1. This value is slightly lower than the mean reported by Katzenburg (1989) of 5.5 for prehistoric deer. Of the other species that Smith (1973) estimated were important food resources for which information was available, only beaver, bear, and noncarnivorous fish had delta ^{15}N signatures low enough to fall within the Powers Phase population values.

With the considerable variation in diet represented by the Powers Phase population, it was difficult to decipher differences by sex. Male diets appear to have been generally more homogeneous than that of females based on collagen results for both carbon and nitrogen (X = 0.05). A number of explanations could account for this situation. Females may have been responsible for food distribution at a household or larger unit area. In this case females would have had access to a variety of food stuffs to eat as they wished. Social position may have been more variable for females than for males. In other words, some females may have had access to better quality and quantities of food resources than others, while males all shared the same access to these food resources. Females may have been the primary food providers, responsible for maize harvesting and gathering as well as hunting. However, some evidence suggests that males may have hunted or eaten protein products different from those eaten by females. When nitrogen values were examined alone, they showed that on the whole, males (with the exception of Turner B30) had delta ^{15}N values that were slightly higher than females. These signatures relate to different dietary items consumed, not different quantities of meat protein as indicated by delta ^{13}C values on gelatin.

Assuming, as Ambrose (1993:109) suggests, that apatite values reflect the dietary whole, females and males appear to have had considerably different diets. Female values were consistently more negative than male values (Figure 6). If the pattern suggested by Krueger and Sullivan (1984)

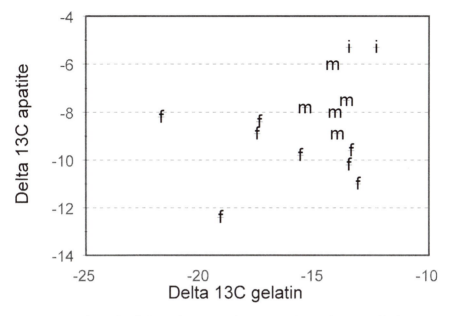

Figure 6.   Delta 13C gelatin and apatite values. Note that males generally have higher δ 13C apatite values than females.

holds, as it appears to, differences in apatite values reflect differential protein intakes and/or metabolic rates. Following the trophic-level differences observed in bone carbonate relative to gelatin in delta ¹³C values, males appear to have consumed less protein on average than females, although this was not statistically significant. Again, male values were more consistent and more often fell within the mean and standard deviation than female values.

Thus, it is likely that at least some females had access to more and better quality food sources than males. It is also likely that females had a more variable social position than males within the Powers Phase social system, since females seemed to have both extremely high quality diets and low quality diets. This extreme is perhaps best exemplified in the comparison of Turner B30 and Powers Fort B6. Male homogeneity is perhaps best exemplified by the similarity of the diet of Powers Fort B3 and all other Turner males, in contrast with the drastic difference in the diet of the only female recovered from Powers Fort compared to the rest of the population.

Conclusions

So where were the males that should have accompanied the females in equal proportions into the Turner cemetery? There does appear to be an abundance of males at the Powers Fort site, but a true sex ratio from this site may never be known. The current sample of six individuals does not make the known sex ratio from the Powers Phase more equal. The Powers Fort material remains do suggest, however, that there was an engendered segregation of space within the Powers Phase. Village sites, at least the Turner and Snodgrass villages, appear to have been culturally allocated space for a gender dominated by females. Powers Fort may have been space allocated for a gender dominated by males.

Within the village context, goods and food resources appear to have been distributed preferentially to females. The diets of males were homogeneous, whereas female diets differed. Grave goods with males were more numerous in single burials than in multiple burials (averaging 1.5 in single burials and 0.6 in multiple burials). Fewer individuals were interred singly than in multiple burials, and most were interred with females. Grave goods with females numbered the same (averaging 1.4) whether females were buried alone or with others. In multiple burials, artifacts clustered around the females, and females were placed in the center of the grave, so females may have been socially characterized with material culture and by important relationships with others.

The pattern of grave-good association in multiple burials suggests that female social identity was an important part of group identity. These groups were probably familial groups, the identity of whose members was seen in the female or matriline. Female identity did not change when they were recognized apart from others; however, when males were recognized individually, their social identity appears to have changed. Only seven of the twenty-eight males from the Turner site were in single graves. Inclusions of grave goods increased for males buried by themselves. More males than females have been found at the Powers Fort site. Male status in this situation may have been partly achieved rather than simply ascribed through the matriline, hence some males were recognized individually both at the Powers Fort site and at the Turner cemetery site.

There is evidence of surplus food production from the Turner site in that a maize-storage structure was found (Price and Griffin 1979:140). It is possible that communal redistribution of food resources was overseen by a powerful matriline. Such redistribution would explain the difference in female diet, although it is more probable that dietary differences represent food distribution that was performed on a daily basis by females who were in constant association with dietary items. Simply by being in charge of food processing and/or procurement, females would have had greater access to a variety of foods than males.

It is also possible that the difference in female diets was related to social status, which may have varied by and within each matriline. There was considerable variability in the number and quality of grave goods interred with females, ranging from zero to six items per individual, while none of the males had more than three items included in their grave. Grave goods may also have reflected different social status among and within matrilines.

Acknowledgments

I wish to thank Dr. Harold Krueger of Krueger Enterprises, Inc., Geochron Laboratories Division for providing the stable-isotope analysis presented in this essay. I also wish to thank Cheryl Claassen for providing many much needed reviews of this essay. Any errors are my own.

9. The Archaeology of Maize, Pots, and Seashells: Gender Dynamics in Late Woodland and Contact-Period New England

Mary Beth Williams and Jeffrey Bendremer

> Facts, of course, do not speak for themselves, let alone unequivocally for one interpretation or another. We need to ask . . . not simply whether we are interpreting the evidence in a sound manner but also whether or not our understanding of the underlying social dynamics can be placed in a larger theoretical framework.
>
> (Braun 1985)

Introduction

Settlement and subsistence systems in southern New England during the Late Woodland (A.D. 1000–1500) and early contact (A.D. 1500–1650) periods have been a source of continuous discussion for regional archaeologists and ethnohistorians. Recent research has led to increasing dissent rather than consensus, and what should be the least troublesome time period to discern because of its temporal proximity to the present, the Late Woodland, remains perplexing.

This lack of accord largely arises from the theoretical frameworks applied rather than from insufficient archaeological data. With the exception of a few "interpretive" pioneers, New England archaeologists resolutely embrace the "New Archaeology" to the relative exclusion of rival epistemologies. These advocates of ecological determinism place humans as passive bearers of culture, constantly adjusting subsistence strategies to accommodate external forces. Hypotheses have promoted environmental and demographic factors for cultural change such as sea-level stabilization (Perlman 1980; Salwen 1962), the development of inland and tidal wetlands (McBride 1992), fluctuations in mean temperatures (Bendremer 1993), and population pressure (Bernstein 1987; Yesner 1980). Short-term dynamics and "events" are deemed insignificant or invisible in the archaeological record.

The reliance on a single theoretical approach to account for change, both long-term and episodic, is fraught with difficulties (Charles 1992). In contrast to earlier periods, the Late Woodland and contact periods are characterized by diverse and rapidly shifting social conditions. The changes that occur over millennia in earlier periods appear during the Late Woodland as seemingly instantaneous, within centuries or, at times, decades. Both maize and pottery, benchmarks of Western interpretations of cultural change, spread throughout the region within the span of a few hundred years during the Woodland period. In contrast, observers of the dynamic Late Archaic period are more likely to speak in terms of millennia to discern changes within societies (Dincauze 1990). Established cultural-ecological hypotheses, appropriate for viewing long-term variation, fail to explain sufficiently the rapid cultural changes of the Late Woodland period.

In the absence of appropriate models for Late Woodland life, New England archaeologists place undue emphasis on the Eurocentric and androcentric ethnohistoric record without corroborating archaeological evidence. European male explorers and chroniclers, seemingly more comfortable using native male informants, place an undue emphasis on male activities and are, with few exceptions, silent on the role of women and children. Although documents are more easily deciphered than are shattered pots or abandoned hearths, interpretation in the absence of corroborating archaeological evidence, and without identifying inherent biases, is problematic. Ethnohistoric sources often depict the indigenous societies of New England as hierarchical and patriarchal (e.g., Verazzano 1970; Williams 1973). This viewpoint has been adopted by historians and anthropologists. In accepting this androcentric bias, archaeologists consistently ignore the implications of gender-related activities: the contribution of shellfish to subsistence, the initiation of trade with Europeans, and the cultural as well as functional significance of pottery.

More generally, the exclusive employment of cultural-ecological models neglects the internal structuring principles of gender. Viewed as an "ethnographic variable," and thus impractical to reconstruct archaeologically with any reliability, gender is lost in the rhetoric promoting a "systemic paradigm." In some cases, archaeologists have appropriated such feminist-sounding phrases as "household archaeology" in their studies of indigenous lifeways, ironically using such terminology to uphold the traditional view of New England native groups as patriarchal. Archaeologists in New England de-gender women's activities while making those activities the basis for developing models and hypotheses regarding the adoption of aquatic-based coastal subsistence, maize horticulture, trading practices, and ceramic manufacture.

New interpretive ontologies, however, place internally driven dynamics at the center of cultural change and regard humans as active participants in a symbiotic relationship with nature, constrained rather than controlled by their environment. Models that allow for human innovation can incorporate intra-group diversity where humans seldom act completely outside the influences of their environment. The way in which one segment of a group reacts to external dynamics may have profound effects on the group as a whole.

In this essay, we review current models of Late Woodland and contact period settlement and subsistence patterns in light of recent interpretations of regional diversity. In addition, we propose new avenues for research and interpretation of archaeological and ethnohistoric data that more fully take into account internally structuring variables such as gender.

Engendering the Archaeological Record

The debate over gender roles currently rages between schools promoting theories of biological determinism versus those supporting the social construction of gender. Although we view gender as a construct of culture, we acknowledge that in all societies there appears to be a predictable division of labor. In hunter-gatherer populations the distribution of labor generally falls along the following lines (Watson and Kennedy 1991:257):

$$men>hunt>animals$$
$$women>gather>plants$$

This premise, however, becomes more complicated in societies that incorporate marine resources into their diet. New England (Verazzano 1970; Williams 1973) and more general ethnohistoric sources (Claassen 1991a) are very clear on the divisions, which, in essence, follow traditional hunting-gathering strategies. Men's activities surround the "hunting" of large marine and riverine vertebrates, both fish and mammals, whereas women's actions are inclined toward "gathering" shallow-water invertebrates, particularly shellfish. We alter, therefore, Watson and Kennedy's model to incorporate aquatic resources:

men>hunt/fish>vertebrates
women>gather>plants/invertebrates

Ethnographic studies of hunting-fishing-gathering populations occasionally describe inter- and intra-group diversity, with men collecting shellfish, particularly for fish bait (Claassen 1991a, b), and women participating in group-related marine and terrestrial hunting and fishing activities (Conkey 1991). Although this variability may also have occurred in southern New England, lacking explicit evidence to the contrary, the sexual division of labor along the aforementioned model will be utilized in this study.

The Late Woodland and Contact Periods: Conflicting Interpretations of Diversity

The Late Woodland period in New England is characterized by radical changes in indigenous lifeways. Large, semipermanent villages, maize horticulture, and extensive trade networks all become highly visible in the archaeological record. Attempts to interpret these cataclysmic changes, however, have led to dissension within the New England archaeological community. Debate has become more pronounced as prehistoric coastal-settlement patterns, once viewed as a seasonal occurrence, are now thought to have been year-round and relatively sedentary (Bernstein 1987; Dirrigl and Bellantoni 1993; McBride 1984). The small, multi-component seasonal camps (100–1,000 m²) established as the basis for settlement in the Middle Woodland period virtually disappear in coastal areas after A.D. 600, apparently replaced by large (5,000 m²) year-round villages (Figure 1) and highly variable temporary or task-specific "satellite" camps (Bernstein 1987; Gwyne 1982; McBride 1984; McManamon 1983). The latter, very small (10–100 m²) camps seem to be temporarily occupied for the logistical exploitation of important resources (McBride 1984). Reduced mobility in the Late Woodland period appears in conjunction with dramatic changes in food storage, trade, territoriality, social structure, sexually defined roles, subsistence, and demography.

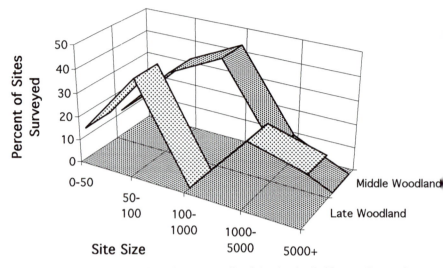

Figure 1.   Changes in Middle and Late Woodland site size (m²). (*Sources:* Bernstein 1987; Bendremer 1993; Bellantoni 1987; McBride 1984.)

In the past, archaeologists attempted to account for these changes in different ways. The adoption of maize horticulture has been cited as a factor in the increase in sedentism and population (Smith 1987; Snow 1980). The areas of New England, however, that exhibit year-round residency and larger populations are those where, according to archaeological evidence, maize played a relatively insignificant role in subsistence strategies (Bendremer 1993; Bendremer and Dewar 1994; Ceci 1982; Lavin 1988; McBride and Dewar 1987). Those groups that adopt horticulture, moreover, reveal few indications of increased sedentism and instead merely incorporate maize into their patterns of "seasonal rounds" (McBride 1984).

At the time of European contact (A.D. 1500–1650), ethnohistoric sources describe the coast of southern New England as populated by complex horticultural economies (Mourt 1866; Verazzano 1970; Williams 1973). These societies, like traditional hunter-gatherers, engendered their divisions of labor, with men hunting and fishing, and women farming and collecting wild resources (Williams 1973). Thus it is critical to understand the gender dynamics behind the transition to horticultural subsistence, where, as Williams (1973:169) described, "women commonly raise two or three heaps of twelve, fifteen or twenty bushell a head" of maize in a season.

Prior to the Late Woodland period there is no archaeological evidence of horticulture in southern New England (Bendremer and Dewar 1994), although groups to the west had initiated the cultivation of chenopodium, sunflower, cucurbits, and maize centuries earlier (Smith 1987). Chenopodium, often seen as a precursor to maize and beans, has been found at a number of sites throughout New England (Bendremer 1993); however, no evidence for human cultivation of the species has been uncovered archaeologically.

Although maize did appear in southern New England around 1000 B.P., it was incorporated into the existing seasonal scheduling and did not visibly alter settlement patterns. Inland groups maintained the seasonal round established in the Archaic period, with spring and summer aggregations in the floodplain, and removal to the terraces and uplands in the fall and winter. The few kernels of maize that have been located in coastal sites may suggest trade with inland horticulturist groups rather than actual intra-site maize cultivation. Pollen cores have failed to detect evidence for maize in Late Woodland sites along Narragansett Bay (Bernstein 1992) and Block Island (Nicholas Bellatoni, personal communication, 1994). Ceramic-wall thickness decreases over time, signaling to some (Bendremer 1993; Bernstein 1987; McBride and Dewar 1987) the processing of new starchy seed foods, such as maize, which require the higher temperatures and longer cooking times afforded by thin-walled cooking pots. Although thin-walled vessels frequently appear in inland sites associated with maize horticulture, they have also been recovered from contemporaneous coastal sites that contain no evidence of tropical cultigens (Figure 2). The debate still rages over a time frame for the intensification of maize horticulture as viewed by early European visitors. Ceci (1990a) has argued that maize horticulture in coastal regions was a consequence of contact with Europeans, whereas the majority of regional researchers still believe maize to be a pre-contact phenomenon.

Some archaeologists have sought to correlate increased sedentism with the adoption of horticulture (Smith 1987), pointing to demographic change as an important factor affecting reduced mobility (Cohen 1977; Yesner 1980). As increasing regional populations caused gathered resources to become scarce, foragers intensified their subsistence efforts by spending more time and energy processing foods, including "less favored foods" such as shellfish (Bellantoni 1987; Bernstein 1987). But did burgeoning populations cause or result from increased sedentism? Highly mobile hunter-gatherer groups, like those in the periods preceding the Late Woodland, would char-

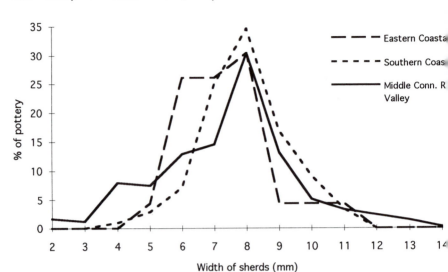

Figure 2.   Differences in Late Woodland pottery-sherd width by region. (*Sources:* Bendremer 1993; Bernstein 1987; Dincauze 1975; Lavin 1988.)

acteristically maintain lower populations (Kelly 1992). At present, a phenomenon that would result in population increase in coastal, but not inland, areas is not evident. Furthermore, this logic overlooks other instances where significant decreases in residential mobility have occurred without agriculture, for example, the Gulf Coast (Widmer 1988) and the Midwestern United States (Brown 1985a).

Changes in environment have recently been proposed as a factor in Middle and Late Woodland settlement and dietary changes (McBride 1992). During the centuries following the stabilization of sea level, silting occurred along various estuaries, creating a fertile band of coastal wetlands that attracted a multitude of faunal species. Due to the increased productivity of this region, previously mobile groups could remain in a particular locale with relatively little risk. This hypothesis maintains that "hunting" determined residential mobility. This view is not consistent with subsistence strategies for most hunter-gatherer populations (see below).

The traditional hypotheses used to explain the complex dynamic of the Late Woodland period fall short for a number of reasons. For the most part, few of the available models consider the growing gulf between coastal and inland populations. Throughout the Late Woodland period, groups in southern New England are treated as homogenous entities, evolving similar social, cultural, and economic traits. As new evidence points to greater variability in southern New England, models that seek to explain the disparate subsistence systems need to be explored. In addition, maize has been consistently advanced as the catalyst for settlement change in the Late Woodland, although this is apparently not the case for coastal areas. Perhaps other critical resources were instrumental in the development and intensification of sedentism. In the following sections these possibilities are explored, and new interpretations of settlement and subsistence patterns offered.

Mobility and Sedentism Among Hunter-Gatherers in New England

Inland sites, although multifunctional, were occupied seasonally as entire groups moved to new resources in a yearly round, supporting a "forager" association. Coastal sites, in contrast, are characterized as either large, year-round base camps or "villages," or small, task-specific locations lending support to an interpretation of coastal populations as "collectors." These divergent settlement systems are inherently gendered. According to optimal foraging theory (see Smith 1983; Winterhalder and Smith 1981), as groups exploit the resources around their encampments, they reach a point of diminishing returns. They are forced to expend more energy by increasing the foraging area, exploiting fewer resources, or exploiting less desirable foods more intensively (Sahlins 1972). While optimal foraging models are frequently genderless, studies of hunter-gatherer populations indicate that "women's foraging activities by and large determine time and frequency of residential mobility" (Kelly 1992:47). This is because gathered plant and animal resources are exploited intensively and reach a point of diminishing returns faster than other, more widely distributed hunted resources.

The subsistence strategies of collectors are also heavily engendered, with women frequently controlling the acquisition, processing, and storing of gathered resources. Ethnohistoric sources describe the management of critical food stores by women, even those resources originally procured by men (Brown 1970).

It is important to remember that subsistence alone may not determine sedentism in hunter-gatherer populations (Bender 1978). Non-environmental factors have also been noted as inducing reduced mobility

among hunter-gatherers (Kelly 1992). However, because increased sedentism is most often linked to subsistence activities, either economically
and/or socially, it is the first avenue to explore when looking for possible
motivation.

The Implications of Shellfishing for
Coastal Sedentism and Subsistence

Surprisingly, many archaeologists have either ignored or underestimated
the importance of the vast expanses of molluscan remains along the
New England coast, failing to recognize fully the role of shellfishing in
the subsistence strategies of indigenous peoples. For example, Bernstein's
(1987:223–224) research points to an absolute increase in shell and a substantial reduction in terrestrial-mammal remains throughout the Middle
and Late Woodland periods in Greenwich Cove, Rhode Island. He concludes, however, that "although the *archaeological* record of subsistence
is visually dominated by the remains of coastal resources in the form of
shell, creatures of the land and air were of equal, if not greater dietary
importance."

Oysters and several species of clams contain high-quality protein, with
all essential amino acids (Borgstrom 1962:124), and are more nutritionally
complete than other "gathered" foods such as hickory and walnut (Claassen 1991b; Waselkov 1987). Mollusks also have higher levels than terrestrial
animal and vegetal species do of iodine, thiamin, sodium, and other trace
minerals critical to human development (Klippel and Morey 1986). In light
of the year-round availability of shellfish, evidence that stable levels of protein are more beneficial than periodic feasting (Meehan 1982) support an
argument for the preference for marine resources over less consistently
available terrestrial species.

Ethnographic observations confirm that women shellfished in southern New England. In his chronicle of Narragansett lifeways, Williams
(1973:215) describes how "at low water the women dig shellfish . . . which
all Indians in our country, winter and summer, delight in." He further
describes in detail the sexual division of labor, where "men only hunted
and fished," while "women from their extraordinary great labour (even
above the labour of men) in the field, in carrying the mighty burdens, in
digging clammes and getting other shellfish from the sea," sustain the
community.

Women's foraging activities in New England also determined the group's mobility. Increased shellfish exploitation was an important factor in increased sedentism in southern New England. The actual degree of sedentism, however, varied among groups within the community, since hunting males, in particular, remained mobile in their activities. This gender-based divergence in mobility would have affected numerous aspects of society, including political organization, territoriality, trade, technology, and economic specialization. In southern New England, as groups increasingly incorporated marine resources and subsequently reduced their mobility, a distinct diversification and elaboration of utilitarian materials and tools developed (Renouf 1984). This diversification and elaboration of materials were particularly evident in the products of women's activities. Lavin (1984) concludes that the previous "relative homogeneity" in ceramics breaks down in the Late Woodland, while projectile points become more homogeneous.

Making Silent Shells and Potsherds Speak: Identifying Gender in the Archaeological Record

Over a period of six hundred years beginning in the late Middle Woodland period (ca. A.D. 900), middens throughout southern New England increased in size and changed in morphology from accretion middens (Bernstein 1987) to blanket middens (Knapp 1973; Waselkov 1987:117). Late Woodland middens consistently contain additional accumulation of shell debris, upwards of 200 percent more than earlier deposits, with the majority of the later levels dominated by soft-shell clam remains (Bellantoni 1987; Boissevain 1943). In her study of post-contact shell midden utilization, Ceci (1984) argued for substantially larger middens than are currently reported, because decaying shell was harvested as a resource by Europeans for everything from furnace flux to lime for golf courses.

Responses to subsistence risk are never limited to the mechanics of subsistence alone (Braun 1985). In southern New England, the shifting patterns of shellfish collection and shell midden distribution evident in Late Woodland middens spark interpretations that move beyond ecology and demographics. Women may have initially exploited shellfish primarily for food; however, this focus upon subsistence changes radically during the Late Woodland and contact periods.

In his writings on the Narragansetts, Williams (1973:215) describes an extensive trade network: "among them they trade their Corne, skins, Coates, Venison, shellfish, etc." This movement of raw and manufactured materials is very visible in the archaeological record. Non-local lithics and diverse ceramic styles have been found throughout southern New England, and local shell beads have been uncovered in contemporaneous sites in upstate New York (Ceci 1990b).

Trade in shellfish is noted extensively in the ethnohistoric literature. Wampanoags reportedly traded "basketloads" of dried shellfish to the English in their first year of settlement (Mourt 1866). The Algonkians of the Northeast Coast dried oysters and clams for their own winter consumption as well as for trade to inland groups (Kalm 1966:127; Rau 1872: 373). Marine shell fragments and shell-tempered ceramics found in Late Woodland inland sites (Bendremer 1993; Lavin 1988) imply extensive organized trade with coastal groups. Although evidence is lacking in the archaeological record, we can probably assume that dried shellfish was also an important trade commodity well before contact with Europeans (Waselkov 1987:108).

Although trade in shellfish and shell may have been widespread throughout the Woodland period, who controlled such trade is less clear. Because power and prestige often derive from the control of desired materials, control of shell and dried meat may be a critical key to understanding gender relations during the period. In his study of indigenous groups in the Susquehanna Basin, Handsman (1989) hypothesized that "as some men shifted their labor to the production of commodities needed for trade with white colonists," the "position and power of Susquehannock women intensified," due in part to "their control over the production, allocation, and redistribution of critical agricultural surpluses." In the Northeast, Williams (1973) described in detail the control Narragansett women maintained over the food supplies of the group, including meat procured through hunting. As men became increasingly active in the fur trade, a shift in power and control over resources may have occurred. Further research into this dynamic may prove very productive in developing a clearer resolution of gender relations during the period.

It is conceivable that coastal women purposely arranged to produce ample supplies of dried shellfish in order to trade such stores to inland groups for maize and/or other commodities. At this time, small amounts of tropical cultigens began to appear in coastal contexts, although there is little evidence of any corresponding characteristics of extensive horticulture (e.g., maize storage). Although relatively scarce and highly controversial (see Claassen 1990, 1991b for critiques of Northeast seasonality studies), scheduling models may clarify the relationship between maize cultivation and large-scale shellfish processing.

Ceci (1982, 1990a) has argued that maize was a late addition to coastal lifeways. Indigenous groups, desiring to increase opportunities for trade with Europeans, established year-round villages along the coast. The archaeological record of coastal regions supports the late intensification of maize horticulture. Sedentism, however, was established centuries earlier, and may have occurred in response to the increased use of shellfish for subsistence and trade. Intensive maize horticulture, although presumably a familiar practice to coastal groups due to trade and interaction with inland groups, was not a necessary or desired addition to coastal subsistence strategies prior to the contact period. The advent of trade with Europeans, however, may have added impetus to the adoption of maize horticulture among coastal populations. In addition to trade in shellfish, ethnohistoric sources describe maize as an extensively traded resource (Mourt 1866; Williams 1973). As horticultural activities are extensively attributed to women (Verazzano 1970; Williams 1973), the decision to adopt tropical cultigens must have been a highly engendered one. Besides altering subsistence strategies, the shift to maize horticulture in coastal areas apparently led to a shift in settlement patterns, with many groups mirroring the seasonal mobility of inland horticulturists (McBride and Bellantoni 1982). Whether this was a widespread phenomenon or limited to specific groups or individuals is unclear because the pool of early contact period archaeological sites is still very small. As more data become available, however, research correlating changing subsistence and settlement patterns to changes in material culture, such as ceramic form and function (as described below), may also be productive in developing interpretations of gender dynamics.

Shell-tempered ceramics and shell beads are found in Late Woodland and contact period sites throughout New England, indicating extensive intra-group trade. Although archaeologists in the region have linked changes in ceramic morphology to changes in subsistence strategies, studies of the dynamics of decorative and stylistic changes are general and sparse (Dincauze 1975; Lavin 1980). Braun (1985), in studies of small-scale societies in the Illinois Valley, used changes in the diversification of pottery decoration and style to claim greater interaction and cooperation within and among groups. Handsman (1989) concluded that "Susquehannock women expressed their resistance [to growing patriarchy] through the production of a distinctive pottery style." These frameworks linking changes in ceramic styles to intra-group dynamics may be equally useful in studying changes in New England. In the Thames River valley, a very distinctive style of pottery, Shantok Incised, developed at the height of the fur trade in the region. By engendering pottery production, models may in the future be used to describe women's roles in intra-group communication and power relations in southern New England.

The production of shell beads, or wampum, offers a clear example of the disparity between pre- and post-contact control over production and distribution. Although used as a monetary unit in post-contact trade, wampum continued to be imbued with its former ritualistic and communicative properties (Ceci 1990b). As late as the mid-seventeenth century, ethnohistoric sources describe the seasonal collection of periwinkle and quahogs by women for shell bead production in winter months (Williams 1973). The association of wampum drills (muxes) with women in contemporaneous mortuary sites also suggests a connection between women and shell bead production (Robinson 1990). The intensification of the economic role of wampum during the early contact period must have had profound effects on men's and women's roles in shell bead production and trade, leading to the renegotiation of power in indigenous societies.

Conclusion

Interpretation of the Late Woodland and contact periods in southern New England have been shaped largely by cultural-ecological models. Within this framework, the advent of maize horticulture or population pressure have been offered to explain the intense cultural dynamics of the period. These models fail, however, to take into account the diversity of settlement patterns in the region (seasonal mobility inland versus year-round sedentism along the coast). Non-subsistence-based explanations of cultural change have not been thoroughly explored.

Cultural-ecological models, in particular optimal foraging theory, offer explanations for long-term subsistence and settlement patterns. These models may account for the extensive exploitation of shellfish as a dietary resource among Archaic and Early Woodland coastal populations. Processual models, however, do not explain the changes in shellfish utilization during the Late Woodland and contact periods. In order to do this, we need to look to internal structuring dynamics. Because shell middens are usually the products of women's activities, models incorporating gender as a variable may offer a much clearer understanding of these dynamic social and economic transformations.

Finally, although the women of coastal New England may have produced many of the common trade goods, such as dried shellfish, shell, wampum, and pottery, whether they retained control of the exchange of these materials is currently unclear. In order to understand more fully the motivations for the intensive increase in shellfish exploitation during the Late Woodland and contact period, we must determine who within society directed trade, both with Europeans and with neighboring indigenous groups. Future research exploring men's and women's roles in trade, intragroup negotiation and cooperation, and the communication of ideas and social status through pottery and shell beads may offer more insightful interpretations of cultural change in southern New England.

Acknowledgments

Several individuals provided us with support, analysis, and assistance during the many stages of this essay. Nick Bellantoni offered both humorous commentary and unlimited access to the Connecticut State site files. Earl French offered his many years of editing experience, and Elizabeth Dougan, her exceptional organizing skills to help compile the references for the bibliography. Kelli Costa, besides proffering critical bibliographical information and judicious comments, provided excellent companionship and support during the Boone conference. Cheryl Claassen's invaluable editing and suggestions helped pull the final version of this chapter together. And finally, Doug Charles furnished thoughtful insight, critique, prodding, and support, as well as hours of stimulating discussion and ample reference suggestions, throughout the many drafts of this essay.

PART III

The Symbolic Construction of Gender

10. Weaving and the Iconography of Prestige: The Royal Gender Symbolism of Lord 5 Flower's / Lady 4 Rabbit's Family

Byron Hamann

Around the year A.D. 1280, Lord 5 Flower, a Zapotec prince, married Lady 4 Rabbit, a Mixtec princess (Figure 1). Their wedding marked the foundation of the noble house of Zaachila. Three hundred years later, at the time of the Spanish conquest, Zaachila was the most powerful dynasty in the Valley of Oaxaca (Acuña 1984:2:158). This is a study of the imagery created by and for that lineage.

Four sources of imagery are used: the contents of Monte Albán's Tomb 7, pages 33–35 of the Codex Nuttall (1975), the contents of Tombs 1 and 2 at Zaachila itself, and the palace architecture of Mitla. The visual culture from all of these sources, although preserved in different media and contexts, is extremely interesting for an engendered study because of the prominence of references to spinning and weaving. Spinning and weaving were stereotypically gender-female tasks throughout pre-Columbian Mesoamerica, and so their prevalence in the royal iconography of the Zaachila dynasty deserves a closer look.[1]

This study of weaving and the iconography of power progresses through three parts. It begins with an introduction to pre-Columbian spinning and weaving tools. This provides the reader with a background for the following section, an iconographic analysis of textile imagery at the four sources introduced above. Finally, explanations for the Zaachilan nobility's focus on an imagery of female production is suggested.

1. A discussion of the engenderment of spinning and weaving in Mesoamerica is beyond the scope of this essay. The topic is discussed by McCafferty and McCafferty (1989, 1991, 1994c) and Cordry and Cordry (1968). Also note that all of the illustrations of spinning and weaving in this chapter depict women engaged in the practice. This is not the result of a careful selection of images. Males are seldom, if ever, depicted as spinners and weavers in pre-Columbian visual records.

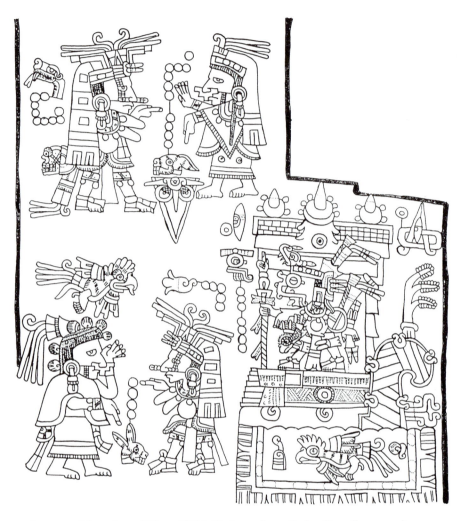

Figure 1.   The rulers of "Bent Hill." (Redrawn from Codex Nuttall 1902:33.)

The Mesoamerican Textile Kit

In addition to the imagery of finished cloth, four types of tools used in textile production are encountered in the Zaachila dynasty iconographies. Two are used in spinning: the spindle whorl and the spinning bowl. Two are used in weaving: the batten and the pick.

Figure 2.   Mixtec woman spinning. (Redrawn from Codex Vienna 1929:9.)

Figure 3.   Aztec girl spinning with spinning bowl. (Redrawn from Codex Mendoza 1925:30r.)

Figure 2, from the Codex Vienna (1992), depicts a Mixtec woman spinning. In her raised hand she holds a wad of unspun fiber, and in the other hand she twirls the end of a spindle. The spindle consists of two parts, the spindle shaft and the spindle whorl. The shaft is a pointed stick of wood about 11 to 16 cm in length and is thrust through the center of the whorl, a circular weight that can be made from a number of materials, including wood, ceramic, bone, or gourd (Cordry and Cordry 1968:27). The shaft-

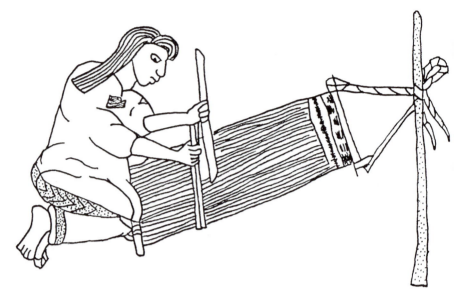

Figure 4.   Aztec girl weaving with batten. (Redrawn from Codex Mendoza 1925:32r.)

and-whorl unit acts much like a top, and when set in rotation, the spindle's twirling motion helps to draw out the raw fibers into yarn.

In Figure 2, the spindle shaft rotates on the ground. This is in contrast to the image in Figure 3, from the Aztec Codex Mendoza. Here the spindle shaft rests in a hourglass-shaped "cup." This cup-like support is called a spinning bowl. As depicted, the spinning bowl is quite small, usually having a rim diameter ranging from 6.5 to 8 cm (McCafferty and McCafferty 1994b: 148). Spinning bowls are usually ceramic, although different support surfaces may be used and can be as simple as a ceramic plate or concave slice of a dried gourd (Cordry and Cordry 1968:28). The purpose of the spinning bowl is to give the spinner greater control of the spindle's rotation, usually when a finer thread is desired (McCafferty and McCafferty 1991:23).

Another image from the Codex Mendoza depicts the next step in cloth production: weaving (Figure 4). The girl is harnessed into a back-strap loom, and in her raised hand she grasps a long flat stick tapered at both ends. This is a weaving batten. Weaving battens are made from wood or bone and range in length from under 40 cm to over 1 meter (Sperlich

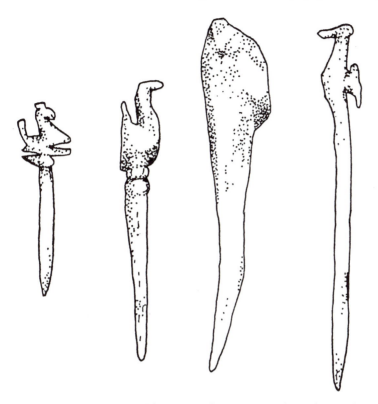

Figure 5.   Bone weaving picks, twentieth century. (Redrawn from a photograph in Cordry and Cordry 1968; courtesy University of Texas Press.)

and Sperlich 1980:32–33). The batten is used first to separate the warp threads, allowing the shuttle to pass between them. The batten is then pulled towards the weaver, compressing the newly deposited trail of yarn into the cloth already woven.

The fourth weaving tool is the pick (Figure 5). This is used in finessing the weaving and allows the weaver to adjust individual threads and smaller areas of the cloth. An image from the Codex Nuttall depicts a Mixtec woman using a turquoise mosaic weaving pick in a ritual context (Figure 6).

These four types of spinning and weaving tools are encountered in a variety of ways in the discussion of the four iconographic sources that follows. Actual tools were included in grave offerings. Some of these were functional, and others were carefully made out of expensive materials, sug-

Figure 6.   Mixtec woman holding turquoise
mosaic weaving pick. (Redrawn from Codex
Nuttall 1902:15.)

gesting that their purpose was sumptuary or ritual (as shown in Figure 6)
and not strictly technological. Spinning and weaving tools were painted in
manuscript pictures, and their product—cloth—was referenced in paint
and stone mosaic. Regardless of the form these references take, all draw
attention to the stereotypically gender-female task of textile production.
I stress both the artifactual and engendered aspects of cloth production
here because at two of the source sites—Monte Albán's Tomb 7 (Caso
1969) and Zaachila's Tombs 1 and 2 (Gallegos Ruiz 1978)—the identity of
strangely shaped objects as spinning and weaving tools has been pointed
out only in the last five years, decades after their original discovery.

Before beginning iconographic analysis, I discuss the relationships
among the four sources. Tomb 7, located at the summit of Monte Albán,
served as an elite burial cave for the settlement of Sa'a Yucu, which was
located at the mountain's base (Marcus and Flannery 1983:221; Marcus
1983:282; Kowalewski (1983:289). According to legend, the Mixtec settlement at Sa'a Yucu was founded as a direct result of interactions between
Mixtec immigrants and the nobility of the Zapotec center of Zaachila. Five

generations of Zaachila's nobility are depicted on pages 33–35 of the Codex Nuttall (Jansen 1982; Paddock 1983). Portraits of two of these rulers in the Codex Nuttall—Lord 5 Flower and his son 9 Serpent (Figure 1)—correspond to the stucco portraits of the same two men on the walls of Tomb 1 at Zaachila (Gallegos Ruiz 1978; Jansen 1982; Paddock 1983). The relationships between Sa'a Yucu and Zaachila are further corroborated in the Lienzo de Guevea. All three of these sources are discussed in Paddock (1983). Tombs 1 and 2 at Zaachila are located beneath that site's main palace. After their construction, both tombs seem to have been opened and used only once (Gallegos Ruiz 1978:115). This corresponds to ethnohistoric accounts of the mummy bundles of the Zaachila nobility being taken to Mitla at the time of the conquest (Burgoa 1989:123; Pohl n.d.). There they were interred in a special chamber beneath the Palace of the Columns, and the spirits of the deceased were consulted by the *Vuijatao*, Mitla's oracular "Great Seer" (Pohl 1994a:75–76).

Iconographic Analysis

MONTE ALBÁN'S TOMB 7
The first of these iconographic sources, one of the two where the presence of spinning and weaving tools had been entirely overlooked until recently, is Monte Albán's Tomb 7. Discovered in 1932 by Alfonso Caso, Tomb 7 proved to be one of the richest archaeological finds ever made in Mesoamerica (Caso 1932a, 1932b, 1969). Beneath the floor of a Classic period building just north of the main acropolis at Monte Albán, a two-chambered rectangular tomb with nine skeletons and a trove of Postclassic period offerings was uncovered. More than five hundred grave goods were found, made of such costly materials as gold, turquoise, amber, coral, silver, and jade. Included in the treasure were examples of all four of the above-mentioned spinning and weaving tools. Of these, the original excavator was able to identify only the six spindle whorls as objects tied to textile production (Caso 1969:157). A recent reinterpretation of the tomb (McCafferty and McCafferty 1994b) has provided identifications for the other thirty-eight tools. These include five spinning bowls, four made of onyx and the fifth of rock crystal. Twenty-five weaving battens and eight weaving picks were also discovered. These are intricately carved from eagle and jaguar bones, with narrative scenes and calendric glyphs quite compa-

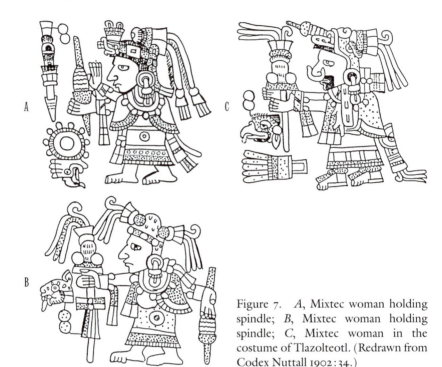

Figure 7. *A*, Mixtec woman holding spindle; *B*, Mixtec woman holding spindle; *C*, Mixtec woman in the costume of Tlazolteotl. (Redrawn from Codex Nuttall 1902:34.)

rable to those found in the Mixtec codices (Figures 7B-C). In total spinning and weaving tools account for around 10 percent of the tomb's contents. Judging by their costly materials and detailed workmanship, they were clearly objects of great importance.

SA'A YUCU, ZAACHILA, AND THE CODEX NUTTALL

The settlement of Sa'a Yucu was located in the shadow of Monte Albán, some 300 meters below Tomb 7 (Kowalewski 1983:289; Paddock 1983:54). Indeed, its Mixtec and Zapotec names (Sa'a Yucu and Xaquietoo, respectively) mean At the Foot of the Mountain and Below Mountain-Great (Paddock 1983:54). The location of a Mixtec settlement at the base of a mountain near the summit of which was located a tomb containing Mixtec-style artifacts suggests that the two may be related, especially since this spatial patterning of settlement and mortuary shrine was common in the Mixteca (Spores 1967:96–97). When Tomb 7 was first discovered, the presence of a trove of Mixtec-style artifacts in the Valley of Oaxaca, a region assumed to be ethnically Zapotec, came as a great surprise (Caso 1932a, 1932b). Ethnohistoric research has since provided an explanation for this "anomalous" presence. The 1580 *Relación de Teozapotlan* (Zaachila) documents the reasons for Mixtec presence in this part of the Valley of Oaxaca. According to the *Relación*, two Mixtec-Zapotec marriage alliances had brought Mixtecs to the Valley. The first, over three hundred years before the conquest, had joined a Mixtec princess and a lord of Zaachila. Only a few Mixtec retainers were reported to have accompanied the princess to Zaachila. The second alliance, which brought many Mixtecs to the Valley, occurred shortly before the conquest. A Mixtec lord of Yanhuitlan married the Zapotec daughter of the lord of Zaachila, and the two were granted the territory centered around Sa'a Yucu by the bride's father (Paddock 1983:8). Sa'a Yucu and Tomb 7 were thus located in lands first controlled by Zaachila itself and later granted to a branch of the Zaachilan dynasty headed by a Zaachilan princess.

Two and a half pages of the Codex Nuttall depict five generations of the rulers of the site of Zaachila, beginning with a marriage scene between the Zapotec Lord 5 Flower and the Mixtec princess Lady 4 Rabbit (Byland and Pohl 1994:178). The codical image in Figure 1 therefore corroborates the *Relación* account of the wedding of a Zapotec prince and a Mixtec princess, corresponding both in content and in the circa A.D. 1280 date at which the wedding took place. The pages that follow this image document five generations of the Zaachilan nobility, and as at Tomb 7, spinning and weaving imagery is prevalent.

Two of these Zaachilan women, Lady 2 Reed and Lady 2 Jaguar, hold yarn-wound spindles (Figures 7A and 7B). Two other women, both named Lady 2 Vulture, wear the costume of goddesses associated with spinning and weaving. One has black mouth paint, a spindle in her hair, and unspun cotton around her head and around her neck—the basic traits of the Aztec goddess Tlazolteotl (Figure 7C; McCafferty and McCafferty 1991:26–27). The second wears a dress of elaborately woven cloth, an unusual bundle at the back of her neck, and a quetzal helmet (Figure 8A). The only other appearance of the quetzal helmet combined with the odd neck bundle in the Codex Nuttall is on page 19. There it is worn by Lady 13 Flower, one of a procession of deities attending a wedding (Figure 8B). Lady 13 Flower is shown associated with spinning and weaving; she holds both a spindle and a weaving batten.

A final reference to spinning and weaving on the Nuttall's Zaachila pages is in the tufts of cotton worn in the hair of Lady 4 Rabbit, similar in

Figure 8.   *A*, Mixtec woman in the costume of Lady 13 Flower (redrawn from Codex Nuttall 1902:34); *B*, Lady 13 Flower (redrawn from Codex Nuttall 1902:19).

concept to the fillet of cotton worn by the first Lady 2 Vulture (Figures 1
and 7C). Cotton's major use in Mesoamerica is as a fiber for spinning and
weaving, and Central Mexican weaving goddesses like Tlazolteotl are often
shown wearing cotton in their hair (McCafferty and McCafferty 1991:26–
29). The tufts worn by Lady 4 Rabbit may therefore be yet another reference to cloth production.

The frequency of spinning and weaving imgary on these pages is
unique for the Mixtec corpus. No other sections of any other codex contain so many depictions of spinning and weaving items, and in no other
dynastic representation are these items so prevalent, again suggesting that
spinning and weaving was particularly associated with this royal family. The
relationships between cloth and kingship is perhaps encapsulated in the
headdress worn by four of the men and one woman on these pages and
interpreted by John Paddock as a symbol of rulership (1983:60–63). This
headdress, worn in Figure 1 by Lord 9 Serpent, Lady 11 Rabbit, and Lord 5
Flower, is made of several sumptuous yards of red and white cloth. This
striking headdress is found nowhere else within the Mixtec corpus, and
further emphasizes the importance of textile imagery for both female and
male members of the Zaachilan nobility.

TOMBS 1 AND 2, ZAACHILA
Besides being painted on page 33 of the Codex Nuttall, the husband and
son of the cotton-haired Lady 4 Rabbit are also sculpted in stucco on the

walls of Tomb 1 at Zaachila (depicted in Paddock 1983:69; Jansen 1982). Both Zaachilan tombs were discovered by Roberto Gallegos Ruiz in 1962 beneath the floor of the palace crowning Zaachila's Mound A. The tombs consisted of an antechamber and a main chamber, the latter of which had niches in three of the walls. In Tomb 1, eight skeletons were placed in the antechamber and three in the main chamber (Gallegos Ruiz 1978:77–78). In Tomb 2, six bodies were placed in the antechamber, and ten in the main chamber (1978:99).

As at Tomb 7, four types of spinning and weaving tools were found in Tomb 1. An unspecified number of spindle whorls was associated with the skeleton and offerings grouped in the northeast corner of the main chamber (1978:77). This skeleton, and the items placed around it, were interpreted as offerings made when the construction of the tomb was first completed.

When the ruler for whom the tomb was built died, this initial deposit was pushed into the corner to make way for the two principal interments in the center of the chamber (1978:77–78). A miniature "cup" with a hummingbird perched on the rim was associated with one of these two primary burials (1978:79; see also Arturo and Romas 1987:126). This "cup" is quite comparable in size and form to the spinning bowls found in Tomb 7, and I propose that it is an effigy spinning bowl. The hummingbird on the rim, although rendering the bowl useless as a functional spinning bowl, stresses the symbolism inherent in spinning and weaving.

As Jill Furst points out (1994:158), small birds are frequently associated with spinning and weaving iconography throughout Mesoamerica. A hummingbird pierced by a spindle whorl occurs as women's nicknames in both the Codex Nuttall and the Codex Selden. Maya Jaina figurines of the moon goddess and patron of childbirth Ix Chel often depict her weaving at a backstrap loom on which a small bird perches (Cordry and Cordry 1968:48, Figure 22). In the *Primeros Memoriales,* a depiction of the Aztec Atamalcualitzli ceremony shows a cloud of small birds hovering around a woman weaving (Furst 1994:158). This association continues into the twentieth century; in Figure 5, tiny birds perch atop three of the weaving picks. The basic symbolism of this bird-textile association is one of conception and childbirth. The tiny bird represents the soul of the child, and the sexually coded acts of spinning and weaving—the spindle in the spinning bowl was a metaphor for coitus, as was the in-and-out thrusting movement of the batten (Sullivan 1982:14)—attempt to ensnare the soul-child. "The woman accompanied by a bird or birds wove the body of a child, which acted as a net, entrapping the bird-soul and entangling it in the flesh" (Furst 1994:158).

The last group of spinning and weaving items in Tomb 1 includes the three carved weaving picks and two carved weaving battens placed in the northern niche of its main chamber (Gallegos Ruiz 1978:83 and 86, Figure 54). More bone weaving picks and battens were found in Tomb 2. Five carved *plegaderas* were found on the threshold between the chamber and antechamber, and four more plegaderas—three uncarved—were found in the southeast corner of the main chamber between two skeletons (Gallegos 1978:105, 107, 109). Unfortunately, Gallegos lumps both battens and picks under the term "plegaderas" in his report, so it is impossible to determine the specifics of batten and pick distribution. Also associated with the plegaderas located on the jamb area between the two rooms in Tomb 2 were lumps of bitumen, a black tar used as a paint. One of its uses, as Gallegos notes, is to decorate spindle whorls (Gallegos Ruiz 1978:107); however, he does not record the presence of any spindle whorls themselves in Tomb 2.

In total, a minimum of fifteen spinning and weaving tools were found at Zaachila, and as at Tomb 7, their importance is evident in their high degree of craftsmanship. A final point of interest is the extreme stylistic similarity between the picks and battens from Zaachila and Tomb 7. The similarity was so close that Alfonso Caso even suggested they were created by the same artist. He proposed that the person buried in association with a Mixtec polychrome olla found in Monte Albán in 1936—which contained copper carving tools and fragments of carved bone—may have been the artist who made both sets of bones (Caso quoted in Marcus 1983:283).

MITLA
Roughly 40 kilometers east of Zaachila lie the ruins of the palaces of Mitla. There are five groups of palaces, all consisting of a series of long buildings arranged around a central courtyard. Two of these groups are of interest here, both dating to the Postclassic period and the era of Zaachila's ascendancy. They are the three courtyards of the North Group and the two buildings of the Group of the Columns. The Group of the Columns was the home of the oracle of Mitla, and it was in one of the tombs beneath the floor of his palace that the mummy bundles of the Zaachilan nobility were being interred at the time of the conquest (Burgoa 1989:123; Pohl 1994a:

75). The outstanding feature of the North Group and the Group of the Columns, including the aforementioned tombs, is that their walls are encrusted with greca friezes of mosaic stone. Every surface, inside and out, is so decorated—the friezes are a hallmark of Mitla style. Although the use of greca decoration is not unique to Mitla—it is found at the contemporary site of Yagul and is often depicted on temples in the codices—Mitla is unique for the extent to which these patterns encrust almost every surface. One of the interpretations for these panels is that they represent textile patterns (Seler 1993:264; John Pohl 1994b:11). Their long, narrow proportions are quite comparable to those of fabric produced on the backstrap loom, and their patterns have direct parallels to textile patterns depicted in the Mixtec codices (compare Figures 8A and 10A, and 9 and 10B). Indeed, the palaces of Mitla do not seem so much buildings built of stone as giant tapestries woven from cloth.

Although the mummies of the Zaachilan nobility interred at Mitla have not survived to the present day, it is perhaps not a coincidence that they were buried in tombs hung with unrotting weavings of stone. And while we do not know if the grave goods placed with these elite were comparable to those at Tomb 7 and Tombs 1 and 2, it is interesting that the Spanish chronicler Burgoa noted that the Zaachilan mummies were

Figure 9. Mixtec woman in patterned skirt. (Redrawn from Codex Nuttall 1902: 30.)

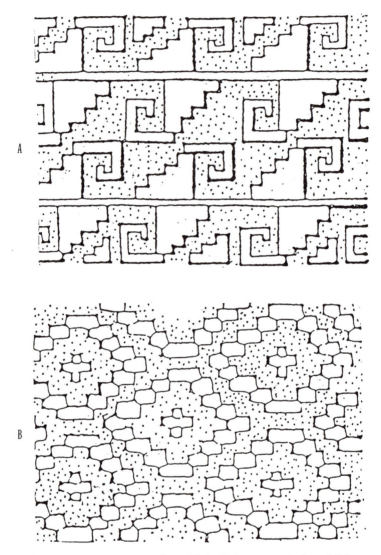

Figure 10.   *A*, Stone mosaic from Mitla; *B*, Stone mosaic from Mitla.
(Redrawn from León 1901 : 68–69.)

"brought thither richly dressed in their best attire" (Flannery and Marcus 1983:296).

Weaving and the Iconography of Prestige

Why is the imagery of spinning and weaving so important in all four of these sources? Were references to spinning and weaving a standard aspect of all Oaxacan elite iconography during this time? Or does the stereotypically female act of textile production have specific symbolism for Lord 5 Flower's family? Lack of comparative iconographies from other Oaxacan ruling families makes this a difficult question to answer either way, and so both possibilities are explored.

One possibility is that spinning and weaving were stressed in the Zaachilan imagery because of the extreme importance of textile production in the Oaxacan elite-class gift economy. Recent work by John Pohl has pointed out the great importance of the creation and distribution of sumptuary items in the interaction of the Oaxacan elite. Codical and ethnohistoric sources show that the exchange of textiles was a fundamental aspect of noble marriages and feasts, both of which were major arenas for elite interaction and alliance building. An obvious question is where did all of these sumptuary items come from? Today, weavers and markets are a ubiquitous, seemingly traditional aspect of the tourist's visit to Oaxaca. This is in strange contrast to conquest period accounts, which say very little about the existence of specialized classes of craftsmen and merchants or the presence of markets (Pohl 1994c:4). This silence may be due to the fact that members of the elite class itself served as the principal craft producers. Pohl cites the Spanish historian Herrera, who said that the lesser wives or concubines of Mixtec noblemen "spent their time spinning to make the cacique and his lady their clothes" (Herrera 1945:167). "Considering that Mixtec kings might have had as many as fifteen wives, a single royal household could have produced hundreds of garments each year" (Pohl 1994c:4). A similar case of elite production was noted by the chronicler Motolinía in Central Mexico. He credited the practice of polygamy by the Aztecs in part to the need of the elite to maintain a large labor pool of women for producing textiles for ritual gift giving (Motolinía, cited in McCafferty and McCafferty 1991:23).

It is possible that the political importance of cloth production may be embodied visually in the Zaachilan textile imagery. Indeed, Pohl interprets the greca frieze panels at Mitla as weaving patterns displayed as advertisements of the palace's skill in the production of these commercial crafts (Pohl 1994c: 11). This type of visual propaganda is not unknown in Mesoamerica; a similar economic/iconographic interrelationship has been suggested in Veronica Kann's study of figurines in Matacapán, Veracruz (Kann 1989). She links the Late Classic appearance and increasing frequency of female figurines wearing lavish clothing and jewelry to the fundamental importance of textile production at the site during the same period. Along the same lines, it is perhaps not unusual that spinning and weaving were appearing as prominent artistic themes in Oaxaca during a time when textile exchange was a basic aspect of elite interaction and alliance building.

A second interpretation for the interest of Lord 5 Flower's family in imagery symbolic of female production assumes that this interest is particular to that dynasty's history. At the beginning of this study, it was noted that at the time of the conquest, the Zaachilan royal house was viewed as the most prestigious lineage in the Valley of Oaxaca. It has been suggested that this preeminence has its origins in a marital alliance three hundred years earlier, the marriage presented on page 33 of the Codex Nuttall (Figure 1). There, the Zapotec prince Lord 5 Flower marries the Mixtec princess Lady 4 Rabbit. We know nothing about Lord 5 Flower's background, from either ethnohistoric or pre-contact documents. However, we do know Lady 4 Rabbit's ancestry, which in the Codex Nuttall is traced back through centuries of the two most powerful lineages in the Mixteca to a quasi-mythical progenitor-ancestor, Lord 12 Wind. The Nuttall clearly depicts Lady 4 Rabbit as the heir to centuries of prestigious Mixtec bloodlines. Indeed, the Codex Nuttall has been interpreted as a document of Mixtec-Zapotec alliance building, in which nineteen pages of Mixtec genealogies are crowned by the founding of the Zaachila dynasty at Lady 4 Rabbit's marriage (Pohl 1994a: 143). Her wedding, and her descendants depicted on pages 33–35, are presented in the Codex Nuttall as the culmination of more than 300 years of Mixtec history. It is through this marriage that Lord 5 Flower's family gained its political clout and authority (Byland and Pohl 1994: 179–180). In an elite culture based on political alliances and ancestry, the Zaachilan emphasis on female production may have served as a continual reminder of the cotton-haired Lady 4 Rabbit, the source of Zaachila's prestige.

This interpretation can be pushed one step further, and in so doing it considers Lady 4 Rabbit not merely as a passive reference point but as an active participant in the creation of the Zaachilan tradition of artisanry. This tradition of artisanry (or taste in goods acquired through trade or exchange) is unified by its Mixteca-Puebla style. Although the artifacts from Monte Albán's Tomb 7, Tombs 1 and 2 at Zaachila, and the stonework at Mitla have all been used as evidence for Mixtec presence at these sites, in actuality the Mixteca-Puebla style that these artifacts were created in was a "horizon style" shared by numerous cultures throughout Postclassic highland Mesoamerica (Caso 1932a; Gallegos Ruiz 1978:127; Paddock 1983:41, Byland and Pohl 1994:3–5). Because of this widespread distribution, it is extremely difficult to attribute most Mixteca-Puebla artifacts to a single region or ethnic group. Even the ostensibly Mixtec Codex Nuttall may be a "forgery" created in a Mixtec style by Zapotec artists; its pro-Zaachila message certainly makes this a possibility (Furst 1987).

The style of the artifacts discussed above presents a key question. Is the (textile-oriented) form and subject matter of these artifacts the only bearer of information, or is the *style* of these artifacts meant to signify specifically Mixtec links as well? Although we don't currently possess enough information on the history of the Mixteca-Puebla style in the Postclassic to be able to source artifacts to specific regions of highland Mesoamerica, this does not mean that regional variations in this horizon style were not important or recognized by the people who created and used such artifacts. While we cannot uncritically assume that Mixteca-Puebla artifacts offer proof of a Mixtec presence, neither can we dismiss the possibility that the style of the objects and architecture discussed above *was* created by Mixtecs or meant to specify Mixtec links. The Mixteca-Puebla horizon is often treated as a monolith, a single stylistic umbrella thought to embody the shared ideals and goals of highland Mesoamerican elite culture. While this may certainly be partially true, it is quite probable that artifacts created in this style were imbued with very specific local meanings by each of the polities that participated in this pan-elite stylistic culture. Concomitant with specific, localized symbolic meanings, Mixteca-Puebla artifacts and stylistic innovations probably had very specific vectors of transmission. The Mixteca-Puebla style did not, in a single day, appear in all cultures throughout highland Mesoamerica. Rather, this horizon style probably had multiple centers of development out of which artifacts and images traveled and were traded. How, when, and from whom a polity received and traded Mixteca-Puebla style goods probably had a very localized history, and the political relations created by these trade vectors would have been super-imposed over the artifacts' overall value and meaning as pan-highland Mesoamerican elite goods.

Acknowledging the near-impossibility of archaeological verification, I would like to suggest how such localized meanings and vectors for Mixteca-Puebla style artifacts could potentially be at work in the Zaachilan iconography. Like textile imagery, the adoption of a Mixtec artistic style by the Zaachilan royal family might have been used to stress the source of Zaachila's prestige in Mixtec alliances. If Mixtec-style artifacts suggest the presence of at least some Mixtec artists, it is plausible to argue that Lady 4 Rabbit may have had an active role in bringing Mixtec artists from her homeland to Zaachila, and in commissioning artworks from them. If the elite class was Oaxaca's major craft producers, she may have even been a creator of Mixtec-style objects herself.

An analogy can be drawn to Eleanor of Aquitaine's role in the creation of the French Gothic style in Europe in the twelfth century. A study by Eleanor Greenhill notes that the expansion of the Cathedral of St. Denis, viewed as the most important founding example of the Gothic style, was begun at exactly the same time Eleanor of Aquitaine married King Louis VII (Greenhill 1976). This expansion was halted around 1252—the same period Eleanor divorced King Louis to marry Henry II of England (1976:97). Greenhill argues that Eleanor was the most probable source of the enormous sums of money "miraculously" provided for the cathedral's construction (1976:82), and she notes that unusual architectural and icono-graphic features of St. Denis have direct parallels in buildings already existing in Spain and southern France, Eleanor's homeland (1976:86, 87, 90). This suggests that Eleanor may have brought workers from her own court to build the cathedral, and that she may have even been involved in its planning (1976:89, 96–97). In both European and Mesoamerican examples, the arrival of a politically important queen is accompanied by the importation/creation of a distinctive artistic style, and in neither case should this relationship be dismissed as mere coincidence.

Conclusions

In this study, I havĕ argued that the prevalence of textile imagery referring to female production in the iconography of the most powerful dynasty in Late Postclassic Oaxaca suggests that women had an especially prominent role in that family's politics. In one interpretation, this iconography is viewed as emphasizing women's role in the creation of textiles needed for elite politics. In another interpretation, this iconography is viewed as an emphasis on the woman who first brought Zaachila into allegiance with powerful Mixtec families.

But what are the ramifications for women in contexts where their economic production has been placed in high demand, whether symbolically or in lived actuality? Does the textile imagery of Zaachila necessarily correlate to high status for women? I would argue that it does. We know that the Mixtecs, at least, practiced bilateral descent and inheritance. Both codical and ethnohistoric sources depict Mixtec women who are actively involved in the political sphere as warriors, queens, and oracles. In a system of elite gift exchange, an elite woman creating textiles in her palace may have been working directly to further her own political goals, creating the literal fabric of alliances. And at the same time elite women were creating textiles, elite males may have been creating goldwork or lapidary objects for the same exchange system.

I would end by returning to page 33 of the Codex Nuttall and arguing that it presents the founding of the Zaachilan royal house in terms of male-female complementarity and equality. The Zaachilan genealogy begins with a Temple-and-Bent-Hill place glyph (Zaachila itself) and the first two ruling couples of Zaachila: Lord 5 Flower / Lady 4 Rabbit and Lord 9 Serpent / Lady 11 Rabbit. This presentation of wedded couples breaks standard Mixtec conventions for such scenes. Typically, weddings are depicted by showing the man and woman seated on a mat, facing each other, the woman holding a cup of cacao. On page 33 of the Codex Nuttall, the two couples stand, and they inhabit an open space, unimpeded by the intrusion of a boustrophedic red line. The presentation of these two pairs mimics exactly the "poetic couplet"–like presentation of figures in other sections of the codices. The Mixtec codices were created not as books to be referenced by a single reader in private, but as scripts to be recited and enacted. Recent work on the codices has examined whether the way information is presented reflects the oral transmission of this information. One major aspect of oral performance throughout Mesoamerica is a poetic structure based on the literary device of the couplet. In the couplet, two lines of text present the same idea in a slightly different way. Ideally, the combination of the two lines resonates with additional insights. Both King (1990) and Monaghan (1990) have suggested that paired series of figures in the codices may reflect sections of the narratives that are to be recited in couplet form.

This is exactly how the two pairs of couples are presented on page 33 of the Codex Nuttall. A poetic reading of these figures emphasizes their parallel and complementary presentation:

Male—Female
Female—Male

Upper face paint—Lower face paint
Lower face paint—Upper face paint

Arms crossed—Arms extended
Arms extended—Arms crossed

Nose bar—Nose step fret
Nose step fret—Nose bar

I argue that this complementary, paired presentation of male and female rulers is suggestive of an official message of gender equality. We may never know whether this official message transferred to lived actuality—just as we may never know the Zaachilan lineage's motivations for creating an iconography stressing textile production. But whatever their reasons, Lord 5 Flower's/Lady 4 Rabbit's family was engaging in a complex politic, intertwining weaving, gender, iconography, and prestige.

11. The Third Gender in Native California: Two-Spirit Undertakers Among the Chumash and Their Neighbors

Sandra E. Hollimon

In the 1770s, when the Spanish chronicler Costanso visited the Chumash of the Santa Barbara area, he noted that "In all of their towns there was noticed a class of men who lived like women, associated with them, wore the same dress, adorned themselves with beads, earrings, necklaces, and other feminine ornaments, and enjoyed great consideration among their companions" (Hemert-Engert and Teggart 1910:137). Fages, another eighteenth-century Spanish traveler in Chumash territory, reported having "substantial evidence that those Indian men who, both here and farther inland, are observed in the dress, clothing, and character of women . . . are called joyas, and are held in great esteem" (Heizer and Whipple 1971:259).

These Europeans were among the first to describe "two-spirits" (*berdaches*) among the native people of California (see also Wilbur 1937:192–193). Like many groups in North America, Chumash society had not merely two genders, but three. In a multiple-gender paradigm, two-spirits could be viewed as a third gender, a status that encompasses occupational, religious, and sexual elements (Jacobs and Thomas 1994; Roscoe 1995).

The third gender of the Chumash and their neighbors, the Yokuts, Mono, and Tubatulabal, is the focus of this discussion (Figure 1). Two-spirits in these societies were occupational specialists who were responsible for undertaking and other funerary activities. Their position as corpse handlers and mourning-ritual practitioners highlights the spiritual power with which these individuals were invested by members of their societies.

Two-Spirit Studies

The study of two-spirits is appropriate in archaeology for three reasons. First, any attempt to reconstruct or understand prehistoric gender systems

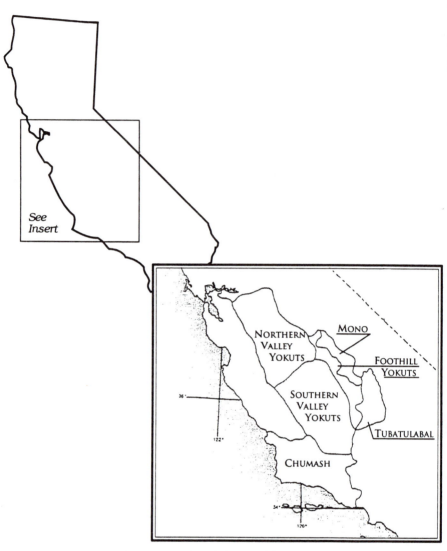

Figure 1.   Location of the Chumash and their neighbors.

must take all genders into account. The gender dynamics of prehistoric societies cannot be fully understood unless all genders are considered. Second, two-spirits formed part of the archaeological record, both as individuals and in their specialized activity as undertakers. The third aspect concerning prehistoric two-spirits is their identification in the archaeological record. How can archaeologists identify and study these pre-historic people?

Recent examinations concerning alternative gender roles have included reviews of historical and anthropological accounts of North American two-spirits (Callender and Kochems 1983; Katz 1976; Roscoe 1987; Williams 1986), theoretical discussions of the two-spirit "institution" (Blackwood 1988; Callender and Kochems 1986; Fulton and Anderson 1992; Jacobs and Cromwell 1992; Roscoe 1994; Whitehead 1981) and examples of two-spirit activities among particular North American groups (Greenberg 1986; Hauser 1990; Roscoe 1988, 1990, 1991). This discussion seeks to complement recent two-spirit studies by focusing on the occupational specialization of two-spirits among the Chumash and their neighbors, and examining the duties unique to the two-spirit gender in these societies.

Two-Spirits in Native California

The study of two-spirits in Native California societies is fraught with the same difficulties encountered by research concerning North American two-spirits in general. Confusing terminology, the conflation of many distinct statuses, and bias on the part of observers have hampered attempts to describe and examine the many aspects of two-spirit and alternative gender roles (Callender and Kochems 1983:443–444; Roscoe 1987:154).

The different sources of data contribute to the confusion about two-spirit undertakers. For example, some information comes from detailed ethnographies written by trained anthropologists (e.g., Gayton 1948a, b). Other data, which are much less complete, were recorded in the culture-element distributions. These lists are compilations of standardized traits, and the ethnographer would note the presence or absence of a given cultural feature (e.g., Harrington 1942). The third source of information is ethnohistoric sources, in which Europeans recorded their observations of native societies (e.g., Fages in Heizer and Whipple 1971). These sources' treatments of two-spirits vary widely in the degree of accuracy and thoroughness.

The bias (of unknown proportions) on the part of Spanish explorers, missionaries, and chroniclers has lent particular difficulty to the study of two-spirits among Native California societies in contact with the mission system. Although references to two-spirits in California by the Spanish are among the oldest in North America (e.g., Alarcón in Hakluyt 1904:286), the influence of the Catholic Church did much to disrupt native practices, especially with regard to sexual mores (Roscoe 1990:170–176; Williams 1986). The Spanish padres had *confesionarios* translated into native languages in order to interrogate the neophytes about their "sinful" habits (Katz 1976:287). In the Chumash area, these questions included those directed at sinning with same-sex partners (e.g., Beeler 1967:53). Such males were identified in mission documents as *joyas*, the Spanish word for "jewel" (John Johnson, personal communication, 1994; see Roscoe 1995: 201–204 for a discussion of the origin of this term for California two-spirits).

Among the groups discussed here, most of the detailed information about two-spirits was collected during the first four decades of the twentieth century. By that time, cultural disruption and assimilation had obscured this gender and its manifestations. The lack of obvious features, such as transvestism, and its denial by native consultants made investigation of alternative genders extremely difficult. For example, the gender of Yokuts undertakers was contradicted repeatedly during Anna Gayton's fieldwork. Some indicated that they were big, strong women (Gayton 1948b:236), while others stated that there were mixed burial parties, consisting of two-spirits and "normal men" (Gayton 1948a:46).

Two-Spirit Undertakers in Native California

Two-spirits were professional undertakers among a number of neighboring California groups. They were paid for their services and in some cases belonged to secret societies or guilds (e.g., the Chumash [King 1982:74]). Two-spirit funeral activities included gravedigging, transportation of the body to the grave, and singing or making speeches at the graveside. In addition to these tasks at the time of death, two-spirits performed in the periodic or annual ceremonies commemorating the dead.

Descriptions of two-spirit participation in funerary rites are available for the Chumash, Yokuts, Mono, and Tubatulabal. The major features of these activities are summarized in Table 1. These accounts highlight the confusion surrounding the gender of native undertakers and probably reflect influencing factors such as cultural disruption and Western attitudes toward the institution (see Gayton 1948a:106).

The virtual or actual synonymy of words used to denote two-spirits

TABLE I. Features of two-spirit undertaking in Native California groups.

	Chumash	Yokuts	Mono	Tubatulabal
Two-spirit undertaker	+	+	+	+(?)
Sings or speaks at graveside	+	+	+	
Performs in annual mourning ceremony		+	+	
Purifies by washing	+	+	+	
Position inherited	+	+	+	
Occupation choice influenced by dream			+	
Belonged to society or guild	+	+(?)		
Synonomy of two-spirit and undertaker	+	+	+	

and corpse handlers reflects the strong association between the two roles in these societies and is perhaps an indication of the conflation of two-spirit status and this specialized occupation. Examples of this principle can be found in studies of Chumash languages. Applegate (1972:155) recorded the word ('aqi) that translates as homosexual or transvestite, while King (1969: 48) noted the similarity between words in several Chumash languages; terms are remarkably similar for gravedigger (Heizer 1955), homosexual (Applegate 1972; Beeler 1967), and celibate medicine man (Yates 1957). In addition, the root 'aqi is found in a Chumash word glossed as "the fancy ones" (Applegate 1972:128).

CHUMASH

Paraphrasing J. P. Harrington's linguistic notes, King (1969:47–48) describes the role of the Chumash two-spirit undertaker. Women undertakers were called 'aqi by the Chumash. Harrington's consultant always thought they were women, despite the fact that they must have been very strong to carry the dead. These women devoted their lives to the duty of burying, and the job descended from mother to daughter. When Harrington asked the consultant about homosexuals, she stated that they were called 'aqi. The consultant realized that it was strange that women buriers and homosexuals were known by the same term, and that the women were strong enough to lift bodies. Harrington had heard that these women never married, contradicting other information that the office descended from mother to daughter (King 1969:47–48). The undertakers belonged to a secret initiating society, suggesting that this was an occupational specialization (King 1982:74).

The gender of Chumash undertakers is somewhat unclear. Harrington collected information indicating that the undertakers were a class of women who did nothing else and were respected for their work (King 1969: 47). In an oral narrative, undertakers were identified as old women; one says that she has "followed this occupation from youth on up" (Blackburn 1975:271). The Chumash undertaker has also been identified as male, because Kroeber reports that at funerals a man dug the grave and carried the body to it (Kroeber 1908:17). It should be noted that Kroeber's information was not based on direct observance but comes from his review of mission documents whose authors may have intentionally or mistakenly misidentified the undertaker's gender.

The Chumash burial consisted of the following elements. Professional undertakers tied the corpse with a tule mat (Hudson and Blackburn 1986: 250). The undertakers buried the remains after the graveside mourning ceremony, and they were purified by washing upon its completion (Harrington 1942; King 1969:50).

The undertakers were overpaid for their service to insure good luck for the deceased's journey to *similaqsa* (the afterlife) (King 1969:50). They were paid with the baskets used to dig the grave (King 1982:74). Wealthy families could afford more of these baskets, and therefore their deceased relatives had deeper graves; this practice was confirmed with archaeological evidence from the Medea Creek cemetery (King 1982:92–93). One of Harrington's consultants stated that the old woman undertaker would carry the body to the grave and say to the body, "Do not return. Take heed, do not frighten your family. You are now another kind of being" (King 1969:50).

YOKUTS

Early observers in the Yokuts area described individuals who may have been two-spirits. In 1819, the Spaniard Estudillo described a group of Yokuts he encountered, including a "hermaphrodite whom they called Joya," the generic term used in Spanish California for a male transvestite or homosexual (Gayton 1936:81; see also Roscoe 1995:203–204). During the 1850s, a white man named Thomas Jefferson Mayfield lived with the Yokuts and later recounted that a man dressed as a woman lived on the edge of the village (Mayfield 1993:107).

Despite these comments from the ethnohistoric literature, Yokuts culture certainly had been disrupted by the time of Gayton's ethnographic work in the twentieth century. Gayton's information highlights the difficulty in identifying two-spirit undertakers in the ethnographic literature. While all the corpse handlers were called *tono'cim*, some consultants disagreed as to whether they all were transvestite males. One of Gayton's consultants described the corpse handlers as "big women" and gave *tai'yap* as their name or title, but he denied the presence of two-spirits in his culture (Gayton 1948b:236). Some indicated that those dressed as women were usually two-spirits, but others stated that there were male undertakers who dressed as, and performed the tasks of, traditional men.

Still other consultants stated that some of the undertakers were actually women with children. According to Gifford's consultants (in Gayton 1948a:31), two-spirits had no established functions at funerals, but this contradicted older data reported by Kroeber (1925:497). Gifford considered Kroeber's data more reliable, and assumed that with a scarcity of two-spirits, women would probably function as substitutes (in Gayton 1948a:31). There were merely a few women who normally undertook burials, even in a tribe of more than one village. If there was only one undertaker available, the chief would appoint other women to help her, and these women were also referred to as *tono'cim*. If a burier had female children, they would carry on the profession (1948a:106). It was said that Yokuts undertakers were women who "grew up that way, with a desire to get rid of the dead" (1948b:168).

This information undoubtedly reflects the disruption of Yokuts culture by the time of Gayton's fieldwork. It is probable that transvestism among two-spirit undertakers had lapsed or been suppressed by Western influences. It is also possible that the common factor among undertakers was not cross-dressing but, perhaps, homosexuality. Gayton provided support for this notion by suggesting that male undertakers dressed as traditional men were in homosexual relationships with those who assumed the two-spirit role (1948a:46).

Although Gayton discussed the confusion surrounding the gender of Yokuts undertakers, she considered it a moot point. In her opinion, if any of the undertakers was a two-spirit, it was probably the one who carried the corpse to the grave. All of Gayton's consultants indicated that this individual was "a big strong woman." Gayton also questioned the number of two-spirits living in any village or group, suggesting that there would only be a few (1948a:106–107).

Despite unclear information about the gender of undertakers, detailed descriptions exist concerning their role in the annual mourning ceremony and their method of payment. The undertakers performed in long false hair, projecting over the forehead like a beak, representing long-billed birds. They were allowed to take any property at the fiesta for themselves. They symbolically captured audience members as hostages, extracting payment for their release. *Tono'cim* played the same role in the annual mourning ceremony—with crying, dancing, and singing—as they would over unburied dead at the graveside ritual. On the last night of the festivities, property of the deceased was destroyed by burning. The *tono'cim* stood in a circle, singing, while the relatives swayed with effigies of the dead. At the end of each song, the *tono'cim* clapped and the mourners burst into wails. After daybreak, the effigies were burned, and the beads, baskets, and other goods were given to the *tono'cim*, despite the fact that they had already been liberally paid (Kroeber 1925:500–501).

The significance of undertakers in ritual settings is perhaps reflected in the Yokuts Ghost Dance of 1870. One of Gayton's consultants stated that a Yokuts man nicknamed "*Tono'cim*" was one of the singers who traveled the Ghost Dance "circuit" (Gayton 1948a:133).

MONO

As among the Yokuts, the Mono term for undertaker was the same as the term for two-spirit (Driver 1937:99). While working among the North-fork Mono, Edward Gifford attended a funeral at which a woman gave a ceremonial speech. Gifford remarked that her voice was very loud and masculine, and he suspected that this individual was a two-spirit (1932:44), although his Western Mono consultant insisted that the corpse carrier was not a two-spirit.

One consultant said that undertakers were married and had children, perhaps indicating that non-two-spirit undertakers were women (Driver 1937:138). These women were called *onotim* and were responsible for digging the grave.

Gayton collected information indicating that the gender of the deceased determined the gender of the undertaker. A man would bury a man, but if the dead person were a woman, she would be buried by a woman (Gayton 1948b:236). The profession was said to run in families (1948b:

237), and among the Western Mono the position was apparently inherited patrilineally (Driver 1937:99).

A consultant of Gayton's stated that the corpse handler's dream help always came from dead people, "that is why they were not afraid of the dead" (1948b:236). The undertaker was paid because a relative was not supposed to touch the corpse. Two-spirits were also paid performers at the annual mourning ceremony (Driver 1937:101).

The Western Mono corpse carrier led a procession of mourners to the burial site. This person made speeches during the mourners' wailing, to both the assembly and the corpse. All the possessions of the deceased were placed in the grave, and the mourners filled it in with dirt. At the conclusion of the burial, the corpse carrier announced, "Go home!" (Gayton 1948b:237).

The Northfork Mono held similar mourning ceremonies. The individual whom Gifford suspected to be a two-spirit was the leader of the funeral singers. These singers accompanied male and female dancers who performed at the mourning ritual. The singing leader kept time for the singers and dancers and did not allow a rest of more than a minute between singing/dancing episodes. Gifford remarked that she appeared not to be mourning, but rather joked and laughed during the proceedings (1932:44).

TUBATULABAL

Driver (1937:90, 99) reported that Tubatulabal two-spirits performed some functions at burial and the mourning ceremony, but he did not elaborate. This information contradicts Voegelin's consultants, who denied that two-spirits were undertakers (1938:47). As among the neighboring groups, it was said that every village had two old women whose regular job it was to take away the bodies and bury them. Other consultants indicated that these individuals were men. Whether female, male, or two-spirit, the undertaker was a professional who was paid for the service (1938:47).

Male transvestites were reported among the Tubatulabal, despite the denial that they were undertakers. The transvestite wore a woman's apron, and his mother taught him to gather, to prepare acorns and tobacco, and to make baskets and pottery. The transvestite would "stay around with women," but Voegelin's consultant did not know of any married two-spirits (1938:47).

After death, the body was kept in the house overnight while relatives and friends wailed. The following day, the corpse was wrapped in tule mats and taken away by two old, women corpse handlers. Each corpse handler carried the body about one-sixteenth mile away from the village, where they dug a shallow grave and buried the corpse. Upon returning to the village, they washed themselves well and were paid by the relatives of the deceased (Voegelin 1938:47).

The Undertaking Gender

The confusion surrounding the gender of undertakers among the Chumash, Yokuts, Mono, and Tubatulabal may result from the conflation of the two-spirit gender and the undertaking occupation. The fact that some ethnographies identify women, men, and two-spirits as undertakers may indicate that the gender of the undertaker was modified while performing those tasks (Will Roscoe, personal communication, 1994). After completing mortuary duties, the undertaker might return to his or her "original" gender.

Some cultures recognize the ability of an individual to change gender (Jacobs and Cromwell 1992). Among the Chukchi of Siberia, seven gender categories are identified, including those that could be considered "intermediate" between male/man and female/woman in a binary gender system (1992:50–53). Any of the genders can be adopted at any time during an individual's life, and transformation need not be permanent; indeed, some gender "transformations" are specifically said to occur when shamans enter trance states or perform particular ceremonies (1992:51).

Perhaps among the Yokuts and Mono, individuals temporarily occupied the "undertaking gender" while performing ritual activities. Support for this idea comes from Gayton's notes on the Yokuts and Mono. Some of her consultants indicated that there were mixed burial parties of women, men, and two-spirits (Gayton 1948b:236). Both Yokuts (1948a:106) and Mono (Driver 1937:138) consultants indicated that the children of female undertakers would carry on the profession and that, as an occupation, undertaking ran in families (Gayton 1948b:237). Undertakers in these societies may have been considered "gender variant" (sensu Jacobs and Cromwell 1992:63–64) only while performing mortuary duties.

A parallel may be found among the Yurok of Northern California. At the time of Kroeber's fieldwork during the 1910s and 1920s, all Yurok two-spirits were considered to have supernatural power enabling them to perform shamanistic duties. Although the position was open to men, women, and two-spirits, there appears to have been a particularly close association between shamanism and two-spirits (Kroeber 1925:46). Although this situation does not appear to have been an actual conflation of two-spirit and shaman roles, as among Yokuts undertakers, it may indicate that the supernatural power of Yurok two-spirits made them logical candidates for shaman status.

According to published ethnographies, the Chumash, Yokuts, Mono and Tubatulabal lacked a linguistically marked female gender category analogous to male two-spirit. Perhaps no such female role existed among these societies. Alternatively, such roles may have existed but were perhaps more subtle than those of male two-spirits, or may not have constituted true gender categories that were recognized by natives or ethnographers. If females were considered to be gender variant only while performing undertaking duties, a linguistically marked role might not exist. Female gender variance of this kind might still be associated with supernatural power. Examples include the "female berdache" shamans among many Northern California groups (see Roscoe 1987) and the gender-variant females who were allowed to participate in the otherwise male *kuksu* cult rituals among the Maidu (Loeb 1933:175).

Two-Spirits and Supernatural Power

Two-spirits have been associated with supernatural power in native societies throughout North America (Callender and Kochems 1983:448, 451–453; Fulton and Anderson 1992:608–609; Hauser 1990:52; Roscoe 1988:51; Whitehead 1981:99–100; Williams 1986:35–38). In many of these groups, the intermediate gender position of two-spirits was viewed as a reflection of their spiritual position between the earthly realm and the supernatural, allowing two-spirits to mediate between human and divine worlds. Fulton and Anderson (1992:609) suggest that North American two-spirits were in a unique position to act as spiritual intermediaries during three liminal events in human life: birth, marriage, and death. Because these events were fraught with supernatural danger, the two-spirit's main purpose in society was to maintain order and continuity.

In some cultures outside North America, two-spirit status or mixing of traditional male and female roles is roughly equivalent to shaman status. This suggests that many societies recognize spiritual power in those who belong to alternative gender categories (Callender and Kochems 1986:

170–171). Roscoe (1987) documents North American groups in which two-spirits performed religious functions, and provides evidence from oral traditions that justify two-spirit spiritual roles (Roscoe 1988:77–93). Such a view was espoused by a Sioux two-spirit (*winkte*) with whom spiritualist John Fire Lame Deer conversed. The *winkte* observed that "if nature puts a burden on a man by making him different, it also gives him a power" (Fire/Lame Deer and Erdoes 1972:149).

In addition to the undertakers described here, two-spirits among many Native California groups performed shamanistic or other spiritual/ritual activities (see Roscoe 1987). The belief that two-spirits were supernaturally powerful was not limited to those groups in which they participated in funerary rites.

In many Native California societies, people had ambivalent reactions to spiritual power. Power could be used wisely or imprudently, for good or evil purposes. Therefore, shamans and others who possessed extraordinary power were often regarded with a combination of admiration and fear (Bean 1976). Native California two-spirits were probably viewed in this way, making it difficult to separate native opinions about them into a simple positive/negative dichotomy (see Greenberg 1986:180).

Two-Spirits and Power: The Oral Traditions

Among many Native California groups, two-spirits were explicitly linked to supernatural events or states through mythology or cosmology. Examples include the Nisenan spirit who is both man and woman (Powers 1976:345) and the Kamia (Tipai) culture heroine/hero who is a female transvestite. According to Kamia oral traditions, this individual was greatly admired for introducing many aspects of their culture, including agriculture. However, in a Kamia origin myth, the people were said to have dispersed from their ancestral Salton Sea territory because they were afraid of her/him (Gifford 1931:56).

Additional evidence of this explicit spiritual link can be found in the native attributions of two-spirit status. Like many North American groups (Callender and Kochems 1983; Whitehead 1981), some Native California societies believed that the adoption of two-spirit status was influenced by spiritual guidance. This could take the form of dreams or spirit possession. Such beliefs were documented among the Mono (Gifford 1932). Although Gayton's Western Mono consultant had not experienced such a dream, she thought that the spiritual guidance came from specific deceased individuals, not transient ghosts of the unknown dead (Gayton 1948b:236).

Two-Spirits and Cannibals in Myths

Examples of the association between two-spirits and power can be found among the oral traditions of the Western Mono (Monache). A myth describes a character named Berdache (*tono'cim*) who is an ogre and cannibal. His supernatural power came from two talismans; the winnowing tray and pestle, both tools traditionally used by women. Berdache caught people and cooked them, but revived their bones after they died (Gayton and Newman 1940:34, 73).

Perhaps significantly, other Western Mono and Yokuts myths include cannibalistic characters. One is a giant bird, one is an old woman, and another is a walking skeleton or a basket carrier who steals children and eats them (Gayton and Newman 1940). In most myths, the basket carrier is female. Occasionally the character is male, and in one instance is a two-spirit (Gayton and Newman 1940:96). Even when the cannibal is male, his supernatural tools include the mortar and pestle, implements usually associated with women (Gayton and Newman 1940:48–49). In the story "Transvestite Steals Cougar's Child," the character steals the children of many mythical animal-people and, when caught and bound by them, attempts to work magic with a pestle, without success (Gayton and Newman 1940:86–87).

Similarly, cannibalism is associated with supernatural power in Chumash oral traditions (Blackburn 1975; Hollimon n.d.). In addition to the general "bogeyman" nature of mythological cannibals such as the basket carrier, an encounter with the spiritual power of the cannibal transforms ordinary people (Tafoya 1981). The cannibal acquires power by eating his or her victims, while those who survive an encounter with a cannibal acquire some of his or her power (Tafoya 1981). This principle is illustrated in the Yokuts cannibal myths discussed above.

Yokuts, Chumash, and Tubatulabal oral traditions also describe the perilous journey to the land of the dead (Blackburn 1975; Gayton and Newman 1940; Hollimon n.d.). The association of two-spirits with supernatural power explains their unique ability to guide spirits to the afterlife. As undertakers or funerary specialists, two-spirits were able to call upon their special attributes to help the deceased through the difficult journey to the afterlife. This association is demonstrated by the linking of two-spirits with cannibalism, bone reviving, and talisman use in myths.

Two-Spirits in Archaeology

The examination of two-spirits in archaeological contexts is important for a number of reasons. First, the analysis of gender in the archaeological record of a given culture must take all genders that were in existence prehistorically into consideration. Second, as individuals, two-spirits were responsible in some part for the formation of the archaeological record. In the specific cases discussed here, two-spirits contributed to the archaeological record by performing as undertakers.

In the case of the Chumash, payment of two-spirit undertakers was said to be in the form of previously unusued baskets, which were then used to dig the grave. Although preservation in archaeological sites from the Santa Barbara Channel area is generally quite good, it is difficult to identify baskets used for gravedigging from fragments or impressions. An examination of burial accompaniments in prehistoric graves from this area showed that as many males (14/210) were buried with portions of baskets or basketry impressions as were females (15/210) (Hollimon 1990 : 123). Either all these individuals were two-spirits and/or undertakers, or this burial accompaniment was not solely indicative of the two-spirit/undertaking occupation (1990 : 162–163).

An analysis of sex differences in degenerative-joint-disease patterns from this area has provided tentative identification of two-spirit burials (Hollimon 1996). Degenerative joint disease is often an activity-induced pathology reflecting habitual motions and postures (Merbs 1983). Studies of the skeletons of males and females from the Santa Barbara Channel area showed marked differences in the location of arthritic joints. Females displayed much greater degeneration in the spine as compared to males, even when the sample was controlled for age (Hollimon 1988; Walker and Hollimon 1989). The presence of two males, both about eighteen years of age, with severe spinal arthritis may indicate that these individuals were engaged in habitual activities that placed their spines under great mechanical stress. One such activity could be the use of digging sticks, either for harvesting tubers or digging graves. Burial accompaniments support the latter activity, as these individuals were buried with digging-stick weights and basket fragments, known from ethnographic accounts to be the tool kit of two-spirit undertakers. In addition, while a number of males were buried with either basket impressions or digging-stick weights (see above), these two skeletons were the only males to be buried with both items (Hollimon 1996).

As in any archaeological analysis, sampling problems must be considered. In a sample of roughly two hundred burials with associated artifacts, how many two-spirits might one expect to find? Despite ethnohistoric sources that indicate up to three two-spirits per village among the Chumash (Fages in Heizer and Whipple 1971:259), Gayton was probably more accurate when she noted that one would expect few two-spirits relative to the rest of the population (1948a:107).

The identification of two-spirits in mortuary contexts relies on hypotheses that can be tested with archaeological data. Two such hypotheses are provided here (Table 2). If the test implications of the second hypothesis were met, one could possibly identify two-spirit burials.

In practice, however, it might be more productive to differentiate clothing, ornaments, or burial accompaniments that are unique to a third

TABLE 2.   Hypotheses for identification of two-spirit burials.

Hypothesis 1:
    Gender is not symbolically marked in mortuary contexts.
    Test implications:
      a. High or moderate (51-100 percent) overlap in burial accompaniments of males and females.
      b. No spatial differentiation between female and male burials.
      c. No stylistic differences (material, form, color, etc.) of clothing or ornaments.

Hypothesis 2:
    Gender is symbolically marked in mortuary contexts.
    Test implications:
      a. Dichotomous treatment of male and female burials (artifacts buried with males are never found with females and vice versa).
      b. Spatial segregation of male and female burials.
      c. Stylistic differences between male and female clothing and ornaments.

Two-spirit burial can be identified when:
    a. A male burial is associated with female artifacts.
    b. A male is buried in the female portion of the cemetery.
    c. A male is buried with female or third-gender clothing and/or ornaments.
    d. An individual is buried with tools used in a third-gender craft or occupation (e.g., digging sticks and baskets). These tools must be sufficiently uncommon among other burials to indicate specialized use.

gender rather than simply look for "males in female clothing." One point bears repeating: in most North American societies, two-spirits were not simply men who adopted women's clothing or work. They were members of a third gender with clothing, ornaments, and occupations unique to the gender. These individuals probably would be numerically less frequent than "true males" in cemetery populations, and statistically rare burial accompaniments found with male skeletons might point to an occupational specialization or status associated with two-spirits. Of course, caution must be exercised during interpretation of mortuary remains; any number of social variables, such as status, occupation, or rank, may be symbolized in a mortuary context and may not be simply a reflection of gender.

We might hope for a situation encountered by Elsie Clews Parsons, who described the burial of a two-spirit among the Zuñi. In situations where cloth is preserved, the following sort of burial could be identified in an archaeological context.

> When prepared for burial the corpse of a *la'mana* [two-spirit] is dressed in the usual woman's outfit, with one exception, under the woman's skirt a pair of trousers are put on. "And on which side of the graveyard will he be buried?" I asked, with eagerness of heart if not of voice, for here at last was a test of the sex status of the *la'mana*. "On the south side, the men's side, of course. (Is this not a man)?" And my old friend smiled the peculiarly gentle smile he reserved for my particularly unintelligent questions. (Parsons 1916:528)

Acknowledgments

I thank Will Roscoe and Daniel Murley for information and editorial assistance.

12. Gendered Goods: The Symbolism of Maya Hierarchical Exchange Relations

Susan D. Gillespie and Rosemary A. Joyce

In many Southeast Asian societies it is common practice for a group of men to refer to another group of men by kin terms that refer to biological females. These men are called "our sisters" or "our daughters," or more generally "women of our clan" (Barraud 1979:152; Clamagirand 1980:141; Cunningham 1965:374; Forman 1980:156; McKinnon 1991:115; Rodgers 1990:324; Sherman 1987:867 after Leach 1965:80 n. 14; Valeri 1980:185), although by definition they must be of a different descent line. George Sherman (1987:867) raised the obvious question: " 'Why are men called by a term for women?' "

This practice has nothing overtly to do with biological sex, gender roles, or gender identity. Instead it reveals the active use of a "gender ideology" (Conkey and Spector 1984:15)—the "culturally construed difference" between "male" and "female" (Boon 1990:211)—as both a construct and a code for social (and other) relations. Gender is one of many possible organizing principles, but it has characteristics that make it distinctive. As a mode of classification, gender comprises a complementation of opposites that must be united for both biological and social production. At the same time, paired members can historically take on different values, so that gender can express asymmetry and hierarchy as well as complementarity (Hoskins 1990:275; Traube 1986:4).

This chapter presents a model of gender ideology expressed in social action among the ancient Maya of Mesoamerica. Monuments and hieroglyphic texts dating from the Classic period (ca. A.D. 200–1000), as well as documents from the early Hispanic period and contemporary ethnographic information, are brought together to create a coherent picture of Maya social organization. These data are examined against the comparative backdrop of ethnographic material from Southeast Asia, and especially Eastern Indonesia, where gender classification operates overtly in conceptualizing sociocosmic categories and relationships. The Southeast Asian comparison helps to explicate the organizing principles of Maya gender

ideology, revealing insights into the social, economic, and political relationships of that pre-Hispanic civilization.

Gender and Alliance

The example of gender ideology that opened this chapter—with men
calling other men their sisters or daughters—is based on marital alliances
between specific kin groups. Paired family groupings, composing a "wife-
provider"/"wife-receiver" dyad (Sherman 1987), refer to one another by
terms that are glossed at a basic level as "male" and "female." This gender
symbolism connotes the complementarity of the two groups, which, once
united by marriage, form a larger totality. At the same time, gender coding
also indicates that this relationship is asymmetric, and the two kin groups
are differentially valued. The difference between them is hierarchical in nature and is manifest in social interactions, when one group must be defer-
ential to the other.

In Eastern Indonesia in particular (Errington 1990), gender symbolism is also extended to the classes of goods that the allied groups proffer to
one another, this exchange both establishing and maintaining their relationship. The objects therefore also form a complementary set, and they
are treated explicitly or implicitly as "masculine" and "feminine" goods.

The assignment of gender to material objects in this way should be of
interest to archaeologists, who more frequently gender-code artifacts by
inferring which sex made, used, or possessed the items; by identifying
which sex was represented iconically by items; or by inferring how items
were employed in relationships between actual men and women (e.g.,
Claassen 1992a; Conkey and Spector 1984; Hodder 1991; Spector 1991).
Those issues are pertinent as well to the assignment of a specific gender to
these exchange items, but the ethnographic data can broaden our understanding of how and why objects are laden with this particular set of meanings as part of larger social processes. The linking of gender to material
objects within the domain of social action is a topic that needs more attention from archaeologists (e.g., Hodder 1991:13; Sørensen 1991:128).

Although we are dealing with gender as a symbol system, and not specifically with gender roles or identities, the employment of gender classification to facilitate social relationships cannot be divorced from the use of
gender as a structuring principle in other domains within these societies
(Conkey and Gero 1991:9). We emphasize how gender may better be un-

derstood as a *relationship*—defined in the cases we discuss by an opposition of "male" and "female"—that structures organizing concepts and operations in these other domains, rather than as an *objectification* of two separately defined identities.

Indonesia as a Comparative Example

Within Southeast Asia, Eastern Indonesian societies are especially explicit in their use of gender ideology to facilitate social relationships. We begin by isolating features of Indonesian gender coding of allied kin groups in terms of a model that explains the different manifestations of this usage. We then apply that model to evidence from the Maya civilization.

Ethnographic research in Eastern Indonesia has long focused on symbolic issues that include gender ideology. Beginning with the crucial work of Wouden in 1935 (Wouden 1968), many Indonesian ethnographers have taken the perspective that a "single classification . . . orders both social life and cosmos" (Barnes 1980:93). This sociocosmic classification is founded on a principle of dual organization that is apparent in all domains of life. Among the many manifestations of duality, gender symbolism is pervasive (Hoskins 1990:274). The same emphasis on dual organization, and specifically on gender complementarity, has been demonstrated for the ancient Maya, who strongly contrasted "male" and "female" identities as a complementary opposition using costume and other icons (Joyce 1990, 1992b).

Another important parallel between these two regions is their social organization. Although larger social groupings may exist, the fundamental cultural and social category in Eastern Indonesia is the "house" (Cunningham 1964; Fox 1980a:10–11). The house was explicitly defined by Claude Lévi-Strauss (1982:174) as an enduring social unit that acquires and maintains an estate through both descent and marriage ties. The estate includes material and immaterial property, the latter consisting of such things as names, titles, and performance rights. In many instances, the native term for this social unit actually means "house" (1982:172), and this is true for Eastern Indonesia.

Some members of the house perpetuate it by their life-long residence and their recruitment of new members via descent. Other members (usually females) marry out to form alliances with other houses, binding together the larger society. Women thus serve a "unique and crucial social role" as mediators between houses (Sherman 1987:873; see also Barraud 1990:202; Cunningham 1964).

From this latter perspective, the house is also the unit of alliance (Fox 1980b:115; Lévi-Strauss 1987:155), and houses are sometimes definable only in terms of the alliances formed between them (Barraud 1990:202). Marriage alliances go far beyond simple "woman exchange" (1990:198). They are the basis for long-lived relationships between houses that create a network of social ties within and beyond a single society. These relationships extend outside the social domain, influencing and signifying ritual, economic, and political behaviors as well.

Data on Maya kinship principles from the colonial to the modern periods indicate that, as is frequently the case, the basic social grouping is often misinterpreted as a descent group (Gillespie 1994). An exhaustive study by Richard Wilk (1988) concluded: "Every ethnographic and ethnohistorical account of the Maya seems to point away from the lineage, clan, or *barrio* as the primary social group, at least in the minds of the Maya themselves; the [extended family] household, in contrast, was important in every region and class," and its persistence and pervasiveness indicate that this was "an ancient pattern" (1988:137, 139). Furthermore, this basic social unit, which we posit is the "house" and not just a "household," is still referred to by some Maya peoples by a native term that means "house" (e.g., Vogt [1969:127] for Tzotzil Maya; Wisdom [1940:248–249] for Chorti Maya).

Thus, the ethnographic information on the Indonesian house, as a unit of alliance and exchange, has the potential to elucidate our understandings of Maya social organization stretching back into the pre-Hispanic past. In particular, the embedded gender complementarity that, linked to these kinship ties, is part of a sociocosmic model of Eastern Indonesian alliance was an important component in conceptualizing and operationalizing Maya social relationships.

ALLIANCE BETWEEN HOUSES: THE INDONESIAN MODEL

In most Southeast Asian societies, the wife-provider houses are "male" to their "female" wife-receivers. A single house will be engaged in numerous alliances and so will have several "male" wife-providing houses and several "female" wife-receiving houses with whose members it will interact.

Susan McKinnon (1991:93) has demonstrated how the gender coding of alliance relationships can be explained according to an elegant model that is grounded in certain widely held principles. Her analysis of data from the Tanimbar Islands of Eastern Indonesia indicates that each house is conceptually androgynous. A house is represented by male and female symbols, united on an altar dedicated to male and female ancestors, and is composed literally of male and female members.

Because each house has the same characteristics, they are equivalent. In order to establish a relationship, the houses must be differentiated from one another in the context of social interaction (McKinnon 1991:34, citing Louis Dumont). Gender is the mechanism for symbolically differentiating members of one's allied houses, forming both a contrast and a complementarity with them (Fox 1980a:13). The androgynous houses therefore act in ways that introduce a sexual dimorphism, transforming them into single-sex (male or female) entities for the purpose of establishing or maintaining a productive relationship. The relationship with a cross-sexed house recreates the same gender-totalizing unity that each individual house ideally incorporates (McKinnon 1991:35, 95).

As a part of this process, the houses are differentiated from one another by the assignment of opposing genders to the objects used in the ritual exchange transactions between them (Weiner 1992:10). These obligatory prestations are outward signs of the relationship between the houses (Needham 1980:37), the exchange of "male" goods for "female" goods signifying both the complementarity of the two allied houses as well as the larger gender unity created by the relationship. Once such a relationship has been established by a marriage, it is continued for many years, even generations, by the on-going exchange of male and female goods on numerous occasions outside of marriage, especially at life-crisis rites (McKinnon 1991:112).

In Eastern Indonesia the male wife-providers usually give female objects to their female wife-receivers, who in turn offer male objects. This inversion between the gender of the house and the gender of the goods it is obligated to exchange with its allies has been explained by McKinnon (1991:165) as a product of the conceptual operations inherent in her model. In providing a sister or daughter to their wife-receivers, the androgynous wife-providing house "exteriorizes" its feminine aspect, remaining essentially "masculine." It further exteriorizes its femininity by proffering female goods along with the bride. This out-movement of "femininity" is how the house splits off one of its genders, transforming itself from a totality to a single-sexed entity.

By the same process, and as a necessary part of it, the wife-receivers, in receiving the woman, are endowed with her femininity. From the point of view of the wife-providers, the wife-receivers are seen as a female off-shoot of their house, like a sister or daughter. Becoming essentially female, the wife-receivers exteriorize their masculine aspect in the male objects they give to the wife-providers (Figure 1).

The actual items that are assigned reciprocal genders for the purposes of these highly ritualized exchanges vary from culture to culture. In some instances, gender is assigned on the basis of who typically makes the item or, in the case of adornments and costume, wears the item. Cloth, for example, is often considered "female" in contrast to "male" objects made of metal. Women are associated with textiles because they weave them, while

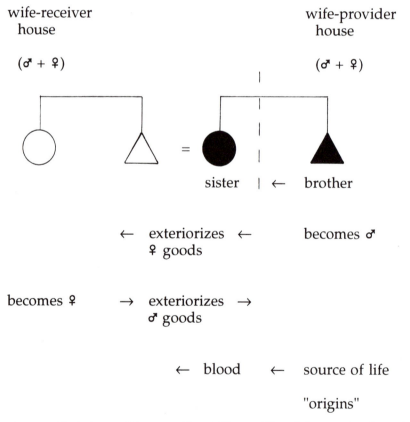

Figure 1.   Tanimbar model proposed by McKinnon. The split between brother and sister precipitates the fracture of androgynous houses into single-sexed entities.

the metal items are used by males (Adams 1980:220). But there are other reasons for assigning gender. Cloth is also female because, like the women of a house who leave it upon marriage, it is an impermanent good. Metal, on the other hand, may be cast as male because it is more enduring, like the men who remain with a patrilineally organized house (Adams 1980: 220; Hoskins 1989:166; McKinnon 1991:177–178; see Weiner 1992:59). Still other goods are assigned gender for reasons that are more abstract or historical (e.g., Valeri 1980:189) and have to do with the perception that they constitute opposed categories (Fox 1971:230).

THE ASSIGNMENT OF GENDER TO HOUSES

It is usual in Indonesia for wife-providers to be male and wife-receivers to be female. This gender assignment is also predicated on a sociocosmic principle, explicated in mythology and cosmology, that underlies the alliance ideology. In juxtaposing a gender opposition for the two allied houses, the model is itself based on a particular cross-sexed relationship, whose two members then represent the two cross-sexed houses.

In Island Southeast Asia, the relationship that is given emphasis in sociological and cosmological contexts is the brother-sister tie (Errington 1989:237, 243–244). There is a widely shared belief that the cosmos was initially characterized by an undifferentiated primordium that was shattered, resulting in the sequencing of differentiations that constitute the cosmogony. This primordial unity was represented by a brother-sister pair, and it is this unity that continues to lie at the "heart of all kinship relations" (McKinnon 1991:111; see Errington 1987, 1989, 1990; Fox 1980a:12–13).

The essential tie between these cross-sexed siblings was epitomized by the "blood" that they shared. People today who are of the same house are also of the same blood, so the house replicates the primordial cosmic unity. As in the past, however, sisters must still be separated from their brothers. The unity of the house is thus continually fractured, its resulting parts forming a gender opposition.

This sociocosmological principle explains the gendering of houses in alliance relationships. The wife-providers represent the "brother" half of this dyad and take on his male gender. Their sisters and daughters go to the wife-receivers, carrying with them the "blood" of their natal house, and thereby bestow upon that house their female gender (McKinnon 1991:111). The wife-receivers are both literally and figuratively endowed with the women's "blood," which provides them with life in the form of future progeny.

The brother-sister tie is one of several possible cross-sexed relation-

ships that could be used to indicate the gender of the allied houses. Indonesian scholars recognize that other societies focusing, for example, on
the husband-wife pairing, would reverse the gender assignments of the
houses (McKinnon 1991:111 n). Logically, the wife in this instance would
represent her natal house, endowing it with her female gender, and her
husband would represent the wife-receivers, rendering them masculine
(Valeri 1980:185).

THE SOURCE OF HIERARCHY

The superior/inferior relationship of wife-providers/wife-receivers is well
known in the literature of Southeast Asia (especially following Leach 1965).
However, the superiority of the wife-providers, so typical of Indonesia, is
not inherent to their male gender (cf. Boon 1990:222). Instead, hierarchy
is predicated on other factors.

Wife-providers in Eastern Indonesia are superior because of what they
possess and provide to their wife-receivers, namely, life itself (e.g., Barnes
1980:79; Clamagirand 1980:144; Erb 1987:118; Fox 1980b:116). Life-force
is epitomized as "blood," and blood flows through females as mothers
(Fox 1980a:12). The wife-providers, source of those mothers, are therefore the "source of life," and "it is the relative value accorded to the source
of life and its issue that differentiates houses" (McKinnon 1991:32). As
Sherman (1987:868) noted, this is a specific example of a more general pattern described by Leach (1971a:25) of an "*uncontrolled mystical influence*
[that] denotes a relation of alliance" extending from the wife-providing
house to the wife-receiving house members, through the women who entered the latter house. This asymmetry is apparent in the contrast between
the types of influence exerted over persons by members of their own house
and their wife-provider houses. The wife-providing house has control over
the well-being of persons who share in its "blood" or physical substance
(Sherman and Sherman 1990:95). The mother's brother, as the quintessential wife-provider, thus has the power to cure his sister's children when
they become ill. By the same logic, he can curse his sister's children if they
fail to show respect, for he controls their life functions (e.g., Barnes 1980:
79–80; Erb 1987:118).

In contrast, a house exerts jural control over its own members and is
concerned with shaping them into social beings. This difference between
types of influence is summarized for the Island of Roti as follows:

> From his father, a person derives his enduring social person embodied in
> his genealogical name and represented by his bones, which survive the de-

cay of his flesh; from his mother, a person derives his flesh and blood, and he is dependent on his maternal relations for the rituals that sustain his life. (Fox 1980b:119)

As the "source of life," the wife-providers are associated with "origins" (Fox 1980b:117). They are identified with "the original totality, the prior unity" (McKinnon 1991:36) of the cosmos. For example, on Roti the phrase meaning "mother's brother of origin" refers to all the wife-providers. The notion of origin is also the basis for botanic metaphors used to refer to kin relationships. The term for mother's brother means "trunk" or "stem," and his sister's child is the "plant," the offshoot of that stem (Fox 1971:221; also McKinnon 1991:111).

As this botanic metaphor indicates, another source of hierarchy in the alliance relationship derives from the fact that the wife-providers encompass the exteriorized females that issue from their house and their progeny, all of whom share in the blood of the wife-providing, or mother-providing, house. By encompassing its issue, the wife-provider house is necessarily of higher value (McKinnon 1991:111).

UNITY AND DIFFERENTIATION

To form relationships with other units, the androgynous house reconceptualizes itself as either male or female and then engages in subsequent gender-totalizing actions. Thus there is a constant alternation between these two extremes: unity–differentiation–unity. This dialectic is a key process in sociocosmic classification in Indonesia (McKinnon 1991).

This alternation also explains the importance of the brother-sister pair and the motivation behind marriage alliance. The initial primordial unity was exemplified by "an ancestral brother-sister pair whose sexual relationship, or lack of it, and their eventual parting, is equivalent to the original fracture of unity that brings about the world's events and begins human history" (Errington 1990:51). This original unity is replicated in the relationships of all brothers and sisters, differentiated beings who, nevertheless, "as zero-degree siblings, are *already* one" (Errington 1987:429).

A corollary to this belief is the implicit or explicit notion that although the original brother-sister pair was separated, there is the promise of their reunion in the future. This promise is fulfilled by their descendants as their surrogates, a female descendant of one marrying the male descendant of the other. Just as every brother-sister pair represents the original totality fated for separation, so every husband-wife pair exemplifies their reunification. It is a common practice in Southeast Asia for spouses to address one another as brother and sister (Gordon 1980:53), the spouse being a ritual substitute for the sibling (Errington 1989:237).

While unity and fracture form a dialectic, different societies may emphasize one over the other in cosmology, myth, and ritual, as well as social practice. Shelly Errington (1990:54) has demonstrated that within Island Southeast Asia, some societies "are preoccupied with unity" and associate fracture or disunity with failure and misfortune. Eastern Indonesian peoples, however, do the reverse—they "represent themselves as irremediably fractured into pairs" (1990:55). This extreme is exemplified by the gender coding of wife-provider/wife-receiver pairings and their exchanges of complementary goods. The emphasis on the fracturing of the primordial brother-sister unity should also explain the focus on the movement of the woman away from her natal house as the act that initiates the gender differentiation of allied houses. This "exteriorizing" of the female aspect from the wife-providers structures the gender assignments to the two houses.

All the symbolic representations incorporating gender coding associated with marriage alliance in Eastern Indonesia are therefore explained in terms of a single model predicated on key cosmological concepts and processes. This same synthesizing model can be applied to the Maya data to reveal how they, too, used gender to organize their equivalent social practices.

The Gendering of Maya Alliance Relationships

Available information for alliance and exchange among the ancient Maya, though fragmentary and scattered among the different Maya peoples, indicates that gender ideology may have been used in the same way as in Eastern Indonesia to motivate and conceptualize social relationships, according to very similar structural principles. There is an essential difference, which is itself inherent in the Indonesian model. Unlike Eastern Indonesian societies, the Maya emphasized unity over difference (keeping in mind that both are the endpoints of a dialectical process and that each requires the other to have any meaning).

This contrast with our Old World example is best revealed in Maya cosmology. Surviving cosmological narratives dating to the early colonial period, such as the Quiche Maya *Popol Vuh* (see Tedlock 1985), relate that the primordium was characterized not by an original unity but by a pre-existing separation into two parts. Cosmic history proceeded as a series of halting steps to combine these dichotomous segments correctly in order to create a unity that was productive both biologically and socially. It was initially achieved in the union of a man and the woman who left her natal house to join his. The explicit motivation for this union was the engendering of children, namely, the Hero Twins who set about creating cosmic order.

In emphasizing unity over fracture, this text downplays the brother-sister relationship (although it is not absent) to highlight the husband-wife, or better stated, father-mother union. Applying this principle to Maya society, according to the model developed for Southeast Asia, the emphasis on husband-wife unity rather than brother-sister separation should reverse the gender assignments of the allied houses. In the wife-provider/wife-receiver relationship that is implicit in this Maya father-mother pairing, the wife-provider should be represented by the wife or mother who comes to the marriage. Wife-providers should be externally female, while the wife-receivers, represented by the husband, would be male. The available data on Maya marriage alliance shows this is precisely what occurred.

The inherent character of the wife-providers is unchanged, and Maya concepts in this regard are remarkably similar to those of Indonesia. Wife-providers are still superior because they are the "source of life." As in Indonesia, this concept is represented by the "blood" of the wife-providers that flows to their receiving houses through women. The female protagonist of the *Popol Vuh*, who left her own house to effect the union of husband-wife, eponymously incarnated blood. She was literally named "Blood," and her father's name "Blood Gatherer," indicates that this characteristic was inherited from her father, the head of her house (Tedlock 1985:114), who was the wife-provider. In Yucatec Maya, *ts'ak* as a noun refers to a curative liquid as well as a poisonous liquid; as a verb it can mean to cure or to kill. It is also the root of *ts'akab*, referring to offspring through the mother's line (Barrera Vásquez 1980:871–873). Following from this concept is another parallel with Indonesia, that the mother's line of kinsmen are associated with the physical well-being of her children, both for good and for ill.

However, the change in gender assignment for the two houses does reverse the symbolic representations of the alliance. For example, the wife-providers are still the source or origin, but instead of being represented by the mother's brother, this notion is embodied by the woman herself, as mother. In Tzotzil Maya, *me'*, the word for "mother," "carries a causative element of meaning, which has to do with the origins of things" (Devereaux 1987:92). The word for mother in Yucatec Maya, *na'*, has a similar extension of meanings (Barrera Vásquez 1980:545).

As in Indonesia, evidence for the gender coding of Maya alliance relationships is most apparent in the context of marriage exchanges. This evidence is available in documentary materials describing social interactions in the colonial period, as well as in ethnographic descriptions of contemporary Maya peoples. While these data are sparse and reveal the incorporation of Spanish customs, they nevertheless meet the expectations of this sociocosmic model.

In Maya marriage negotiations of the past as well as the present, the greater economic burden was typically placed on the wife-receiving groups. This pattern indicates the inferior standing of the wife-receivers (Leach 1971:102). For example, wife-receivers in early colonial Yucatán were obligated to provide a considerable period of bride-service (Landa 1982:43; Roys et al. 1940:15), as well as specific goods. The latter consisted of clothing for the bride and groom, chocolate beverage, and precious stone beads used in necklaces. The taking of chocolate drink by the groom's father to the potential bride's father was the custom known as *tak ha'* in Yucatán (Barrera Vásquez 1980:759). *Ha'* is literally "water," but was also used to refer to chocolate beverage (e.g., *ah haa'*; see 1980:165). The payment of stone beads was part of the formal petition for the bride (*tsa*, 1980:848) and was a gift for the bride (*ximila'*, 1980:944). Landa (1982:43) mentioned the bride-price (which was *mu'huul;* Barrera Vásquez 1980:533) without stating what it was, and noted that the groom's mother made clothing for the bridal couple.

It is possible to associate these items with a specific gender. Cloth was a quintessential female good in the Mesoamerican culture area (McCafferty and McCafferty 1991). As for chocolate, a red liquid, it is iconically linked to blood (Sahagún 1969:256), the life-giving fluid that flows through females. It is more difficult to assign a gender to the precious stone beads, but we suspect that it is not the beads themselves that are important in this context, but the fact that they are part of a necklace, probably a female adornment. This supposition is supported by the fact that in modern Yucatán, the necklace worn by women (now in the form of gold chains) constitutes the most important item of the bride-price, a custom that retains its pre-Hispanic name (*muhul*) (Redfield and Villa Rojas 1962:193). A Tzotzil Maya groom in Zinacantán is also expected to provide his bride with a necklace as well as a ring (Collier 1968:158).

While there was a reciprocal obligation for the bride's father to provide a dowry (*mek'*) to the wife-receivers, in sixteenth-century Yucatán it was paid in cacao beans (Barrera Vásquez 1980:518). Cacao beans were used as currency well into the colonial period (Thompson 1956), so it is uncertain whether this "money" payment replaced an earlier type of valuable. The bride's family was also responsible for the wedding feast, and a wife was obligated to provide food for her husband as a "sign" of their married state (Landa 1982 : 43). Similarly, the modern Tzotzil Maya of Zinacantán conduct a long courtship during which the prospective bride must feed her fiancé cooked food in return for the raw food he brings her family (Collier 1968 : 158). Thus, the wife-providers did offer specific valuables— prepared food—to the wife-receivers as part of their exchange obligations, both as part of and long after the marriage rites.

More information on colonial period marriage exchanges comes from the central Chol-speaking Maya, a people of the southern lowlands area where earlier Maya rulers had erected monuments with hieroglyphic texts. Documentary evidence records that a simple exchange was customary: a man gave his new wife skirts, a gender-identifying part of costume (Joyce 1990), while she in turn gave him his stool (Thompson 1938 : 602). Among these same Chol speakers, stools were placed over the graves of men exclusively (1938 : 597). The gender association of the stool continues among some modern Maya groups, most explicitly in the practice whereby men customarily sit on stools, while women sit on the ground (Gossen 1972 : 141). Thus the stool or seat may be assigned a male gender in terms of these uses.

In sum, among these items of bride-price and dowry, we see the wife-providers giving the woman herself, who carried the "blood," the life-giving liquid. In addition, the wife-providers offered such things as cooked food (another life-sustaining substance), the man's stool, and cacao beans. As for the wife-receivers, they provided the labor of the groom as well as items actually commonly used as standards of exchange—cacao (but in the form of a beverage), cloth, and precious stones—all of which may be gendered as female in these exchange transactions.

As valuable as these data are, they refer to exchanges between allied houses only in the context of marriage. Because bride-price was paramount in these negotiations, it receives more attention than the reciprocal and complementary goods that should have been exchanged in the other direction. The Southeast Asian ethnographic data indicate that prestations of complementary goods continue long past the marriage itself and occur at many other occasions, especially ritual and life-crisis events.

Fortunately, pre-Hispanic Maya archaeological materials reveal additional items that the wife-receivers may have obtained from their wife-providers at occasions other than marriage. This information is derived from depictions preserved on stone monuments erected during the Late Classic period in the southern Maya lowlands. Some monuments at political centers in the western Maya area—such as Palenque, Yaxchilán, and Piedras Negras—portray women in the act of proffering items to men. We suggest that these women may do so as representatives of the wife-providing house into which they were born, because they are frequently stated in accompanying hieroglyphic texts to be the wives or mothers of the men depicted. Some of the items held out by the women should therefore be part of the ritual exchange obligations owed by the wife-provider to the wife-receiver, represented by the husband or son.

The men shown in these artworks were either paramounts of a major political center or other important nobles, those with the authority and means to erect stone monuments. Thus we are not looking at evidence for average individuals; on the contrary, these data are exclusive to persons of very high status. Nevertheless, the scenes on these monuments can be considered exemplary of a conceptual system whose organizing principles structured the larger society. We do not interpret these monuments as mere records of singular events idiosyncratic to the moment and individuals portrayed, but as icons that manifest the sociocosmic classification.

According to the model that has been presented, the objects held out by the women were construed as male in opposition to the female goods given by the wife-receivers. Among the identifiable objects that women give to men are shields and eccentric blades. A striking example is the Palace Tablet from Palenque, which depicts a paramount in the act of receiving from his mother a shield paired with an eccentric flint (Robertson 1985:59, Figure 277). As Joyce (1990) has demonstrated, these objects as icons are dramatically gendered male in Maya art. They also likely disappeared from the cultural inventory of exchange goods following the Spanish conquest.

Furthermore, the male-gendered seat is also present in these pre-Hispanic data, not in the imagery so much as in the use of certain titles by which royal persons themselves became objectified. As in hierarchical societies of Southeast Asia, these persons literally *are* the sacred regalia (Errington 1989:240). Instead of being actual objects in the exchange, these goods are shown to coincide symbolically with the women themselves.

There are instances where a title given to the mother of the paramount reveals that she herself represented the man's seat, in the same way that the legendary first woman to represent all subsequent wives and mothers was literally named "Blood." For example, the mother of a Late Classic ruler of Tikal has a title string that includes the pictographs reading "jaguar seat," while the ruler's father's name includes a shield (Jones 1977:41–42), an item that, as noted above, has male associations.

It was the wife-providers who were symbolically "female" and ritually superior to their wife-receivers; both meanings are embedded in the word *ihtan*. The hieroglyphic text on a monument from Naranjo (Stela 23, Schele and Freidel 1990:191) provides a rare explicit confirmation of this extended meaning of the *ihtah* relationship. The protagonist, the paramount of Naranjo, refers to a man of the city of Dos Pilas as his *ihtah*. In an embedded phrase he explains that his own wife was a woman of Dos Pilas. (His mother was also apparently from the ruling house of Dos Pilas.) Thus, Dos Pilas was the "female" wife-provider to the ruler of Naranjo, and a particular personage from that city is referred to as the Naranjo paramount's "elder sister."

Here is an example of a man calling another man by a female kin term, just as occurs today in Southeast Asia in connection with wife-provider/ wife-receiver relationships. *Ihtan* is a kin term that encodes a cross-sexed relationship, because it is used by a male ego to refer to his sister, but more importantly, it also encodes age superiority. In Maya kinship terminology, relative age is a more important criterion than gender for classifying people as social persons (Danziger 1991).

By metaphoric extension, Dos Pilas was the "source of life" for the Naranjo paramount and his ruling house. In this instance, the ritual superiority attached to the wife-providers was also more literally a political superiority. At this time, Dos Pilas was a powerful center, and Naranjo was struggling to regain its former glory (Culbert 1988:146–147). By claiming wife-receiver status to the sacred center of Dos Pilas, Naranjo became its offshoot or extension, sharing in its access to authority.

The specific use of a sibling term for the female half of the marital alliance indicates that for the Maya, as in Southeast Asia, the sociocosmic concept underlying the alliance relationship is the reunion of brother and sister as husband and wife. This principle survived into traditional Tzotzil Maya weddings of Zinacantán, in which the bride and groom addressed each other as "elder brother" and "younger sister" (Laughlin 1975:63, 321).

All these lines of evidence suggest that among the ancient Maya, the wife-providers, the source of blood and life, were gendered female with respect to wife-receiving houses. The cosmological principle structuring this gender complementarity was the union of husband and wife, the cross-sexed relationship that motivated the assignment of male and female genders to the wife-receiver and wife-provider houses, respectively. In turn, the obligatory exchange transactions consisted of the prestation or "exte-

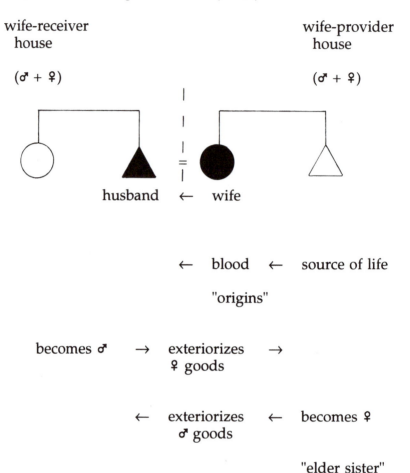

wife-receiver house

(σ + φ)

wife-provider house

(σ + φ)

husband   ←   wife

←   blood   ←   source of life

"origins"

becomes σ →   exteriorizes   →
φ goods

←   exteriorizes   ←   becomes φ
σ goods

"elder sister"

Figure 2.   Maya model using Indonesian analogy. The reunion of husband and wife configures the gender assignment of the allied houses.

riorizing" of male goods by wife-providers in return for female goods from wife-receivers (Figure 2).

Summary and Implications for Maya Studies

Information compiled from ethnohistoric, ethnographic, and archaeological sources reveals how gender ideology facilitated social relationships among the ancient Maya. These data are organized into a coherent model, one that is derived from similar Southeast Asian societies but that also contains within itself the explanation of why Maya sociocosmic classification differed in essential respects from its Asian counterpart.

Marriage was the critical bond that established relationships among family groups, organized as "houses." The allied houses were construed as male and female, a gender code that simultaneously indicates the complementarity of the relationship as well as its asymmetry and hierarchy. The gender assignments for the Maya are the reverse of those typical of Southeast Asia. The Maya wife-provider house was gendered female, and offered goods to its allied houses that were considered masculine in opposition to the feminine items that composed the bride-price owed by the male wife-receiver houses. As in Indonesia, houses were actually a gender totality, androgynous units that stood as "male" to some allied houses and "female" to others. The gender of the house was fluid, expressed through performance in particular relationships.

The implications of this model for understanding ancient Maya civilization are significant. Southeast Asia is the same part of the world from which Maya scholars have recently been borrowing political models, such as galactic polity, segmentary state, and theater state (e.g., Ball and Taschek 1991; Demarest 1992; Houston 1993). But the sociological concepts that would link "people" (social groups) to these various forms of "polity" (political units) have been missing in Maya studies. We have demonstrated the applicability of Southeast Asian types of social organization to the Maya. It is also necessary to indicate where the Maya are unlike their Asian counterparts when using these borrowed models. As our research has shown, there are crucial differences in the basic principles that structure the sociocosmic classifications of Mayan and Eastern Indonesian peoples.

The identification of the "house" as the main social unit for the Maya, and the emphasis on examining social organization in terms of asymmetric relationships between houses are initial steps in this process. Evidence indicates that the paramount, at the top of the political organization, came from a ruling house organized according to the same sociocosmic principles that structured and interrelated all houses. Social actions taking place at the elite level of society, preserved in stone monuments, are homologous to those at the non-elite level.

The Southeast Asian data reveal that social and political organization are predicated on the same principles and processes, so that the ritual hierarchy of wife-providers and wife-receivers is mirrored in the expression of political authority. According to Edmund Leach (1971:74; see also 1965:136):

> The status relations between wife givers and wife receivers must conform to the status relations implicit in other (non-kinship) institutions: e.g., when wife givers are socially superior to wife receivers, one can predict that the political and territorial rights of wife givers will be superior to those of wife receivers, etc.,—and *vice versa*. In other words, . . . it is part of the political structure.

Among the Maya, the ritually superior wife-providers received as bride-price the same items that Maya vassals paid as tribute to their politically superior overlords. The payment made by the bride's father to the groom's father in early-colonial Yucatán was known as *mek'* (Barrera Vásquez 1980:518). It is the root of a series of words referring to governance; for example, *mek'tantah* meant to govern a people or a town. The Yucatec Maya bride-price, *mu'huul* (1980:533) shares its root in colonial Tzotzil Maya (Laughlin 1988:I:261) with the word *mu'nil,* which was the tribute paid by vassals to their overlord, a tribute paid in cloth. Thus there seems to be a pattern whereby the wife-provider was aligned with the ruler, and the bride-price paid by the wife-receivers to their ritual superiors was equated in the political realm with the tribute paid by subjects to their political superiors.

In the Classic period, the Maya paramount, who had ritual as well as political powers, was aligned with the superior wife-providers' side in the dyadic division of society. He was the "source of life," responsible for the physical well-being of his people, and receiving from them the economically costly consumer goods and labor that were his due.

Furthermore, the specific values attached to the complementary categories of male and female, which manifest the asymmetry of this sociopolitical model, should be found in other domains of Maya society, including related concepts of gender roles and gender identity. They more broadly exhibit the opposition of male and female "kinds of agency" or "modes of action" (Hoskins 1987). The implication from the Classic Maya data is that higher ranked paramounts were wife-providers to lesser lords and vassals, *and* that this position was in some way gendered female. The role and context of female kinds of agency in the diarchical construction of "power," as has been described for Southeast Asia (Cunningham 1965; Errington 1990:18; Francillon 1980:261), warrants further investigation of the connections between political and ritual authority, as well as those between political and social action, among the ancient Maya.

Beyond the specific suggestions we have made for the study of the ancient Maya, what implications does our study have for the archaeology of gender? By examining how gender is symbolically assigned to material goods, we have shown that there is no simple association between specific items and gender that can be assumed cross-culturally. Instead, the gendering of objects is part of the complex negotiations through which social relations are formed in any particular society. At the same time, our analysis demonstrates that attempts to understand past social systems without addressing gender ideology and gender relations fail to deal with major arenas of social complexity.

Taking seriously the independence of gendering variables from the sex of their users will not provide a simple key to identifying gender in action, and, in fact, makes all arguments about gender and its material symbolism more complex and thus more realistic. In the absence of the kinds of linguistic, textual, and iconographic data that are available for the Maya, we would, nevertheless, suggest that there are particularly fruitful contexts for the possible understanding of gender ideology. These are contexts in which symbolically charged material goods—those that are assigned gender symbolism in our two examples—are used in stereotyped ways stemming from their social significance. Burials, shrines, and other archaeological deposits resulting from formal social action should be examined as sites where gender symbolism may have been used, and their symbolism given explicit form in social relations. Analyses of such socially charged arenas that do not examine how gender ideology and symbolism may be involved will always be inadequate.

Acknowledgments

The authors are greatly indebted to Professor Clark Cunningham and Amanda Grunden for their invaluable assistance with the gathering and interpreting of the Indonesian literature.

PART IV

The Material Construction of Gender

13. Earth Mothers, Warriors, Horticulturists, Artists, and Chiefs: Women Among the Mississippian and Mississippian-Oneota Peoples, A.D. 1000 to 1750

Lyle Koehler

Much has been written about Mississippian society, but little attention has been paid to women. In fact, to my knowledge, women in Mississippian times have been briefly examined by only two scholars—one of whom is unpublished (Brown 1982; Lumb 1992). While some might throw up their hands and say, "There's nothing we can learn about the status of women in prehistory," I believe that the ceramic imagery, carvings/paintings on various rock faces (most notably the forty-one sites and 1,283 images in southern Illinois and adjacent Missouri that I have examined), and ethnographic material gleaned from early French and Spanish sources (in conjunction with the archaeological record) can flesh out attitudes toward women among Mississippians and the Mississippian-Oneota mixture that occurred after A.D. 1400 in Illinois and Missouri.

In contrast to the European fascination with dichotomies of male gods and female witches, many tribal peoples thought that females had an important positive role to play in the cosmic dynamic as the tribal analogs of the Earth Mother, using her "techniques of maximizing life" (Foucault 1980:123), awesome power, and transforming ability to ensure survival of the individual, family, and society, not only during the lushness of spring-summer but also through the harshness of fall-winter. Earth Mother provided the procreative force to produce all of human, animal, and plant kind. Woman was therefore the creative agent, reproductively, productively, and cosmologically. Because of this, American Indians often traced descent through the mother, as illustrated by the Mississippian-Oneota Illiniwek and the Mississippian Cenis, Alabama, Tunica, Houma, Taensa, Yuchi, and Natchez (Bossu 1962:132; Hennepin 1698b:54; Le Page du Pratz 1976:331, 346; Speck 1909).

There is considerable evidence for Earth Mother figures. Between

A.D. 1050 and 1100, inhabitants of the BBB Motor site near Cahokia, Illinois, buried the Birger figurine, with her plant-serpent associations, and the Keller effigy in separate pits. Both possess elongated noses, flattened foreheads, prominent chins, and wrap-around skirts rolled and fastened at the waist. The Keller effigy has a mano and metate on a stand, plus long straight hair pulled back to expose the ears. She is small-breasted and wears moccasins. Emerson (1982) has pointed out that the Birger figurine may represent the Corn Mother common in Eastern Woodlands mythology, because just as that Mother scratches her body to produce corn, so does the Birger Mother scratch the back of the Earth Serpent. In the Natchez version of this myth, Corn Mother tells others, "Kill me and burn my body. When summer comes things will spring up on the place where it was burned and you must cultivate them, and when they are matured they will be your food" (Swanton 1929:230). Could the fact that both the Birger and Keller figurines were broken prehistorically and buried in pits—the latter in a burned area—represent variations of this legend? (See also Prentice 1986.)

Other Earth Mothers or Corn Goddesses existed as well. A brick-red bauxite figure from the eastern bluffs of the Illinois River near Eldred has a serpent coiled once around the base of a pipe bowl that also serves as a bag. The pipe may also represent a gourd. The figure possesses straight long hair, a skirt, and a pelt or small animal skin over the right shoulder (Emerson 1982:15–18). A buxom figurine from Missouri has pronounced breasts and a lower body that is extremely globular, appearing to be a huge earth womb (Holmes 1903:Pl.27). A Vincennes, Indiana, effigy, quite eroded, is of a woman working on a pot—again an object made of earth (clay) and perhaps bearing figures of fertility in its prospective design imagery (Holmes 1903:Pl. 28). Female effigies from Arkansas, Missouri, and Tennessee possess both breasts and backpacks and sometimes skirts (Fundaburk and Fundaburk 1957:Pl. 118, 119, 120). One long-haired female figure from Etowah, Georgia, appears to be pregnant (Holmes 1903:41).

Good evidence exists that such effigies were not only Earth Mothers connected to the transforming powers of nature, but also goddesses of the home. The French observer La Harpe (Margry 1875–86:VI:247) reported that "their household gods are a frog and a figure of a woman, thinking that they represent the sun." Since the frog is also a notable fertility figure in Mesoamerica, the female effigies in association with sometimes copulating frogs may have served to produce fruitful homes. La Source (Shea 1861: 81) affirmed that "earthen figures" were the Tunica Indians' "manitous," or powerful nature spirits. Tadpoles appear quite commonly in the rock art of southern Illinois-Missouri, and at Piney Creek, Jackson County, Illinois, one woman gives birth to a tadpole while others wriggle about her (Figure 1A). This may be an Earth Mother figure as well.

Historic mythology of the Creek, Hitchiti, Alabama, and Natchez support the idea that women are more closely connected with nature and transformation than men. Women transform into deer, often underground. They also have sex with panthers and earthworms, delivering mixed babies. In Alabamu mythology, a man has to jump on his wife's back so that she can "go through the earth" with him. He cannot do it himself (Swanton 1929:21–22, 28–29, 30–34, 38, 89–91, 144–145, 193).

Male effigies exist as well, some with apparent shamanic character, but the male and female figures are somewhat different, making it possible to distinguish effigies by sex. Male hairstyles focus on ponytails or buns, whereas female hair is usually, but not always, straight. Male chests, even when they bear nipples, are easy to distinguish from female chests. Men are nude—although penises are not generally depicted (some of these may have been slashed off by nineteenth-century moralists)—but women almost always have skirts. (The one exception to this is a Kincaid effigy bottle in the form of a woman with vulva delineated, and a similar effigy from an unspecified location [Cole et al. 1951:336; Fundaburk and Fundaburk 1957: Pl. 98].) Men do not have plant associations, but women do. With one exception, women do not appear on Mississippian pipes, while men do (although both sexes fairly commonly appear on Fort Ancient pipes [Converse 1973]).

The absence of clothing on men (and, to a lesser extent, women) indicates that the images were made to represent warm-weather times. This is consistent with warm-weather ceremonies. The French, in fact, reported among the Illiniwek and southeastern Mississippians exactly the same type of dress as appeared on the Mississippian figurines. The Illiniwek called the skirts *alkonan* (Bossu 1962:82). Hennepin (1698b:106), Marquette (1698: 210), and St. Cosme (Shea 1861:73) stated that the Illiniwek men went "stark naked" in summer and wore only buffalo robes and moccasins in winter, while the "half-naked" women wore skin skirts in warm weather. Women's skirts, bark blankets, feathered mantles, and tanned deerskins covered with colored designs—in effect winter as well as summer dress—

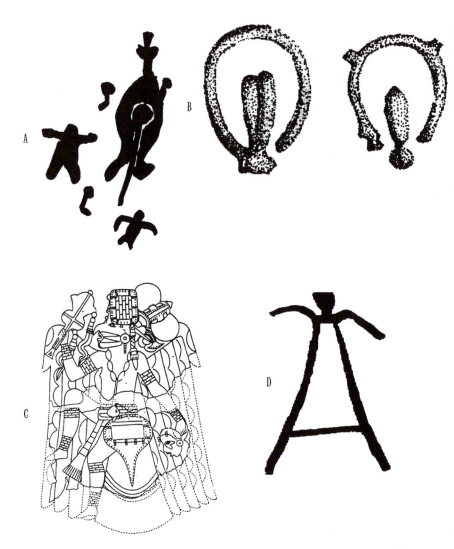

Figure 1. *A*, Earth Mother giving birth to a tadpole, on Piney Creek cliff face, Jackson Co., Illinois (drawing by Lyle Koehler); *B*, vagina symbols on boulders near Miller's Cave, Pulaski Co., Missouri (drawing by Lyle Koehler); *C*, female falcon god on shell, Temple Mound, Etowah, Georgia (from Warren King Moorehead, *Etowah Papers: Exploration of the Etowah Site in Georgia* [1932], p. 34; courtesy of the Robert S. Peabody Museum, Phillips Academy, and Yale University Press); *D*, skirted woman on Piney Creek boulder, Jackson Co., Illinois (drawing by Lyle Koehler).

were stored in *barbacoas*, along with maize and dead bodies (Gentleman of Elvas 1933:93). The rolled-up top of the Earth Mother skirts are similar to the girdles the French described.

Because they were Earth Mother analogs, maturity for women became associated with marriage and creativity. As fully acknowledged "social" beings, they then could "create" a harmonious home and village, nurturing children as Earth Mother and Sun nurtured all growing things. The skirt of Mississippian women served as a symbol of that new creativity, since they donned it only at marriage. An astounded La Source (Shea 1861:80–82) commented that a few Natchez women of twenty-five or thirty years—presumably unmarried—went totally nude. La Source, then, makes it relatively clear that the skirt symbolized more than a passage into adulthood/fertility because women not wearing them were often old enough to conceive.

The association of women and creativity may have been borrowed by Mississippians from their earlier Hopewellian ancestors. At Knight Mound in west-central Illinois, McKern, Titterington, and Griffin (1945) discovered a seated male figurine, and two standing and two seated women. One seated and one standing woman carried nude infants. All figurines bore paint, including one female who possessed one red moccasin and one black (both decorated with white speckles), a broad red belt, and a black skirt decorated with white stripes at the top and bottom. All of the women have bare breasts, pronounced ears, skirts, and black or red moccasins. Three of the four have black and white arm bands and long hair reaching beyond the waist in back. Seven female and two male Hopewellian figurines found in a field along the Illinois River are dressed similarly (Converse 1993). These female carvings are similar enough to the later Mississippians in "social"—perhaps even familial—emphasis, dress, hair, and ear exposure to be considered progenitors.

Women's reproductive status certainly was important apart from Earth Mother associations. At Miller's Cave, Pulaski County, Missouri, petroglyphs cut into a bluff facing the Gasconade River may represent female genitalia. A rounded, womblike oval surrounds either a vaginal opening with interior passageway or a representation of two lips (Figure 1B). Some of these are a half-meter tall. They are similar to those found in sections of the Great Plains, where they have been perceived as fertility figures (Varney 1990), but at Miller's Cave they occur in an area where Mississippian house mounds, pottery, flint, and mortars exist. Caves have much symbolism which a vagina might suggest, and perhaps these vagina symbols were intended to facilitate the flourishing of the entire community, since large numbers of infant skeletons were found in the cave (Fowke 1922:60–97). These infants had not had a chance to thrive and continue the community. The womb/vagina thus celebrated woman's power to ensure that continuity.

Pit-and-groove art has been described by Grieder (1982) and others as a fertility-enhancing symbol. Mississippians carved the long groove with a pit attached, or a pit without a groove (representing vaginas), in numerous places at the Bushburg-Meisner site south of St. Louis. Ellis (1969:53–54) believes these are phallic instead of vaginal, but the usual association of women with fertility suggests a female-based explanation is more credible. The sheer number of such pits and grooves there may indicate a shrine to which women went to ensure that they would become pregnant. As such, these shrines were testaments to women's mysterious power for the growth and sustenance of the lineage, the tribe, and humanity itself.

The Sun cooperated with Earth Mother in providing warmth and light for growing things and human activity. The Taensa, Yuchi, Chitimacha, and Cherokee later considered the nurturing sun female. They also prayed to it for success in war (Swanton 1928b), perhaps because they believed that the blood of captives or servants in major settlements was necessary to feed the sun and ensure continued growth; thus, as the death of winter passed into the life of spring, so may the death of sacrifices have passed into the life of the new maize crop. Hence it was fitting that the gender that bled periodically should have an important role in such activities. The Yuchi believed that a drop of the sun's menstrual blood had awesome creative force (Speck 1909). There is, however, no evidence that Mississippians feared woman's menstrual blood as enervating or dangerous to men, as many historic North American tribes did. Joutel (1714 [1962: 137]) stated that the Cenis women did *not* isolate themselves in menstrual huts to avoid "weakening" their men.

It is, in fact, probable that the prehistoric Mississippians may have viewed the sun as blending male and female characteristics in a dualism suggested by Natchez sun chiefs of both sexes. There is a strong evidence to suggest that even the warfare function of the sun may have had a male and female referent as well. The shell and copper engravings of the Etowah inhabitants, as Catherine Brown pointed out in 1982, show a winged goddess carrying a mace in the right hand and sometimes a head in the other. Both Brown (1982) and Lumb (1992) recognized that a "female" breast may well be depicted on such winged beings, although Phillips and James

Brown (1978:95) asserted that "recognizable sexual characteristics are non-existent in the figural art of Spiro, as in the Southeast generally. The present writers incline to the opinion that this means the identification of human figures as to sex was not considered necessary because it was taken for granted that none was female." The latter androcentrically believe that the relatively small size of the winged-goddess breast makes it male, even though in engravings it is more pointed than representations of male breasts are and has underlying breast tissue (Figure 1C). It is incredibly similar to the small breasts on some clearly female figurines. If such were intended as male gods, then it is unclear why some figures have them and others do not. A notable comparative example appeared in the Temple Mound at Etowah, where two nearly identical figurines, with the same positioning of feet and arms, exist on different shell gorgets. One of these has a breast; one does not. The same is true for two Rogan, Missouri, tablets with such deities, which have different headdresses as well (Phillips and Brown 1978:188). The depiction of only one breast on all such "female" gods suggests that an effort is being made to symbolically distinguish the female from the male winged being. The male god often also possesses horns, which the female does not (Willoughby 1932:34–36, 54–58). Such imagery suggests that the blended dualism of Sun also existed among other divinities.

In one case, two winged beings with swords and bird feet are fighting on an eastern Tennessee gorget (Willoughby 1932:55). Each of these "falcon" gods has a small, pointed breast. This could represent some conflict between goddesses of the air—perhaps between the powers of light and darkness. If the falcon gods were both male and female, and such gods helped warriors, then women were also ceremonially implicated in warfare. Howard (1968:78) has hypothesized that the Green Corn Dance to insure the fertility of the corn crop was originally a Scalp or War Dance. One early account described the Creek Green Corn ceremony as the Women's War Dance (Lumb 1992:7). In modern Green Corn Dances, Howard (1968: 126) observed, women leading the dance carry white-painted *atassa*, or "ceremonial knife-shaped clubs," which resemble the maces on Mississippian engravings. Interestingly, the Aztec goddess Xochiquetzal is described as a courtesan, an Earth Mother, and a War Goddess (McCafferty and McCafferty 1994a). Were the Winged Goddess and Xochiquetzal the same—the end result of a Mesoamerican import into Mississippian locales?

In the rock art of southern Illinois-Missouri several female figures exist. It is not known how many are goddesses, other than the woman at

Piney Creek who gives birth to a tadpole. A number of "skirted" anthropomorphs do appear in the art (Figure 1D). One Oraville, Illinois, carving
duplicates the hairstyle on Hopewellian effigies (Figure 2A). Other images
have distinctly rounded bodies, especially in the hip area. Thirty-two "female" figures have been identified at eight sites, and twenty-four "men"

Figure 2.   *A*, Skirted woman on boulder, Graville, Jackson Co., Illinois (drawing
by Lyle Koehler); *B*, female "chief" leading Green Corn dance (?), on shell gorget,
Moundville, Alabama (courtesy of National Museum of the American Indian,
Smithsonian Institution, New York); *C*, warrior woman, on Piney Creek cliff face,
Jackson Co., Illinois (drawing by Lyle Koehler); *D*, ceramic breasts, Mitchell Ko-
rando site, Jackson Co., Illinois (drawing by Lyle Koehler from Illinois State University–Carbondale archaeology site files).

(linear figures with larger upper bodies and sometimes with penises) at five sites. Forty other figures could not be sexed. Thus, of *all* anthropomorphs, at least one-third appear to be female, a number far higher than in Fort Ancient and Oneota locales.

The strong female-fertility emphasis in Mississippian rock art suggests that it and sexuality may have been widespread concerns among these peoples. The French accounts certainly indicate that feasts were times of searching out eligible mates, and also of considerable sexual activity. Hennepin (1698b:24, 128) reported that "the common Discourse both of Men and Women is down-right bawdy," while La Salle kept his troops distant from "exceeding kind" and "handsom" Cenis women, for fear his men would become "debauch'd." Cavelier (1938:89–91, 103) accused "those prostitutes" of "persecuting" La Salle's men.

Such sexual adventurism might be expected at feasts and times when travelers visited. Women could then engage in sex for material goods, prospective marital partners, erotic need, or transferring power in ceremonial contexts. Some of those nighttime ceremonies where women danced with men, sang lewd songs, and assumed "obscene poses and gestures" may have celebrated the springtime fertility of the soil (Bossu 1962:61; Hennepin 1698b:72).

Female "chiefs" may well have concretely symbolized some of the goddesses represented in art. At Moundville a Mississippian figure with an incredibly female face, hairstyle, and mace (but without wings or head in hand) may be one such "chief" leading a Green Corn dance (Fundaburk and Fundaburk 1957:Pl. 41; see Figure 2B). The breast area is covered by a spotted garment, but some bulge does appear on the right side of the garment. In another case, a "warrior" with two spears in his hand bows before a figure with an elaborate feathered headdress, shield, fringed kilt, picturesque moccasins, and breasts (Holmes 1883:Pl. 31). As late as historic times, women served as chiefs of Illiniwek villages, including at winter-hunting campsites women served as chiefs of Illiniwek villages, including at winter-hunting campsites (Walthall et al. 1992). In 1720 a "Princess of the Missouris" accompanied the Illiniwek "great chief" to France, where she received an audience with the king (Bossu 1962:82–83). When De Soto reached the temple town of Cofitachequi near the Savannah River on May 1, 1540, he found the town governed by a woman who was carried in a special chair and sat on cushions (Gentleman of Elvas 1933:91–102).

The Natchez possessed brother and sister chiefs who may have had separate but equally important functions. The "woman chief," as Father

Gravier called her (Shea 1861:141–42), decided who should supply corn to feed the dead chiefs at the June Harvest ceremony. She smoked the calumet, which was generally associated only with the men. Gravier commented, "The woman chief has much ability and more credit than one would think; her brother is no great genius." The French priest mentioned another Houma woman chief who led several war parties and had "more honor paid to her" than to her brother. When she walked, four young men preceded her, singing and dancing the calumet to her, and "She had the first place in all councils" (Shea 1861:144). Four men also carried the Timucua "queen" on a litter. She covered herself with rare animal skins (Lorant 1946:109).

Lumb (1992:1–9) has pointed out numerous examples of Southeastern women (Catawba, Chickasaw, Tuscarora, Choctaw, Cherokee, Timucua, Creek) who were not chiefs participating in warfare in historic times. They shot arrows over their husbands' shoulders in battle, accompanied husbands into warfare, carried military supplies into war along with male two-spirits, carried medicine bundles into battle, and danced in victory celebrations with enemy scalps. In the mid-eighteenth century, deciding the fate of Natchez and Arkansas captives lay with women who had lost a son or husband in battle. They administered torture, including, among the Natchez and Illiniwek, the burning of enemy penises until the captives died. Among the Illiniwek, women washed their male children in the blood of captives (Cadillac and Liette 1947:160–161). Joutel (1714 [1962:125–127]) reported that the Cenis killed women as well as men in raids, mentioning an instance where one female captive was scalped, wounded, and sent home, whereas another was scalped, stabbed, clubbed, killed, and others of her people were forced to eat her flesh. Consistent with such practices, Natchez mythology contains stories about male and female cannibals (Swanton 1929:218–21, 241–42). Among the Timucua, nursing or pregnant women drank the blood of the dead (Lorant 1946:75).

One female warrior does appear in rock art at Piney Creek, Illinois. She is nude. This female does not possess breasts, but the image is pecked so that a natural opening in the rock face is positioned between her legs. She has a spear in each hand, two other spears associated with her, and a hairstyle unlike that of the usual Mississippian woman and more similar to male styles. She may represent a female two-spirit dressed like a male warrior (or nude) (see Figure 2C). Gravier (Shea 1861:144) corroborated the case of the Piney Creek warrior woman when he described a Houma "woman-chief" who led war parties, dressed like "an Amazon," wore her hair like a man, and enjoyed great honor. We know from the French accounts that the Illiniwek tolerated such "female men," and also "male women" (Marquette 1698:210; Hennepin 1698a:106; Cadillac and Liette 1947:112).

Although female two-spirits did not marry, most women did. Those who married found life was not always egalitarian or harmonious. Marriages could become battlegrounds. Mississippian wives, in certain circumstances, experienced abuse from husbands—sometimes very cruel abuse—although families may have protected them from extreme mistreatment. A woman's adultery might be punished with nose-cutting among the Cenis and Illiniwek. Both the Alabamu adulteress *and* her lover received a whipping with wooden switches on the back and stomach, their hair was cut off, and they were exiled from the village (Bossu 1962:133). A husband's adultery was not similarly penalized, probably because of the three- to four-year postpartum sexual taboo while a woman nursed. Men could, in fact, have several wives, usually sisters, aunts, or nieces (Hennepin 1698b:114, 1698a:106; Cadillac and Liette 1947:127, 135). Among the Illiniwek, the cuckolded husband sometimes got twenty or thirty of his male associates to gang-rape his wife (Cadillac and Liette 1947:117–119).

Not all men agreed with such tactics and could sometimes act to keep husbands in line. Many Illiniwek men objected to gang-rape "errant" wives, instead arguing that the man should simply send his wife away and take another. A wife's relatives who believed she had been treated with too much abuse or abandoned "without sufficient reason" would enter the husband's lodging and destroy all his personal possessions (Cadillac and Liette 1947:119, 139–140). The fact that divorce was also apparently more common than in the twentieth-century, even among chiefs, may have averted beatings as well. (The children chose which parent they wished to live with.) Hennepin (1698b:70), with considerable frustration, declared, "They can't conceive how people can tie themselves indissolubly to one person in Marriage." Jealousy did occur, but Hennepin mentioned only one case of an abusive, jealous male who beat his wife because she danced with other men.

Women had a strong role in marriage negotiations, which could possibly have limited bad choices of husbands. Le Page du Pratz (1976:348) said Natchez Sun women arranged marriages. Illiniwek women carried kettles, animal skins, buffalo meat, and clothing as gifts from a prospective male spouse in their lineage to the cabin of the woman he wished to wed (Cadillac and Liette 1947:114). Women apparently chose older, more mature men for partners, since males under thirty were "look'd upon as Men unfit for War or Hunting" and as "more Woman-like" (Cadillac and Liette 1947:113; Hennepin 1698b:77–81; Marquette 1698:209).

The ease of divorce, association of women with the creative powers of the universe, their participation in warfare, and their singing and dancing in ceremonial events (Hennepin 1698a:125) gave them considerable status. In fact, male and female appear to have been perceived as complementary sexes, without either sex being dominant. Male and female effigies appear together in the same Copena stone box graves in the Tennessee-Cumberland area and Etowah, and in the temples of the Natchez (Shea 1861:141, 144; Garcilaso 1723:60). In northern Georgia, Mississippians equipped shrines with both male and female statuettes (Brown 1985b:104–105). Mesoamerican long-nosed gods are present in male and female form, and the fact that Illinois-Missouri long-nosed gods exist in pairs at several sites may reflect a gendered identity as well (Maxwell 1994). The long-nosed gods, Natchez (and possibly Timucua) brother-sister chiefs, and the feeding of deceased rulers of both sexes all may reflect the complementary equality of male and female.

To a degree, the Suns of the Mississippians recognized female equality—and not only in that women could be chiefs. When male Great Suns died among the Natchez (and probably the Cahokians as well), their wives accompanied them in death, being strangled by a bowstring. Although the French did not report the death of a female Sun, they did indicate that when the female relative of a male Sun died, the people put her spouse to death, too. Others could free persons from this obligation by offering to be strangled instead, for not all spouses wished to die for connubial other-worldly bliss. Old and crippled women often volunteered (Bossu 1962:32–33; Le Page du Pratz 1976:347), considering themselves "honored" to feed and wait on the Suns. The more people, including men and children, who volunteered to sacrifice themselves for him or her, the greater the Sun's prestige (Shea 1861:140).

Women certainly were not limited in their mobility. The French observed them moving freely up and down the Mississippi in canoes, including in one case an old woman of about eighty years who rowed vigorously (Hennepin 1698a:196). We know that such canoes existed during earlier Mississippian times, for one is recorded on shell at Spiro (Fundaburk and Fundaburk 1957:Pl. 27). On trading or hunting trips women hid provisions in "hollow places" on islands in the Mississippi River (Hennepin 1698a:194). The French watched women on the St. Francis River construct "little

Docks to build the new Canou's in" (Hennepin 1698a:184). Apparently, no prohibition existed on females' trading. In fact, much of the trade was carried on by families. Women who had spent much time with other tribes served the French and the Spanish as guides and interpreters (Hennepin 1698a:197; Gentleman of Elvas 1933:251). The French even learned Natchez from the women, who spoke a "softer and smoother" form of the language, causing both the Natchez men and women to ridicule the European males, who were obviously not two-spirits, for speaking women's language (Le Page du Pratz 1976:328).

There were differences between men and women's tasks. Women went with men on buffalo hunts but did not themselves try to kill these dangerous beasts; if they had, the French certainly would have mentioned it. Instead, the women flayed, dried, and packed home the meat. They, along with two-spirits, also carried food and other goods on war parties, while the men kept their arms free for fighting. The French were astounded at how much Mississippian women could tote and how fast they could move. Hennepin (1698a:91–92) stated that the Illiniwek women could carry on their backs "two to three hundred weight, besides their children, and still run as swiftly as our soldiers in arms." He added, "They have no Salt, and yet they prepare their Flesh so well, that it keeps above four Months without breeding any Corruption; and it looks then so fresh, that one would think it was newly kill'd." Since as many as 120 buffaloes might be brought back at a time, women and girls spent considerable time drying meat (Cadillac and Liette 1947:96–97). Timucua men, however, may have done all the meat drying in Florida (Lorant 1946:83).

Women's tasks were not only different from but more diverse than men's. Women cared for children more than men did; made attractive garters of red and white wood rat hair; supplied cabins with firewood; fashioned moccasins for themselves and their husbands; dyed reed mats yellow, red, and black as purses; and spun sacks of buffalo wool, rushes, or bark, which they used as baskets for collecting goosefoot, pigweed, smartweed, nuts, fruits, and berries (Hennepin 1698b:41, 113; Cadillac and Liette 1947:45, 126–128, 152). Carrying baskets were commonplace on the backs of Mississippian female effigies, some of which appeared fused to the bodies in the form of a humped back (Holmes 1903:Pl. 26; Fundaburk and Fundaburk 1957:Pl. 119 and 120). This may have been an Earth Mother representation in the model of the Southwest's *Kokopellimana*, she who brought seeds to be planted and "wild oats" to be sown in springtime. While men hunted, women took care of the corn crop and planted beans, squash, sunflower, marsh elder, and gourd, as well as goosefoot and pig-weed. This task was not strictly gender segregated, however, since old men performed agricultural duties as well (Hennepin 1698b:186). Men also turned the sod while women planted. Drying maize and pumpkins was generally a sex-specific female task, however. Illiniwek women spent time in marshes, their heads under water, plucking a variety of nourishing tubers and sugary-tasting onions (Cadillac and Liette 1947:125–128). During the spring and summer months, women's economic contribution was invalu-able, as was their storage of plant food and meat during the winter and their skilled preparation of tasty meals in all seasons. They quite probably domesticated several local plants. Women did not do all the cooking, how-ever. Among the Timucua at least, women and men both prepared the cooked fare, even on ceremonial days (Lorant 1946:91).

Men and women may also both have performed flint-knapping. One Late Prehistoric 15 × 10 cm clay pipe from near the Arkansas River in New-ton County, Arkansas, shows a seated woman, with a breast bulge and skirt, knapping a stone. The pipe bowl is located in her genital region, and the stem comes out above her buttocks. She is virtually the only con-crete evidence that women did, indeed, work lithics in Mississippian times (Gehlbach 1976; personal communication, 1994).

Women became artists as well. Since ceramics were made of "earth" and held crops, they were associated with women. Natchez women fash-ioned dishes, plates, and pots holding up to forty pints. They also selected iron ore from veins along the Red River's bluffs, and cockle shells from near Natchitoches for tempering the vessels. The French called their work "ad-mirable" for ceramics done without a potter's wheel, finding the red slip and the elaborate shapes of vessels "quite beautiful" (Le Page du Pratz 1976:163–164, 178–179). By placing incised scrolls and meanders on Fatherland Incised, and curvilinear motifs on Bayou Goula Incised pottery, women added artistic decoration to their cooking ware. Women tried many different styles and may have—throughout the Mississippian world—de-clared a form of gender identity through often constructing mammiform lugs or other breastlike features on pots (see Figure 2D). The potter found carved in effigy in Indiana (Holmes 1903:Pl. 28)—the first known female artist of record in Mississippian art—may have been declaring a form of identity as a potter and a woman.

It is not known whether both women and men did rock art, although several places where cliff faces are decorated with such art (including the Washington State Park, Missouri, and Piney Creek, Illinois, sites—each with three hundred images) are located near metates and nutting holes. These probably would have been created and used by women. Perhaps both sexes made petroglyphs, as was true for tattooing. Cenis women tattooed (with bone splinters and charcoal) a streak down their faces and made figures at the corners of their eyes and on their bosoms, while Cenis men placed leaf, flower, and creature tattoos on shoulders, thighs, and other body parts (Joutel 1962:111). Illiniwek, Natchez, Tunica, Timucua, and Houma women also tattooed their cheeks, breasts, and arms (Cadillac and Liette 1947:112; Shea 1861:146–147; Lorant 1946). Such women daubed their temples, cheeks, and chin tips with three different colors at feast times (Hennepin 1698b:88–89). The same may be demonstrated on Missouri head pots, either in paint or tattoo. Particularly exquisite examples of female tattooing exist on the legs and arms of women on Spiro cup fragments (Phillips and Brown 1978: Pl. 21). Equally elaborate are those depicted by John White on the legs, arms, and body of a sixteenth-century Timucua chief's wife (Lorant 1946).

Notwithstanding areas of flexibility in women's and men's tasks, they may have performed these activities in different sections of the home. Along the central Illinois River valley and in the American Bottom, excavators found pottery-making tools, along with food-processing equipment and milling stones, in the northeastern section of burned households. While it appears wives labored in this section of dwelling units, husbands' woodworking tools, large knives, chert-working tools, projectile points, and pipes are found on the southeastern side of structures. Cooking and dining apparently took place in the center of the house, and the western portion was an open area for socializing.

There is no evidence that this division of labor was perceived hierarchically, even among historic Mississippians. Rather, complementarity appeared to be the rule, even in larger, lineage-controlled temple towns. The strong emphasis on fertility in town and country indicates that Turner's (1974:185) "socially inclusive" earth-fertility cults and "politically manipulative cults" could coexist in temple towns. In the former, "access to the relevant spirits is directly available to everyone and denied to no one," while the latter conferred some ultimate authority upon a single individual or a small group. Quite probably, in inland areas distant from large-scale Mississippian settlements, earth-fertility cults had more relevance, since there is more evidence of probable vagina symbols in Illinois-Missouri rock art and at least one petroglyph depicting a tadpole birth from a woman. Even the number of Southeastern Ceremonial Complex images is substantially less in such inland areas. Perhaps significant in this respect is the fact that Liette (Cadillac and Liette 1947:141–142, 147) found both male and female shamans among the more-inland Illiniwek. He also discovered that no "priests" existed, but instead that most elderly men and some elderly women were healer-shamans.

Prohibitions on what women *could* do existed in very few areas, as far as we can tell. Hennepin (1698b:92) reported that women and girls did not play the popular chunkey game, although boys and men did. Women did, however, attend the game, where they returned stray chunkey balls and carried crippled relatives off the field (Cadillac and Liette 1947:124). Women also played their own, less violent game, tossing pieces of cane (like die) (Le Page du Pratz 1976:366). Among the Illiniwek, however, a few women did play lacrosse with the men (Cadillac and Liette 1947:123).

There are no reports of women hunting large game such as elk, deer, buffalo, bobcat, and bear in any of the research with which I am familiar. Warfare was usually the activity of men as well. Women apparently were not prohibited from being warriors, chiefs, or shamans, but they did not seek out such positions as readily as men. Large numbers of male warriors receive mention in the French accounts, but few women.

The important role that women played in horticulture, gathering, religion, and warfare celebrations—as depicted in glyphs, ceramics, shell, and ethnohistorical accounts—reflects a status higher than that of European women of the seventeenth century (see Koehler 1980). Perhaps for this reason, Mississippian women resisted the religious overtures of the French. They refused to be baptized for fear they would go to the land of the "European dead" and lose post-mortem contact with friends and family. They also, the French complained, "most obstinately retain the Traditions of their Ancestors" (Hennepin 1698b:119–121). The women apparently could not conceive of trading a good thing for an uncertain one.

Eurocentric traditions of prehistoric-historic women as "squaw-drudges" must be reexamined, along with social evolutionary beliefs that as society becomes more complex, sex roles and status become necessarily more rigidly defined and segregated. Mississippian art and society clearly demonstrate that women played a strong and valued role in mythology, religion, government, and nutrition, as well as suggests that complementarity, instead of hierarchy, and considerable flexibility may have been cultural norms.

14. Figurines and Social Identities in Early Sedentary Societies of Coastal Chiapas, Mexico, 1550–800 b.c.
Richard G. Lesure

While archaeologists recognize the importance of emic understandings of social categories and differences to the reproduction of social inequality in small-scale societies, such understandings are often impervious to archaeological inquiry. Burial assemblages are, of course, an important source of information on prehistoric social categories. Recent analyses of Mesoamerican figurines, however, show that these form a significant but largely untapped source of data on social differentiation (Guillén 1993; Joyce 1993; Marcus 1989, 1993).

A large figurine assemblage excavated since 1985 in the Mazatán region on the Pacific coast of Chiapas, Mexico, forms the basis for the present study. Research has focused on Early Formative village societies dating from 1550 to 850 b.c. (Blake 1991; Clark 1991, 1994). (Note that "b.c." will be used throughout to indicate uncalibrated radiocarbon years.) Significant changes occurred in the figurine assemblage during this time, but I focus on only the period 1250 to 1100 b.c. During this period two images were commonly moddled into small ceramic figurines: (1) young women and (2) elders wearing masks and ritual paraphernalia. These images probably appeared together in various social and ritual contexts within all households in the community. The juxtaposition of these two images may have been related to an ideological claim that valued the ritual activities of elders over the productive labor of the young, perhaps supporting elders' claims to be able to "give" women away in marriage.

Figurines and Social Identity

Small figurines of clay or other materials were produced at various times and places across the globe, and archaeologists have investigated both the uses to which these were put and the meanings invested in them by their makers and users (Talalay 1993:38). Ethnographic data on figurine manufacture and use could help in generating reasonable hypotheses concerning prehistoric figurines, but, unfortunately, such data are scarce. Talalay (1993: 40–44) has assembled comparative information on the use and meanings of anthropomorphic figurines from a worldwide ethnographic sample. A number of Mesoamericanists have combed the ethnohistoric literature for clues concerning the use and manufacture of figurines in Late Postclassic or early colonial times (Czitrom 1978:21–22; Lee 1969:62–65; Stocker 1991:153–157). However, it is maddeningly difficult to attempt to test individual uses or meanings using archaeological data, especially for assemblages so remote from the ethnohistoric record in time and organization as the Early Formative.

Drawing on figurine and burial data as well as ethnohistoric evidence, Marcus (1989, 1993) suggests that in Early Formative Oaxaca, figurines were used by women in ritual petitioning of recently deceased ancestors. Numerous correspondences between the stances represented in figurines and the positions of burial characteristic of different social categories support this argument (Flannery and Marcus 1978:382; Marcus 1993). The Mazatán figurine traditions discussed here were contemporary with this Oaxacan material, and the kinds of representations in the assemblages are similar in a number of respects. It is possible that Mazatán figurines were used in similar ways, but any correspondences between burial positions and figurine stances are entirely absent in the Mazatán case.

I will assume that there was a range of (still undetermined) uses for figurines in the Mazatán area. Figurines were used, broken, and discarded in household contexts. The representations themselves are stylized human images that seem to depict standard social categories or stereotypes rather than individuals. As representations of social categories, they would have been potential points of reference in the negotiation and reproduction of actual social relationships. In her study of Classic period figurines from Central America, Joyce (1993:257) points out that there would have been a "multiplicity of possible narratives" concerning the social data encoded in figurines, making them "a medium for active constructions of social identity." But she adds that figurines probably also constrained conversations about social identity (see Joyce 1993:256). Because figurines resemble social actors, they appear "natural" and can help make the claim that the categories of social difference represented in figurine assemblages in fact represent the "real" social world and are even "natural" or "inevitable."

Thus, while a multiplicity of narratives concerning figurines would have been possible, the kinds of images that were in fact represented simultaneously limited the scope of these narratives by providing a framework for discussions about social identities, discussions in which different categories of social actors and the relationships between them were negotiated and reproduced. Conversations about figurines would more likely have focused on how images were similar or different, not on how the representational system as a whole ignored certain aspects of social relationships and emphasized others. If figurines really were a medium for active constructions of social identity, then the stereotypes represented in figurine assemblages can provide important clues about what was talked about, and what was not, in conversations about social identity; clues to, in Bourdieu's (1977) terms, the universe of discourse and the universe of the undiscussed. By looking at what was and was not represented, and how social categories were distinguished within figurine assemblages, it is possible to develop hypotheses about the subject matter of conversations about social difference.

The potential of figurine assemblages for indicating the subject matter of conversations about social identity is limited by the possibility that important comparisons may have been drawn not within the figurine assemblage, but between figurines and another system of human representations, or even between figurines and other artifacts altogether. The possibility that Mazatán figurines functioned in a complex way with other artifacts in the ritual system is high, but the outlines of this system are still far from clear. The intent of this paper is thus to use figurine variability to develop hypotheses concerning systems of social identities in the Mazatán region from 1400 to 1000 b.c. Evaluating these hypotheses with reference to other artifactual materials is beyond the scope of this essay; indeed, it will require further fieldwork in the area.

Mazatán Figurines

The Mazatán study area has been known as an important zone of early cultural development in Mesoamerica since the pioneering studies of Lowe (1975, 1977), Green and Lowe (1967), and Ceja Tenorio (1985), who divided the local Early Formative period into four phases: Barra, Ocós, Cuadros, and Jocotal. New investigations by Clark and Blake began in 1985 and have continued over the course of several field seasons (Blake 1991; Clark 1991; Clark and Blake 1993). This work has led to a refined ceramic chronology for the Early Formative period, and the original Ocós phase has been divided into three: Locona (1400–1250 b.c.), Ocós (1250–1100 b.c.), and Cherla (1100–1000 b.c.). The figurines analyzed here date to between 1400 and 1000 b.c., but the patterns identified are most evident during the more restrictively defined Ocós phase, 1250–1100 b.c. During this time period, the population of the Mazatán region, a fertile alluvial fan between the Pacific Ocean and the Sierra Madre, was settled in seven or more large, independent villages. Hamlets, homesteads, and possibly specialized resource-extraction sites surrounded each village (Clark 1994:194–208). There was no marked sociopolitical centralization, though at least some of the large villages may have been organized as simple chiefdoms as early as the Locona phase (Blake 1991; Clark 1991; Clark 1994:467–469).

Data for this study come primarily from 198 solid torsos and torso fragments, 173 solid heads, and 127 hollow figurine fragments from excavations I conducted at Paso de la Amada, a large village site, during 1992 and 1993. In addition, I examined 247 solid figurine torsos and a selected sample of 15 zoomorphic or fantastic heads excavated by John Clark and Michael Blake from 1985 to 1990 and currently stored at the New World Archaeological Foundation laboratory in San Cristóbal de las Casas, Chiapas. Clark and Blake's material is primarily from Paso de la Amada and three other large village sites: Aquiles Serdán, Chilo, and San Carlos.

Three figurine traditions dating to the period 1400–1000 b.c., distinguishable by surface treatment and construction details, have been identified and named by John Clark. All are hand modeled. The first are large, hollow figurines, completely or partially slipped in various colors and well burnished (Naca Group). The second tradition, by far the most common, consists of small, solid figurines that are not slipped or burnished (Paqui Group). Surfaces are carefully smoothed, usually having even, somewhat sandy textures. The third tradition consists of both small, solid figurines and larger, hollow ones that are usually slipped white-to-gray and well burnished (Eyah Group). This last tradition appears in the Mazatán sequence around 1100 b.c., along with other "Early Horizon" artifacts (see Flannery and Marcus 1994:385–390).

These traditions interdigitate in a complex way over time; an interpretation of this in terms of changing representations is presented by Clark (1994:420–429; also 1993). The interpretations presented here focus on the middle portion of the time period to which Clark's more general model applies. My analysis concerns primarily the figurines of the Paqui Group, produced in large numbers from 1400 through 1000 b.c. There are significant changes of style during this time period, and Clark (1994:420–429) proposes significant representational changes as well, such as the replacement of the fat, masked Paqui images with Eyah Group males, but when I broke the Paqui Group sample down by phase, changes within the Paqui Group were not demonstrable, perhaps due to the small sample sizes of figurines from completely unmixed deposits.

For the purposes of this paper, I decided to consider all Paqui Group figurines from deposits dated by ceramic contents to 1400–1000 b.c. (the Locona, Ocós, and Cherla phases) together as a unit. By doing this, it was possible to include a large sample of figurines from a Cherla-phase platform that had Locona and Ocós material mixed into it. In describing some of the rarer costumed and masked representations, I have also included some surface finds that are dated on typological grounds only. Using this expanded sample allows for a high level of confidence that the full range of variability is covered, but it reduces the chronological specificity of the argument. I return to the question of change during the period 1400–1000 b.c., and to a consideration of the two rare figurine traditions (Naca and Eyah Groups), only at the very end of the chapter.

Two Representations

The solid figurines of the Paqui Group usually have a hard, sandy paste, ranging in color from light brown to dark gray. The surfaces are not slipped or burnished, but are carefully smoothed and sometimes painted red or white. Some of the figurines have a fine-grained, soft, and easily eroded paste that may reflect less effort in the preparation of the clay. There is a significant range in the skill or sophistication of manufacture in the assemblage, and the soft-paste figurines are generally cruder than the hard-paste ones. There is some temporal differentiation of the cruder and more sophisticated figurines, with the cruder ones gradually disappearing. It appears, however, that there was a considerable range in the sophistication of figurines in use at any one time. The basic themes represented are the same at all skill levels.

There are two primary themes or representations among the Paqui Group figurines (broken down by site in Table 1). The most common rep-

TABLE I.   Frequency of different representations in excavated samples.

Representation	Paso de la Amada	Aquiles Serdán
Juniors		
Young women	107	41
Young, pregnant women	12	5
Possible young men	11	5
Fragment, gender unidentified	50	23
Elders		
Women, unclothed	5	1
Men, unclothed	5	5
Women in costume	2	0
Men in costume	10	5
Fragment, gender unidentified	19	5
Other		
Unclassified Paqui torso fragments	18	22

resentation is a standing woman with prominent breasts (Figure 1). Some figurines with bare chests and no breasts may have been men, but these are rare and tend to be especially crude or otherwise unusual. No clothing is represented on either the females or the possible males. Primary sexual characteristics, female or male, are also absent. On the best-modeled female figurines, stomachs are flat or slightly rounded and breasts are firm and full, indicating that these are young women of pre-reproductive or early-reproductive age (see Rice 1981:403). Some fat ones in the same style suggest pregnancy. Head shape and eye styles changed over time, and characteristic forms can be identified for each phase. By the Ocós phase, a variety of complicated hairstyles and head ornaments were represented; many heads appear to depict tonsured hair. Earspools and, rarely, nose ornaments are depicted on many figurines of the Ocós and Cherla phases.

On the better modeled examples the most artistic attention was spent in carefully depicting facial features, hair decoration, and head ornaments. It might therefore be possible to argue, as does Harlan (1987:261) for the Chalcatzingo figurines, that the heads were the locus of the primary information being conveyed. However, I do not believe this to have been the

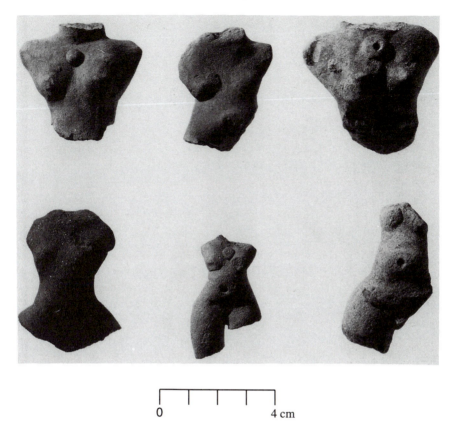

Figure 1.   Carefully modeled young female torsos, Paso de la Amada.

case for Mazatán figurines. The earliest young female images show little attention to facial details (Figure 2), and crude representations with no elaboration of the head were made throughout the period of study, appearing in the same trash deposits as more sophisticated representations. What unites representations of all skill levels is the basic image of a young human female. I suspect that the increasing elaboration of figurine heads was excess information, perhaps related to the social context of figurine production, as figurine makers sought to distinguish themselves in a social world increasingly concerned with personal ornamentation. While all this would have no doubt altered the way people thought of these images, the basic idea—gendered human images—remained the same.

```
┌───┬───┬───┬───┐
0               4 cm
```

Figure 2.   Crude figurine torsos, Paso de la Amada. Heads in the top row are complete, indicating how little attention was paid to facial features. The one in the upper left has no breasts and might be male. All others are female.

The arms of nearly all of the young females (in both crude and sophisticated representations) are depicted only as short, rounded stubs. No hands or fingers are indicated. Careful inspection proves that this was how they were manufactured; there is no evidence that arms have been broken off. A few do have short arms that extend out to the sides, and one figurine with broken arms was actually manufactured first with the usual stubs, whereupon arms were added. Although the sample of figurines with arms is a very small, it appears that arms became more common late in the sequence, amid other changes beginning to occur in the figurine representational system.

The lack of arms might lead one to suppose that these figurines were dressed in perishable materials, but I consider this very unlikely for several reasons. First, patterns painted in red or white on the upper torsos of some females represent body paint and suggest that at least this portion of the body was not meant to be covered by perishable materials. Second, a small set of figurines (discussed below) is actually depicted with clothing; clearly not all figurines were meant to be clothed in separate material. Finally, it is extremely unlikely that Early Formative villagers commonly wore much clothing at all in the intense tropical heat of the Chiapas coast. Clothing was probably not a common part of village life in this area until social differentiation and class formation were much more advanced, providing people with strong social motives to don uncomfortable apparel. During Early Formative times, elaborate clothing would probably have been worn only in special ritual or symbolic contexts, for short periods of time.

The second most common set of representations, where items of clothing do appear, is thus of considerable interest. Comprising 17–18 percent of the torso assemblage is a diverse set of fat to obese anthropomorphic figures. Some are standing, but most are crouching or seated. Some appear to have been seated on stools, though the stool is not clearly differentiated from the body. The characteristic belly form is generally quite distinct from that of the armless females identified as pregnant. In the case of these seated figurines, the belly is flattened from the top so as to protrude out on all sides of the body; in the cruder forms the head is placed practically at the center of a pancake-like torso. Crouching forms are more likely to have a long, cylindrical belly with the knees on each side.

Just over half of the fat figures are unclothed. Neither male nor female genitals are depicted. A few figures have breasts and are apparently female; the rest, though bare-chested, are not represented with breasts. In most cases, the immense belly forms the whole body, so overall torso configuration is not sufficiently detailed to distinguish these unequivocally as males. It is possible that they were gender-neutral images. Alternatively, the lack of female breasts may have been sufficient to mark them as male. This is how they are interpreted by Clark (1994:424).

The other half of the fat figures are depicted wearing elaborate ornamentation. The simplest is a thick neck ornament—a scarf or collar—that sometimes terminates in a large pectoral, possibly representing a mirror. This neck ornament is worn either by itself or with one of the other two forms of apparel. These two forms are quite stereotyped, and both costumes appear at all three of the main sites in the sample. The most common is a set of long tassels that hang down the front of the torso (Figure 3). The tassels are formed from appliqué strips of clay and are decorated with diagonal gouges. Usually the costume consists of three of these tassels, but two recently recovered examples probably had five tassels each. These might represent decoration made of feathers; tropical plumage was abundant in the forests of the Mazatán region. The second costume appears to be a fur tunic covering the whole torso (Figure 4). In this case the clay has been stamped—with the edge of a shell or some other tool—to form a crinkled surface resembling fur.

In contrast to the (contemporary) young females with stubs for arms, the fat figures are generally depicted with arms and hands. Usually the arms rest on either side of the immense belly or on the chest. On a number of the tasseled figurines the arms are short and extend straight out from the body, but even in this case, fingers are represented by a few linear gouges.

The bodies of these figures are entirely anthropomorphic. The heads found attached to eight examples thus come as something of a surprise, since seven of them are zoomorphic or fantastic. The single anthropomorphic head has puffy cheeks and a round nose ornament; it is attached to a fat, standing body with three tassels down the front and no breasts. From the same site (Chilo) is another anthropomorphic body with arms resting

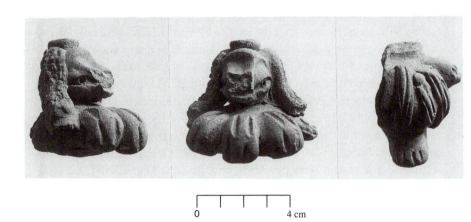

0   4 cm

Figure 3.   Costumed elders wearing tassels. *Left and middle*: Profile and frontal view of same seated figure wearing mask. *Right*: Frontal view of standing figure split down middle of body. Both pieces from Paso de la Amada.

Figure 4.   Figurines of costumed elders wearing tunics and chest mirrors. *Left and middle*: Profile and frontal view of same figure from Paso de la Amada. *Right*: Frontal view of figure from Chilo.

on the fat belly. However, the face, in this case, resembles a fish, though it also wears earspools, and the face emerges from a crinkled cape (see Clark 1991: Figure 6d for a reconstruction). The other bodies with heads have the three tassels, the fur-like tunic, the large neck ornament, or no clothing. Clark (1991:21, 1993, 1994:424) interprets the zoomorphic creatures as representations of humans wearing masks. The single figure with the same costume as the zoomorphic ones but with a human face supports this interpretation, as does a recently discovered piece in which a human face peeks out of a hood that has both mammalian ears and anthropomorphic earlobes with earspools (Figure 5). This representation indicates definitively that these zoomorphic figures are depictions of elaborate costumes with people inside. Part of a clay mask recently discovered by Warren Hill and Michael Blake in an Ocós trash pit at Paso de la Amada shows that masks were used but does not clearly resemble any of the zoomorphic faces represented on the figurines.

Beyond the heads attached to bodies, thirty other zoomorphic or fantastic figurine heads have been recovered since 1985. Four more zoomorphic ones, as well as a second anthropomorphic face on a fat body, all from Paso de la Amada, are illustrated by Ceja (1985: Figure 47d–f and Fig-

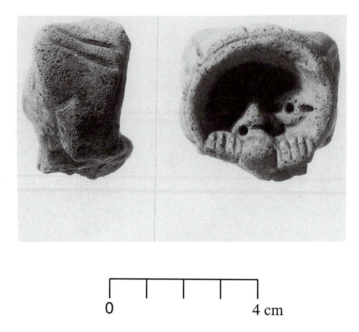

0   4 cm

Figure 5.   Human face peeking out of animal costume from Chilo
site. The figure's hands appear to be placed on the lower rim of the
opening. In the side view, note the animal ears above and the human earlobes below.

ure 49g–h). Of the forty-one known zoomorphic heads, twenty-one can
be classified as examples of four stereotyped images. Although different
examples are executed in different styles and vary in details, recurring features suggest that they represented the same creature. One image (Figure 6, top row) has a long face, flattened from the sides, and a crinkled
hood. The eyes are formed from a punched appliqué disk, and four of the
five examples appear to have a pair of rodentlike teeth jutting up from beneath the snout. Ears protrude from the hood of three of these five examples. All six examples of the second image (Figure 6, middle row) have
large, round, cane-impressed/punched eyes and protruding foreheads
with two deep holes punched into them side by side. The third image (Figure 6, bottom row) has a face usually flattened in the front, with round
eyes. The mouth area is covered with an appliqué disk onto which a cross
is impressed, or else a circle of five punctations. The head gear is compli-

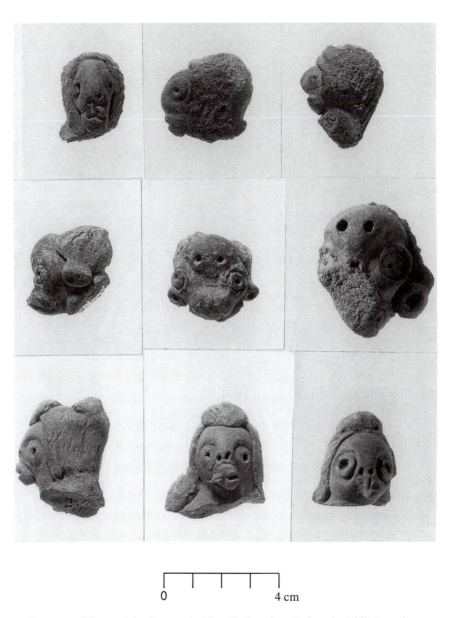

0   4 cm

Figure 6.   Three of the four masks identified to date. Left and middle in each row
are different views of same piece. Figures from Paso de la Amada and Aquiles
Serdán.

cated and variable, but all six examples have conical projections in the back of the head. A fourth, more variable image can only be tentatively identified. It consists of a crinkled hood with large mammalian ears. The face generally has a long snout, but one example has a human face. Among the other heads, several pairs of nearly identical mask and head styles suggest that as the sample of heads is further expanded, new stereotyped images will become evident. Judging from the variability of the other heads, I suspect that at least ten to fifteen distinct masks will eventually be identified.

Masks and Costume

Among the fat, masked figures there is an interesting contrast between the costumes, which consist of two stereotyped patterns with little further variation, and the masks, where a whole range of different images are portrayed. By themselves, the two stereotyped clothing styles, in use throughout the Mazatán region, might suggest particular ritual roles or perhaps be the trappings of offices—denoting a special position in a sodality, the role of ritual specialist, or the status of chief. The combination of a variety of different masks with the same costume style makes the second possibility less likely. There are just too many different masks to suggest that each signified a particular social, political, or religious office in the small villages of the time period. On the other hand, the fact that multiple representations of the same mask can be identified at different sites suggests that these were representations drawn from some sort of shared iconographic system rather than the sort of individualized masks we might expect of chiefly or other high-status offices in separate, independent villages. It seems most likely that the masks and costumes were not the trappings of office but paraphernalia related to ritual or ceremonial roles.

Pernet (1992:77) finds that in indigenous societies of North and South America, "masks are found that represent the totality of living creatures populating the world of their wearers, mythic beings and ancestors, culture heroes, even gods." Particular masks appear in conjunction with other masks and symbols in dramatizations of mythological events or ideas. Pernet (1992:161) concludes that "masks often aim, on the one hand, at expressing a cosmos, a system of the world, and on the other hand, at recalling or dramatizing events, which are in general the founding events of the world, of humanity, of the clan, or of a particular institution."

In light of this comparative ethnography, the fact that the Mazatán figurine masks comprise a significant variety of images that are nevertheless shared among independent communities across the region suggests that these were representations of people reenacting or recalling important mythological events. It would not be surprising if the individuals who put on these costumes and masks were understood to be maintaining balanced interrelationships between human, animal, natural, and supernatural worlds on behalf of their communities. One possible function of the figurines depicting these reenactments would have been pedagogical, like that of Hopi kachina dolls, among which a similar pattern of masked representations appears (Colton 1959; Dockstader 1954).

But comparison to the Hopi also highlights a significant contrast between the Mazatán masked representations and the actors in many ethnographic masked rituals. Masked figures are usually active; they dance or otherwise act out important mythological events. The extreme obesity of the Mazatán figures, on the other hand, suggests passivity. These figures are generally seated, often on stools, in attitudes that suggest respect and authority but not strenuous activity. But I have argued above against their interpretation as representatives of social or political offices based on the appearance of the same masks in different villages. How, then, would the ritual roles indicated by the corpus of masks have been coupled with a sedentary social authority? One possibility is that these are depictions of ritual specialists such as shamans. Another possibility—which I prefer—is that obesity was a symbol of seniority, that the fat, masked figures are depictions of respected elders.

A particularly important seated, fat torso from Paso de la Amada is illustrated in Figure 7. The belly, immense and flattened from the top, is in the characteristic style for this image. The thick scarf around the neck terminates in a large pectoral. Head and seated legs are broken off, as are the arms, though the mark where the right arm broke off from the belly is identifiable on careful inspection. The figure also has breasts. These are carefully enough modeled that the left nipple is depicted, yet the breasts are shown to be stretched and flattened in sharp contrast to the breasts of the standing young woman. Clearly this is a depiction of an older, fat woman wearing an elaborate neck ornament. Generalizing from this case to the other fat, masked figures, I would like to suggest that obesity, and the social authority it implied, were linked to age. These figurines were depictions of elders, perhaps mainly men but also women, who appeared in masked rituals to mediate between human communities and the animal and/or supernatural worlds.

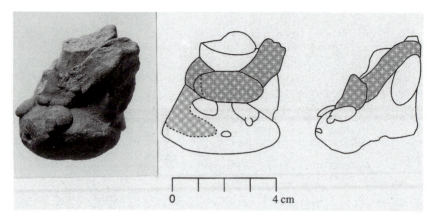

Figure 7. Torso of seated old woman wearing elaborate neck ornament, Paso de la Amada. *Left*: photo; *center*: sketch of frontal view, with neck ornament darkly shaded and place where right arm broke off torso lightly shaded; *right*: sketch of side view, with ornament again shaded.

In the model presented in the next section, I pursue the idea that the obesity of these figurines might have represented seniority, social authority, and a degree of worldly passivity, while the ritual accouterments were a mark of spiritual activity. I assume that the masks and costumes represented ritual roles claimed by some elders—because of their age and respected status in the community. An alternative argument (not pursued here) would view these as images of life-long religious practitioners, such as shamans. The distinction—between a vocational ritual role that only a few individuals ever assume, and a ritual status conferred, at least ideally, on a whole age class—is an important one, but it may be difficult to test archaeologically.

Burial data is a potential arena for testing this distinction, but this possibility depends on the character of the (still poorly known) Early Formative burial assemblage. Some costume elements such as those depicted on the figurines were included in burials, and a seated adult male (an elder?) was excavated at Paso de la Amada in 1995 (John Clark, personal communication, 1995). Distinguishing between elders and shamans in the burial assemblage will be a matter of interpretation, however, since it seems unlikely that mutually exclusive archaeological correlates for elder and shaman burials can be identified.

Gender, Age, and Ritual Status

There were, to summarize the argument to this point, two important sets of representations in the Paqui Group tradition of small, solid figurines. The most common was a young woman, generally standing, depicted in a very stereotyped style that included short, rounded stubs in the place of arms. These figures were gendered images, the basic idea conveyed being "young human female" despite the increasing elaboration of head and hairstyles through time. Some were pregnant, but aside from this there is little variation in the images. The (armless) figurines are never engaged in any sort of activity. Since genitals are never depicted, and pregnant ones are rare, it seems difficult to argue that fertility was an important theme. The lack of variability among the images indicates that Mazatán cannot be compared to Chalcatzingo, where Guillén (1993) was able to identify females in all stages of the life cycle. Perhaps the Mazatán figurines served as stereotyped images of femaleness. If so, then femaleness seems to have been linked to youth rather than to such concepts as fertility and motherhood.

The other set of representations is much more varied than the standing young females, consisting of fat, usually seated elders or ritual practitioners. Most seem to have been masked, and about half wear elaborate costumes. They have arms, and a variety of specific stances of seated and crouching figures are present. They are probably depictions of people as they appeared in public rituals, though they are generally seated and their obesity does not suggest activity. In contrast to the young women, this was not a gendered category. Many of these may be males, since they are not depicted with breasts, but a few are clearly women. Although we have not yet found a female representation with the head intact, and therefore cannot prove that older females were depicted with masks, the match of belly form and ornamentation of such examples as that in Figure 7 with the probable male images strongly suggests that maleness was not a defining characteristic of this category so much as age and ritual status.

If we have two main categories—one gendered, one ungendered—then the question of whether they formed one representational system or two presents itself. The two representations are typically found together in household-midden deposits, though the young females are much more common. Beyond this we have no contextual data on figurine use from the Mazatán region. It is therefore not possible to say for sure whether these two sorts of images were used together—and thus compared directly—or whether they appeared in separate use contexts. However, evidence from elsewhere in Mesoamerica supports the former possibility. A contemporary figurine scene buried under a house floor at San José Mogote, Oaxaca, depicts three prone females and a seated person atop them (Flannery and Marcus 1976:382). Among the burials from Tlatilco in Central Mexico reported by García Moll et al. (1991), partially contemporary with and slightly later than the Mazatán assemblage but from a very similar organizational context, 43 percent of the figurines appearing as burial goods were placed in sets or scenes of two or more figurines. With eleven burials, there were fifteen sets of figurines. Sets consisted of two or more representations of adult females, or of one adult male placed with from one to seven adult females; there was one group that included two standing males and one seated, helmeted male. Unusual forms such as double-headed females and helmeted males were placed in conjunction with more-typical figurines. In a Preclassic tomb in El Opeño, Western Mexico, a pile of eleven complete figurines contained a variety of representations, including male ballplayers and standing and seated women (Oliveros 1974). Formative-period figurines were not often buried in groups, but when they were, a variety of representations were generally placed together. Figurines may have commonly been deployed in such scenes (Flannery and Marcus 1976:382; Marcus 1993).

If, as for other Formative-period figurine assemblages, different small, solid figurines were grouped together and directly compared in social or ritual activities, then what sorts of ideas might have been conveyed by juxtaposing young women with elders wearing ritual paraphernalia? Without knowing more about the use contexts of figurines, it is difficult to answer this in detail, yet some arguments can be developed from the representations themselves. If these two sorts of images were used together, then surely an obvious irony would have been the depiction of arms on the obese elders but not on the young females. Young women would have been actively engaged in productive labor, yet they were depicted without arms, incapable of action. The obesity of the elders, on the other hand, suggests a worldly passivity, yet they were depicted with arms and hands. This latter feature makes elders seem more capable of action than the young females. Perhaps this paradoxical link between passivity and capacity for action in the representations of elders was a deliberate ideological claim by elders that privileged their own (spiritual) activities over the productive material labor of juniors. Depiction of elders with hands and young women without was not a claim that elders did more practical work than young women;

rather, it was a reminder that the productive labor of the young did not matter much in the greater scheme of things. What really maintained the community, and probably made the productive labor of the young possible in the first place, was the ritual knowledge and ceremonial ministrations of the elders. If this analysis is correct, then social dynamics in the Mazatán region seem to have been very similar to the sort of situation Meillassoux (1981:33–49) analyzes as the "domestic community," or to Collier's (1988: 71–141) "equal bridewealth" model.

But why young women and not young men? Surely the labor of young men was also important, and elders would have wanted to control that as well? The absence of young men could have to do with the social contexts in which figurines were used. Thus, household rituals could have focused on femaleness and its relation to the ritual activities of elders, while maleness was represented and defined in contexts outside of the household, contexts that did not involve the use of figurines. Collier's analysis provides an intriguing alternative solution to this problem, however, and in addition, takes us back to a concern with how figurines became involved in establishing social identities. In Collier's equal-bridewealth model, influence over the productive and reproductive capacities of young women is a central issue for elders, since it is the right, claimed by women's kin, to give away women in marriage that makes young men rely on their elders for help in acquiring wives (Collier 1988:230–236). If, in the early sedentary villages of the Mazatán region, the social identities of young women were being reformulated in a way that made them "giveable" by their senior kin in marriage exchanges between kin groups, then perhaps it is not too surprising that people made images of young women without arms, and of elders engaged in important ritual activities, to deploy and discuss in a variety of social and ritual contexts. Perhaps elders would have been much more interested in discussions and public dramatizations (in household contexts) of their relationships with young women than of their relationships with young men, since men would have been forced to come to elders of their own accord to seek help in obtaining wives. Household rituals thus focused on femaleness, and its relation to the ritual activities of elders; perhaps maleness was represented and defined in contexts outside of the household, contexts that did not involve the use of figurines.

Although these observations reflect only vaguely the expectations elaborated by Collier (1988:133–144) for important ritual themes in equal-bridewealth societies, it is important to remember that figurines represent only one aspect of what must have been a complex ritual system. Also, cultural rationalizations of the sorts of social relationships analyzed by Collier could probably take a wide variety of forms, with different dimensions of differentiation (such as age, gender, rank, or ritual role) emphasized in different cases. This was probably the case even within Early Formative Mesoamerica. For instance, the figurine assemblage at Tlatilco, in Central Mexico, contrasts with that of Mazatán, since young men were represented and appeared in figurine sets together with representations of young women (see García Moll et al. 1991). Men and women were depicted wearing different kinds of clothing and engaging in different sorts of activities. Among the social differences signaled by Tlatilco figurines, gender roles appear to have been much more important than the concern with age and ritual role seen in Mazatán.

Other Representations and Change

The model just presented remains static as well as over simplified, since (1) two other figurine traditions introduced other representations beyond those of the Paqui Group to conversations about social identity and (2) the frequencies of these different representations changed significantly over time. Clark (1994:420–429) presents an interpretation of the whole sequence of changing representations through the Early Formative. Early in the time period of manufacture of the Paqui figurines considered here, representations of fat, masked people were scarce (but present) and clothed people without masks were represented in the Naca tradition of hollow figurines. During the period 1250–1100 b.c., representations were nearly restricted to the two analyzed here. However, after 1100 b.c., fat, masked images seem to have been gradually replaced by seated, nude, male figures in what appears to be a chiefly pose (Clark 1994:424; see also Marcus 1993). It may be that at this time an idiom of hereditary ranking was replacing one that had been primarily concerned with the opposition "sacred elders/indebted women" in the construction of social identities.

Conclusions

Whatever their uses in social or ritual contexts within households, the figurines' differences would have been a subject for discussion and reflection. Although a multiplicity of narratives concerning these objects would have been possible, the kinds of images that were in fact represented simultaneously limited the scope of such narratives. Since Formative period Mesoamerican figurines appear to depict stereotyped social categories, the kinds of social categories represented and the ways in which these were distinguished might provide clues about the construction of social identities in these societies; they at any rate provide a basis for constructing preliminary hypotheses about emic definitions of social categories and the relationships between them.

In Early Formative villages of the Mazatán region, two basic representations appeared in the most common figurine tradition: young women, and fat, masked figurines that seem to have been respected elders performing roles in public rituals. If, as was the case elsewhere in Formative period Mesoamerica, different Mazatán figurine representations appeared together in sets or scenes, then the contrast between armless young women and obese elders with arms and hands was surely an intentional irony, probably linked to an ideological claim that valued the spiritual labors of elders over the productive labor of juniors. Such ideological claims are common in small-scale agricultural societies, and some of the structural features of such systems have been analyzed by Meillassoux (1981) and Collier (1988). Important social categories include (1) elders, who generously apply their sacred knowledge to ensure the well-being of the community and who, in return, claim the right to give women away; (2) young women who are "giveable"; and (3) young men who need the help of elders in obtaining wives. The fact that only the first two of these categories were represented in the Mazatán figurine traditions may reflect the particular context of rituals involving figurines (households were the locations for rituals defining femaleness and the debts women owed to elders), or it may reflect the fact that the definition of young women as "giveable" was a crucial ideological claim that gave elders considerable influence over both young women and young men. In this second view, there was no need to portray young men as inherently in debt to elders, since men who wanted to marry would have had to seek out the help of elders of their own accord.

Acknowledgments

Field and lab work in 1992 was supported by a Fulbright (IIE) fellowship; dissertation grants from the Wenner-Gren Foundation for Anthropological Research, the Social Science Research Council, and the University of

Michigan; and the New World Archaeological Foundation, Brigham Young University. Michael Blake generously supported my 1993 work under a grant from the Social Sciences and Humanities Research Council of Canada. Without the guidance and support of John Clark, director of the New World Archaeological Foundation, this whole project would have been inconceivable. I have relied heavily on Clark's unpublished analyses of the Mazatán figurines. Special thanks are due as well to the Consejo de Arqueología of the Instituto Nacional de Antropología e Historia, Mexico, for permission to carry out the fieldwork. Many thanks to John Clark, Rosemary Joyce, Joyce Marcus, John Robb, and Carla Sinopoli for their insightful comments on earlier drafts of this essay. Errors that remain are, of course, my own.

References Cited

Acuña, René
   1984   *Relaciones geográficas del siglo XVI: Antequera.* Vol. 2. México: Universidad Nacional Autonoma de México.
Adams, Marie Jeanne
   1980   "Structural Aspects of East Sumbanese Art." In *The Flow of Life: Essays on Eastern Indonesia*, edited by James Fox, 208–220. Cambridge, Mass.: Harvard University Press.
Allen, Kathleen
   1990   "Gender and Style in the Archeological Record." Paper presented at the annual meeting of the American Anthropological Association, New Orleans.
Ambrose, Stanley H.
   1993   "Isotopic Analysis of Paleodiets: Methodological and Interpretive Considerations." In *Investigations of Ancient Human Tissue*, edited by Mary K. Sanford, 59–130. Langhorne, Pa.: Gordon and Breach Science Publishers.
Applegate, Richard B.
   1972   "Ineseno Chumash Grammar." PhD diss., Linguistics, University of California, Berkeley.
Arnold, Dean E., and A. L. Nieves
   1992   "Factors Affecting Ceramic Standardization." In *Ceramic Production and Distribution: An Integrated Approach*, edited by George Bey III and Christopher Pool, 93–114. Boulder, Colo.: Westview Press.
Arturo, Jean, and López Ramos
   1987   *Esplendor de la Antiqua Mixteca.* Mexico: Editorial Trillas.
Ashmore, Wendy, and Richard Wilk
   1988   "Household and Community in the Mesoamerican Past." In *Household and Community in the Mesoamerican Past*, edited by Richard Wilk and Wendy Ashmore, 1–27. Albuquerque: University of New Mexico Press.
Ball, Joseph W., and Jennifer T. Taschek
   1991   "Late Classic Lowland Maya Political Organization and Central-Place Analysis: New Insights from the Upper Belize Valley." *Ancient Mesoamerica* 2:149–165.
Barber, Russel
   1982   *The Wheeler's Site: A Specialized Shellfish Processing Station on the Merrimac River.* Peabody Museum Monograph, 7. Cambridge, Mass.
Barnes, Robert H.
   1980   "Concordance, Structure, and Variation: Considerations of Alliance in Kédang." In *The Flow of Life: Essays on Eastern Indonesia*, edited by James Fox, 68–97. Cambridge, Mass.: Harvard University Press.

Barraud, Cécille
  1979   *Tanebar-Evav: Une Société de Maisons Tournée vers le Large.* Cambridge: Cambridge University Press.
  1990   "Wife-Givers as Ancestors and Ultimate Values in the Kei Islands." *Bijdragen tot de Taal-, Land- en Volkenkunde* 146 : 193–225.
Barrera Vásquez, Alfredo (editor)
  1980   *Diccionario Maya Cordemex Maya–Español Español–Maya.* Merida, Yucatán: Ediciones Cordemex.
Barth, Fredrik
  1978   "Conclusions." In *Scale and Social Organization*, edited by F. Barth, 253–274. New York: Columbia University Press.
Bass, Patricia M.
  1991   "The Interpretation of U.S. Rock Art: Is It Time to Move to 'Meta-Rules'?" Paper presented at the annual meeting of the Society for American Archaeology, New Orleans.
Bean, Lowell John
  1976   "Power and Its Applications in Native California." In *Native Californians: A Theoretical Retrospective*, edited by Lowell Bean and Thomas Blackburn, 407–420. Socorro, N. Mex.: Ballena Press.
Beauchamp, William
  1900   "Iroquois Women." *Journal of American Folklore* 13 : 81–91.
Beeler, Madison S.
  1967   "The Ventureno Confesionario of José Senan, O.F.M." *University of California Publications in Linguistics* 47 : 1–75.
Bell, Amelia Rector
  1990   "Separate People: Speaking of Creek Men and Women." *American Anthropologist* 92 : 332–345.
Bellantoni, Nicholas
  1987   "Faunal Resource Availability and Prehistoric Cultural Selection on Block Island, Rhode Island." PhD diss., Anthropology, University of Connecticut, Storrs.
Bender, Barbara
  1978   "Gatherer-Hunter to Farmer: A Social Perspective." *World Archaeology* 10 : 204–222.
Bendremer, Jeffrey
  1993   "Late Woodland Settlement and Subsistence in Eastern Connecticut." PhD diss., Anthropology, University of Connecticut, Storrs.
Bendremer, Jeffrey, and Robert Dewar
  1994   "The Advent of Maize Horticulture in New England." In *Corn and Culture in the Prehistoric New World*, edited by Sissel Johannessen and Christine Hastorf, 369–393. Boulder, Colo.: Westview Press.
Bendremer, Jeffrey, Elizabeth Kellogg, and Tonya Largy
  1991   "A Grass-Lined Maize Storage Pit and Early Maize Horticulture in Central Connecticut." *North American Archaeology* 12 : 325–349.
Bernstein, David
  1987   "Prehistoric Subsistence at Greenwich Cove, Rhode Island." PhD diss., Anthropology, State University of New York at Binghamton.

1992   "Prehistoric Seasonality Studies in Coastal Southern New England."
         American Anthropologist 9:96–115.

Biggar, Henry
    1929   *The Works of Samuel de Champlain.* 3 vols. Toronto: Champlain Society.

Binford, Lewis R.
    1970   "Archaeology at Hatchery West." *Memoirs of the Society for American Ar-
              chaeology* 24.

Black, Thomas K., III
    1979   *The Biological and Social Analysis of a Mississippian Cemetery from South-
              east Missouri: The Turner Site, 23BU21A.* Anthropological Papers No. 68,
              University of Michigan, Ann Arbor.

Blackburn, Thomas C.
    1975   *December's Child: A Book of Chumash Oral Narratives Collected by John P.
              Harrington.* Berkeley: University of California Press.

Blackwood, Evelyn
    1988   "Review of *The Spirit and the Flesh: Sexual Diversity in American In-
              dian Culture,* by Walter L. Williams." *Journal of Homosexuality* 15(3/4):
              165–176.

Blake, Michael
    1991   "An Emerging Formative Chiefdom at Paso de la Amada, Chiapas, Mex-
              ico." In *The Formation of Complex Society in Southeastern Mesoamerica,*
              edited by W. Fowler, 27–46. Boca Raton, Fla.: CRC Press.

Blume, Cara
    1990   "A Women's Nutting Camp." Paper presented at the annual Mid-Atlantic
              Conference, Rehoboth Beach, Del.

Boissevain, E.
    1943   "Observations on a Group of Shell Heaps on Cape Cod." *Massachusetts
              Archaeological Society Bulletin* 5(1):6–11.

Bolen, Kathleen
    1992   "Prehistoric Construction of Mothering." In *Exploring Gender Through
              Archaeology,* edited by Cheryl Claassen, 49–62. Madison, Wis.: Prehistory
              Press.

Bonnichsen, Robson
    1973   "Millie's Camp: An Experiment in Archaeology." *World Archaeology* 4:
              227–291.

Bonvillain, Nancy
    1980   "Iroquoian Women." In *Studies on Iroquoian Culture,* edited by Nancy
              Bonvillain, 47–58. Occasional Publications in Northeastern Anthropology
              No. 6. Franklin Pierce College, Rindge, N.H.

Boon, James A.
    1990   "Balinese Twins Times Two: Gender, Birth Order, and 'Household' in
              Indonesia/Indo-Europe." In *Power and Difference: Gender in Island
              Southeast Asia,* edited by Jane Monnig Atkinson and Shelly Errington,
              209–233. Stanford, Calif.: Stanford University Press.

Borgstrom, G.
    1962   "Shellfish Protein: Nutritive Aspects." In *Fish as Food,* vol. 2, edited by
              G. Borgstrom, 115–147. New York: Academic Press.

Bossu, Jean-Bernard
1962   *Travels in the Interior of North America, 1751–1762.* Translated and edited by Seymour Feiler. Norman: University of Oklahoma Press.
Bourdieu, Pierre
1977   *Outline of a Theory of Practice.* Translated by Richard Nice. Cambridge: Cambridge University Press.
Boutton, T. W., P. D. Klein, M. J. Lynott, J. E. Price, and L. L. Tieszen
1984   "Stable Carbon Isotope Ratios as Indicators of Prehistoric Human Diet." In *Stable Isotopes in Nutrition*, edited by Judith R. Turnlund and Phyllis E. Johnson, 191–204. American Chemical Society Symposium Series No. 258, Washington, D.C.
Brandt, E. A.
1994   "Egalitarianism, Hierarchy, and Centralization in the Pueblos." In *The Ancient Southwestern Community: Models and Methods for the Study of Prehistoric Social Organization*, edited by Wirt Wills and Robert Leonard, 9–24. Albuquerque: University of New Mexico Press.
Braun, David
1983   "Pots as Tools." In *Archaeological Hammers and Theories*, edited by James Moore and Arthur Keene, 107–134. New York: Academic Press.
1985   "Ceramic Decorative Diversity and Illinois Woodland Regional Integration." In *Decoding Prehistoric Ceramics*, edited by Ben Nelson, 128–153. Carbondale: Southern Illinois University.
1987   "Coevolution of Sedentism, Pottery Technology, & Horticulture in the Central Midwest, 200 B.C.–A.D. 600." In *Emergent Horticultural Economies of the Eastern Woodlands*, edited by William Keegan, 153–182. Center for Archaeological Investigation Occasional Paper No. 7, Southern Illinois University.
Bridges, Patricia S.
1989   "Changes in Activities with Shift to Agriculture in the Southeastern United States." *Current Anthropology* 30:385–393.
Brock, Sharon L.
1985   "Activity-Induced Shape Change in the Human Lower Limbs Through Time in the Prehistoric Southwest." Paper presented at the annual meeting of the Society for American Archaeology, Denver.
Brown, Betty Ann
1983   "Seen But Not Heard: Women in Aztec Ritual, the Sahagún Texts." In *Text and Image in Pre-Columbian Art: Essays on the Interrelationship of the Verbal and Visual Arts*, edited by Janet Berlo, 119–153. BAR International Series Vol. 180. Oxford: British Archaeological Reports.
Brown, Catherine
1982   "On the Gender of the Winged Being on Mississippian Period Copper Plates." *Tennessee Anthropologist* 7(1):1–8.
Brown, James A.
1985a   "Long-term Trends to Sedentism and the Emergence of Complexity in the American Midwest." In *Prehistoric Hunter-Gatherers: The Emergence of Cultural Complexity*, edited by James Price and James Brown, 201–223. New York: Academic Press.

1985b   "The Mississippian Period." In *Ancient Art of the American Woodland Indians*, edited by David Brose, 94–146. Detroit: Institute of Arts.

Brown, Judith
1970   "Economic Organization and the Position of Women Among the Iroquois." *Ethnohistory* 17(3–4):151–167.

Bruhns, Karen Olsen
1991   "Sexual Activities: Some Thoughts on the Sexual Division of Labor and Archaeological Interpretation." In *The Archaeology of Gender*, edited by Dale Walde and Noreen Willows, 420–429. Calgary: Archaeological Association of the University of Calgary.

Brumbach, Hetty Jo
1985   "The Recent Fur Trade in Northwestern Saskatchewan." *Historical Archaeology* 19:19–39.

Brumbach, Hetty Jo, and Robert Jarvenpa
1989   *Ethnoarchaeological and Cultural Frontiers: Athapaskan, Algonquian, and European Adaptations in the Central Subarctic.* New York: Peter Lang.
1990   "Archeologist-Ethnographer-Informant Relations: The Dynamics of Ethnoarcheology in the Field." In *Powers of Observation: Alternative Views in Archeology*, edited by Sarah Nelson and Alice Kehoe, 39–46. Archeological Papers of the American Anthropological Association No. 2.

Brumbach, Hetty Jo, Robert Jarvenpa, and Clifford Buell
1982   "An Ethnoarchaeological Approach to Chipewyan Adaptations in the Late Fur Trade Period." *Arctic Anthropology* 19:1–49.

Brumfiel, Elizabeth
1991   "Weaving and Cooking: Women's Production in Aztec Mexico." In *Engendering Archaeology: Women and Prehistory*, edited by Joan Gero and Margaret Conkey, 224–251. Oxford: Blackwell.

Buckley, Thomas
1988   "Menstruation and the Power of Yurok Women." In *Blood Magic*, edited by Thomas Buckley and Alma Gottlieb, 188–209. Berkeley: University of California Press.

Buckley, Thomas, and Alma Gottlieb (editors)
1988a   *Blood Magic: The Anthropology of Menstruation.* Berkeley: University of California Press.
1988b   "A Critical Appraisal of Theories of Menstrual Symbolism." In *Blood Magic*, edited by Thomas Buckley and Alma Gottlieb, 3–50. Berkeley: University of California Press.

Buikstra, Jane, Lyle Konigsberg, and Jill Bullington
1986   "Fertility and the Development of Agriculture in Prehistoric Midwest." *American Antiquity* 51:528–546.

Buikstra, Jane E., and James H. Mielke
1985   "Demography, Diet, and Health." In *The Analysis of Prehistoric Diets*, edited by Robert Gilbert and James Mielke, 359–422. Orlando, Fla.: Academic Press.

Burgoa, Francisco de
1989   [1674] *Geografica descripcion.* 2 vols. México: Editorial Porrúa.
Butler, Judith
1990   *Gender Trouble: Feminism and the Subversion of Identity.* New York: Routledge.
Byland, Bruce, and John Pohl
1994   *In the Realm of Eight Deer: The Archaeology of the Mixtec Codices.* Norman: University of Oklahoma Press.
Cadillac, L., and P. Liette
1947   *The Western Country in the Seventeenth Century: The Memories of Lamothe Cadillac and Pierre Liette.* Edited by M. Quaife. Chicago: Lakeside Press.
Callender, Charles, and Lee M. Kochems
1983   "The North American Berdache." *Current Anthropology* 24 : 443–456.
1986   "Men and Not-Men: Male Gender-Mixing Statuses and Homosexuality." In *The Many Faces of Homosexuality*, edited by Evelyn Blackwood, 165–178. New York: Harrington Park.
Canada
1966   *Treaty No. 10 and Reports of Commissioners.* Ottawa: Queen's Printer.
1974   "English River Band, Registered Indians as of June 30, 1974, Meadow Lake District." Department of Indian Affairs and Northern Development.
Cannon, Aubrey
1991   "Gender, Status, and the Focus of Material Display." In *The Archaeology of Gender*, edited by Dale Walde and Noreen Willows, 144–149. Calgary: Archaeological Association of the University of Calgary.
Carr, Lucien
1883   "On the Social and Political Position of Women Among the Huron-Iroquois Tribes." *Report of the Peabody Museum of American Archaeology and Ethnology* 16 : 207–232.
Caso, Alfonso
1932a   "Reading the Riddle of Ancient Jewels." *Natural History* 32 : 464–480.
1932b   "Monte Albán, Richest Archaeological Find in America." *National Geographic* 62 : 487–512.
1969   *El Tesoro de Monte Albán.* Memorias del Instituto Nacional de Antropología e Historia No. 3, México.
Cavelier, Jean
1938   *The Journal of Jean Cavelier: The Account of a Survivor of La Salle's Expedition, 1684–1688.* Translated by Jean Delangley. Chicago: Institute of Jesuit History.
Ceci, Lynn
1982   "Method and Theory in Coastal New York Archaeology: Paradigms of Settlement Pattern." *North American Archaeologist* 3 : 5–36.
1984   "Shell Midden Deposits as Coastal Resources." *World Archaeology* 16 : 62–74.
1990a   "Radiocarbon Dating 'Village Sites' in Coastal New York Archaeology: Settlement Pattern Change in the Middle to Late Woodland." *Man in the Northeast* 39 : 1–28.

1990b   "Native Wampum as a Peripheral Resource in the Seventeenth-Century World System." In *The Pequots: The Fall and Rise of a Nation*, edited by L. Hauptman and J. Wherry, 48–63. Norman: University of Oklahoma Press.

Ceja Tenorio, Jorge Fausto
1985   *Paso de la Amada: An Early Preclassic Site in the Soconusco, Chiapas*. Papers of the New World Archaeological Foundation No. 49. Provo, Utah, Brigham Young University.

Charles, Douglas
1992   "Shading in the Past: Models in Archaeology." *American Anthropologist* 94:1–22.

Claassen, Cheryl
1990   "The Shell Seasonality Technique in the Eastern United States: A Reply to Lightfoot and Cerrato." *Archaeology of Eastern North America* 18:75–87.
1991a   "Gender, Shellfishing, and the Shell Mound Archaic." In *Engendering Archaeology: Women and Prehistory*, edited by Joan Gero and Margaret Conkey, 276–300. Oxford: Blackwell.
1991b   "Normative Thinking and Shell-Bearing Sites." In *Archaeological Method and Theory*, vol. 3., edited by Michael Schiffer, 249–298. Tucson: University of Arizona Press.
1992a   "Questioning Gender: An Introduction." In *Exploring Gender Through Archaeology*, edited by Cheryl Claassen, 1–9. Madison, Wis.: Prehistory Press.
1995   "Mothers' Work Loads and Children's Labor in the Woodland Period of the Midwest-Midsouth Regions." Paper presented at the 1995 Kentucky Heritage Council Meeting, Feb. 25.
1996   "A Consideration of the Social Organization of the Shell Mount Archaic." In *Archaeology of the Mid-Holocene Southeast*, edited by Kenneth Sassaman and David Anderson, 336–360. Gainesville: University of Florida Press.

Claassen, Cheryl (editor)
1992b   *Exploring Gender Through Archaeology: Selected Papers from the 1991 Boone Conference*. Madison, Wis.: Prehistory Press.
1994   *Women in Archaeology*. Philadelphia: University of Pennsylvania Press.

Clamagirand, Brigitte
1980   "The Social Organization of the Ema of Timor." In *The Flow of Life: Essays on Eastern Indonesia*, edited by James Fox, 134–151. Cambridge, Mass.: Harvard University Press.

Clark, John E.
1991   "The Beginnings of Mesoamerica: Apologia for the Soconusco Early Formative." In *The Formation of Complex Society in Southeastern Mesoamerica*, edited by W. Fowler, 13–26. Boca Raton, Fla.: CRC Press.
1993   "Competing Representation of Reproductive Power in Early Mesoamerica." Paper presented at the annual meeting of the American Anthropological Association, Washington, D.C.
1994   "The Development of Early Formative Rank Societies in the Soconusco,

Chiapas, Mexico." Unpublished PhD diss., Anthropology, University of
Michigan, Ann Arbor.

Clark, John E., and Michael Blake

1993   "The Power of Prestige: Competitive Generosity and the Emergence of
Rank Societies in Lowland Mesoamerica." In *Factional Competition and
Political Development in the New World*, edited by Elizabeth Brumfiel and
J. Fox, 17–30. Cambridge: Cambridge University Press.

Clark, Lynn

1987   "Beyond Status: Iroquois Women in the Contact Period." Unpublished
manuscript in possession of author.

Clendinnen, Inga

1982   "Yucatec Maya Women and the Spanish Conquest: Role and Ritual in Historical Reconstruction." *Journal of Social History* 15:427–442.

Codex Mendoza

1925   *Codex Mendoza*. Facsimile. Mexico City: Instituto Nacional de Arqueología, Historia, y Etnografía.

Codex Nuttal

1902   *Codex Nuttall*. Facsimile. Cambridge, Mass.: Peabody Museum of American Archaeology and Ethnology, Harvard University.

Codex Vienna

1929   *Codex Vienna*. Faksirnileausgabe der Nationalbibliothek in Wien. Vienna:
Eingeleitet durch W. Lehman und O. Smital.

Cohen, Mark N.

1977   *The Food Crisis in Prehistory*. New Haven, Conn.: Yale University Press.

1987   "Osteological Evidence for Gender Roles and Gender Hierarchies in Prehistory." Paper presented at the Wenner-Gren Foundation for Anthropological Research: An International Symposium, no. 103, Mijas, Spain.

Cole, Fay C., R. Bell, J. Bennett, J. Caldwell, N. Emerson, R. MacNeish, K. Orr,
and R. Willis

1951   *Kincaid: A Prehistoric Illinois Metropolis*. Chicago: University of Chicago
Press.

Collier, Jane Fishburne

1968   "Courtship and Marriage in Zinacantán, Chiapas, Mexico." *Middle
American Research Institute* 25:139–201. Tulane University, New Orleans.

1988   *Marriage and Inequality in Classless Societies*. Stanford, Calif.: Stanford
University Press.

Colson, Elizabeth

1978   "A Redundancy of Actors." In *Scale and Social Organization*, edited by
Fredrik Barth, 150–162. New York: Columbia University Press.

Colton, Harold S.

1959   *Hopi Kachina Dolls*. Albuquerque: University of New Mexico Press.

Conkey, Margaret W.

1991   "Contexts of Action, Contexts for Power: Material Culture and Gender in
the Magdalenian." In *Engendering Archaeology: Women and Prehistory*,
edited by Joan Gero and Margaret Conkey, 57–92. Oxford: Blackwell.

Conkey, Margaret W., and Joan M. Gero
  1991 "Tensions, Pluralities, and Engendering Archaeology: An Introduction to Women and Prehistory." In *Engendering Archaeology: Women and Prehistory*, edited by Joan Gero and Margaret Conkey, 3–30. Oxford: Blackwell.
Conkey, Margaret W., and Janet D. Spector
  1984 "Archaeology and the Study of Gender." In *Advances in Archaeological Method and Theory*, vol. 7, edited by Michael Schiffer, 1–38, New York: Academic Press.
Converse, Robert N.
  1973 "Another Remarkable Pipe." *Ohio Archaeologist* 23(4):4–5.
  1993 "Hopewell Ceramic Figurines." *Ohio Archaeologist* 43(4):25–27.
Cook, Della, and Jane Buikstra
  1979 "Health and Differential Survival in Prehistoric Populations: Prenatal Dental Defects." *American Journal of Physical Anthropology* 51:649–664.
Cordry, Donald, and Dorothy Cordry
  1968 *Mexican Indian Costumes*. Austin: University of Texas Press.
Costa, Kelly
  1994 "Women's Work: Engendering the Shell Middens of Narragansett Bay." Paper presented at the third Archaeology and Gender Conference, Boone, N.C.
Coyne, James (editor and translator)
  1903 *Exploration of the Great Lakes, 1669–1670, by Dollier de Casson and de Bréhant de Gallinée: Galinée's Narrative and Map*. Toronto: Ontario Historical Society Papers and Records No. 4.
Crown, Patricia, and Wirt Wills
  1995 "The Origins of Southwestern Ceramic Containers: Women's Time Allocation and Economic Intensification." *Journal of Anthropological Research* 51(2):173–194.
Culbert, T. Patrick
  1988 "Political History and the Decipherment of Maya Glyphs." *Antiquity* 62: 135–152.
Cummings, Linda S.
  1990 "Pollen Analysis at the Kite Site." In *The Environmental Context of Decision-Making: Coping Strategies Among Prehistoric Cultivators in Central New Mexico*, by A. E. Rautman, (PhD diss., University of Michigan), Appendix G, 478–495. Ann Arbor: University Microfilms.
Cunningham, Clark
  1964 "Order in the Atoni House." *Bijdragen tot de Taal-, Land- en Volkenkunde* 120:34–68.
  1965 "Order and Change in an Atoni Diarchy." *Southwestern Journal of Anthropology* 21:359–382.
Custer, Jay, Karen Rosenberg, Glenn Mellin, and Arthur Washburn
  1990 "A Re-Examination of the Island Field Site (7KF17), Kent County, Delaware." *Archaeology of Eastern North America* 18:145–212.
Czitrom, Carolyn Baus Reed
  1978 *Figurillas sólidas de estilo Colima: Una typología*. Instituto Nacional de

Antropología e Historia, Departamento de Investigaciones Históricas. Colección Científica, vol. 66. México, D.F.

Dahlberg, Frances (editor)
1981   *Woman the Gatherer*. New Haven, Conn.: Yale University Press.

D'Annibale, Cesare, and Brian Ross
1994   "After Point Peninsula: Pickering vs. Owasco in the St. Lawrence Valley." *The Bulletin* (Journal of the New York State Archaeological Association) 107:9–16.

Danziger, Eve
1991   "Man and Language in Prehistory: Clues to Gender Conceptualization from Semantic Analysis." In *The Archaeology of Gender*, edited by Dale Walde and Noreen Willows, 309–312. Calgary: University of Calgary Archaeological Association.

DeBoer, Warren
1990   "Interaction, Imitation, and Communication as Expressed in Style: The Ucayali Experience." In *The Uses of Style in Archaeology*, edited by Margaret Conkey and Christine Hastorf, 82–104. Cambridge: Cambridge University Press.

Deetz, James
1965   "The Dynamics of Social Change in Arikara Ceramics." Illinois Studies in Anthropology No. 4. Urbana: University of Illinois Press.

Delaney, Janice, Mary Jane Lupton, and Emily Toth
1976   *The Curse: A Cultural History of Menstruation*. New York: E. P. Dutton.

Demarest, Arthur A.
1992   "Ideology in Ancient Maya Cultural Evolution: The Dynamics of Galactic Polities." In *Ideology and Cultural Evolution in the New World*, edited by Arthur Demarest and Geoffrey Conrad, 135–157. Santa Fe, N. Mex.: School of American Research Advanced Seminar Series.

DeNiro, Michael J.
1985   "Postmortem Preservation and Alteration in Vivo Bone Collagen Ratios: Implications for Paleodietary Analysis." *Nature* 317:806–809.

DeNiro, Michael J., and S. Epstein
1981   "Influence of Diet on the Distribution of Carbon Isotopes in Animals." *Geochimica et Cosmochimica Acta* 42:495–506.

DeNiro, Michael J., and Margaret J. Schoeninger
1983   "Stable Carbon and Nitrogen Isotope Ratios of Bone Collagen: Variation Within Individuals, Between Sexes, and Within Populations Raised on Monotonous Diets." *Journal of Archaeological Science* 10:199–203.

Devereaux, Leslie
1987   "Gender Difference and Relations of Inequality in Zinacantán." In *Dealing with Inequality: Analysing Gender Relations in Melanesia and Beyond*, edited by Marilyn Strathern, 89–111. Cambridge: Cambridge University Press.

Diamanti, Melissa
1991   "Domestic Organization at Copan: Reconstruction of Elite Maya Households through Ethnographic Models." PhD diss., Anthropology, Pennsylvania State University. Ann Arbor, Mich.: University Microfilms.

Diaz-Granados, Carol, and J. R. Duncan
  1995   "Female Motifs and Myth in Missouri Petroglyphs." Paper presented at the annual meeting of the Southeastern Archaeological Conference, Knoxville, Tenn.
Dickel, David, Peter Schulz, and Henry M. McHenry
  1984   "Central California: Prehistoric Subsistence Changes and Health." In *Paleopathology at the Origins of Agriculture*, edited by Mark Cohen and George Armelagos, 439–461. Orlando, Fla.: Academic Press.
Dimmick, Frederica
  1994   "Creative Farmers of the Northeast: A New View of Indian Maize Horticulture." *North American Archaeologist* 15:235–252.
Dincauze, Dena F.
  1975   "Ceramic Sherds from the Charles River Basin." *Bulletin of the Archaeological Society of Connecticut* 39:5–17.
  1990   "A Capsule Prehistory of Southern New England." In *Pequots in Southern New England*, edited by L. Hauptman and J. Wherry, 19–32. Norman: University of Oklahoma Press.
Dincauze, Dena, and Robert Hasenstab
  1989   "Explaining the Iroquois: Tribalization on a Prehistoric Periphery." In *Comparative Studies in the Development of Complex Societies*, vol. 3, edited by T. Champion, 67–87. Boston: Allen and Unwin.
Dirrigl, Frank J., and Nicholas F. Bellantoni
  1993   "Comparison of Faunal Assemblages from Fisher's Island, New York, and Block Island, Rhode Island." Paper presented at the 33rd annual meeting of the Northeastern Anthropological Association, Danbury, Conn.
Dockstader, Frederick J.
  1954   *The Kachina Cult and the White Man*. Cranbrook Institute of Science, Bulletin 35.
Douglas, Mary
  1966   *Purity and Danger*. London: Pelican.
Draper, Patricia
  1975   "Cultural Pressure on Sex Differences." *American Ethnologist* 2:602–616.
Draper, Patricia, and Elizabeth Cashdan
  1988   "Technological Change and Child Behavior Among the !Kung." *Ethnology* 27:339–365.
Driver, Harold E.
  1937   "Culture Element Distribution: VI, Southern Sierra." *University of California Anthropological Records* 1(2):53–154.
Drooker, Penelope
  1994   "Representations of Gender in Fort Ancient versus Mississippian Culture Areas." Paper presented at the third Archaeology and Gender Conference, Boone, N.C.
Duke, Philip
  1991   "Recognizing Gender in Prehistoric Hunting Groups: Is It Possible or Even Necessary?" In *The Archaeology of Gender*, edited by Dale Walde and Noreen Willows, 280–283. Calgary: Archaeological Association of the University of Calgary.

Earle, Duncan M.
    1986   "The Metaphor of the Day in Quiche: Notes on the Nature of Everyday Life." In *Symbol and Meaning Beyond the Closed Community: Essays in Mesoamerican Ideas*, edited by Gary Gossen, 155–172. Studies on Culture and Society, vol. 1. Albany: Institute for Mesoamerican Studies, The University at Albany, State University of New York.

Ellis, B.
    1969   "Rock Art in Missouri: A New Discovery." *Central States Archaeological Journal* 16:53–57.

Emerson, Thomas E.
    1982   *Mississippian Stone Images in Illinois.* Champaign-Urbana: Illinois Archaeological Survey Circular No. 6.
    1989   "Water, Serpents, and the Underworld: An Exploration into Cahokian Symbolism." In *The Southeastern Ceremonial Complex: Artifacts and Analysis*, edited by Patricia Galloway, 45–92. Lincoln: University of Nebraska Press.

Engelbrecht, William
    1974   "The Iroquois: Archaeological Patterning on the Tribal Level." *World Archaeology* 6:52–65.

Erb, Maribeth
    1987   "When Rocks Were Young and Earth Was Soft: Ritual and Mythology in Northeastern Manggarai." PhD diss., Anthropology, State University of New York at Stony Brook.

Errington, Shelly
    1987   "Incestuous Twins and the House Societies of Insular Southeast Asia." *Cultural Anthropology* 2:403–444.
    1989   *Meaning and Power in a Southeast Asian Realm.* Princeton, N.J.: Princeton University Press.
    1990   "Recasting Sex, Gender, and Power: A Theoretical and Regional Overview." In *Power and Difference: Gender in Island Southeast Asia*, edited by Jane Atkinson and Shelly Errington, 1–58. Stanford, Calif.: Stanford University Press.

Estioko-Griffin, Agnes, and P. Bion Griffin
    1981   "Woman the Hunter: The Agta." In *Woman the Gatherer*, edited by Frances Dahlberg, 121–151. New Haven, Conn.: Yale University Press.

Farriss, Nancy M.
    1984   *Maya Society under Colonial Rule: The Collective Enterprise of Survival.* Princeton, N.J.: Princeton University Press.

Fenton, William
    1940   "Problems Arising from the Historic Northeastern Position of the Iroquois." In *Essays on Historical Anthropology of North America*, 159–251. Miscellaneous Collections, vol. 100, Smithsonian Institution, Washington, D.C.
    1978   "Northern Iroquoian Culture Patterns." In *Northeast*, edited by Bruce Trigger, 296–321, *Handbook of North American Indians*, vol. 15, William Sturtevant, general editor. Washington, D.C.: Smithsonian Institution Press.

Finsten, Laura, and Peter G. Ramsden
  1989 "The Sociopolitics of Iroquoian Ceramics: Past and Present." Paper presented at the twenty-second Chacmool conference, Calgary.
Fire/Lame Deer, John, and Richard Erdoes
  1972 *Lame Deer: Seeker of Visions.* New York: Simon and Schuster.
Fix, Alan G.
  1991 "Changing Sex Ratio of Mortality in the Semai Senoi." *Human Biology* 63:211–220.
Flannery, Kent, and Joyce Marcus
  1976 "Formative Oaxaca and the Zapotec Cosmos." *American Scientist* 64: 374–383.
  1983 "Urban Mitla and its Rural Hinterland." In *The Cloud People: Divergent Evolution of the Zapotec and Mixtec Civilizations,* edited by Kent Flannery and Joyce Marcus, 295–301. New York: Academic Press.
  1994 *Early Formative Pottery of the Valley of Oaxaca, Mexico.* University of Michigan Museum of Anthropology, Memoir 27.
Flannery, Kent V., and Marcus C. Winter
  1976 "Analyzing Household Activities." In *The Early Mesoamerican Village,* edited by Kent Flannery, 34–47. New York: Academic Press.
Ford, Richard I.
  1972 "Barter, Gift, or Violence: An Analysis of Tewa Intertribal Exchange." In *Social Exchange and Interaction,* edited by Ed Wilmsen, 21–46. University of Michigan Anthropological Papers 46, Ann Arbor.
Forman, Shepard
  1980 "Descent Alliance, and Exchange Ideology Among the Makassae of East Timon." In *The Flow of Life: Essays on Eastern Indonesia,* edited by James Fox, 152–177. Cambridge, Mass.: Harvard University Press.
Foucault, Michel
  1980 *The History of Sexuality: Volume I, An Introduction.* New York: Vintage Books.
Fowke, Gerard
  1922 *Archaeological Investigations: I. Cave Explorations in the Ozark Region of Central Missouri. II. Cave Explorations in Other States.* Washington, D.C.: Government Printing Office.
Fox, James J.
  1971 "Sister's Child as Plant: Metaphors in an Idiom of Consanguinity." In *Rethinking Kinship and Marriage,* edited by Rodney Needham, 219–252. Association of Social Anthropologists Monograph 11. London: Tavistock.
  1980a "Introduction." In *The Flow of Life: Essays on Eastern Indonesia,* edited by James Fox, 1–18. Cambridge, Mass.: Harvard University Press.
  1980b "Obligation and Alliance: State Structure and Moiety Organization in Thie, Roti." In *The Flow of Life: Essays on Eastern Indonesia,* edited by James Fox, 98–133. Cambridge, Mass.: Harvard University Press.
Fox, James A., and John S. Justeson
  1986 "Classic Maya Dynastic Alliance and Succession." In *Supplement to the Handbook for Middle American Indians,* vol. 4. *Ethnohistory,* edited by Ronald Spores, 7–34. Austin: University of Texas Press.

Francillon, Gérard
  1980   "Incursions upon Wehali: A modern History of an Ancient Empire." In
          The Flow of Life: Essays on Eastern Indonesia, edited by James Fox, 248–
          265. Cambridge, Mass.: Harvard University Press.
Fratt, Lee
  1991   "A Preliminary Analysis of Gender Bias in the Sixteenth and Seventeenth
          Century Spanish Colonial Documents of the American Southwest." In
          The Archaeology of Gender, edited by Dale Walde and Noreen Willows,
          245–251. Calgary: Archaeological Association of the University of Calgary.
Friedl, Ernestine
  1975   *Women and Men: An Anthropological Perspective*. New York: Holt, Rine-
          hart, and Winston.
Frison, George.
  1991   *Prehistoric Hunters of the High Plains*. 2nd ed. San Diego: Academic
          Press.
Fulton, Robert, and Steven W. Anderson
  1992   "The Amerindian 'Man-Woman': Gender, Liminality and Cultural Con-
          tinuity." *Current Anthropology* 33:603–610.
Fundaburk, Emma Lila, and Mary Douglass Fundaburk
  1957   *Sun Circles and Human Hands: The Southeastern Indians' Art and Indus-
          tries*. Luverne, Ala.: Emma Lila Fundaburk.
Furst, Jill Leslie
  1987   "Mixtec Narrative Conventions and Traditions: Problems in Defining the
          Codex Nuttal as Mixtec." *Latin American Indian Literatures Journal*
          3(1):9–26.
  1994   "Commentary on Engendering Tomb 7 at Monte Albán: Respinning an
          Old Yarn." *Current Anthropology* 35:158–159.
Gallegos Ruíz, Roberto
  1978   *El Señor 9 Flor en Zaachila*. México: Universidad Autonoma de México.
García Moll, Roberto, Daniel Juárez Cossio, Carmen Pijoan Aguade, María Elena
Salas Cuesta, and Marcela Salas Cuesta
  1991   *Catálogo de entierros de San Luis Tlatilco, México, Temporada IV*. Serie
          Antropología Física–Arqueología. Mexico City: Instituto Nacional de An-
          tropología e Historia.
Garcilosa, Vega
  1723   *La Florida del Inca*. Madrid: Editoria Nacional.
Gardner, Peter
  1991   "Forager's Pursuit of Individual Autonomy." *Current Anthropology* 32:
          543–572.
Gayton, Anna H.
  1936   "Estudillo Among the Yokuts: 1819." In *Essays in Honor of Alfred Louis
          Kroeber*, 67–85. Berkeley: University of California Press.
  1948a   "Yokuts and Western Mono Ethnography I: Tulare Lake, Southern Val-
          ley, and Central Foothill Yokuts." *University of California Anthropologi-
          cal Records* 10.
  1948b   "Yokuts and Western Mono Ethnography II: Northern Foothill Yokuts

and Western Mono." *University of California Anthropological Records* 10:2.

Gayton, Anna H., and Stanley S. Newman
1940 "Yokuts and Western Mono Myths." *University of California Anthropological Records* 5(1):1–110.

Gehlbach, Don R.
1976 "A Female 'Flint Knapper' Pipe." *Ohio Archaeologist* 26(4):13.

Gentleman of Elvas
1933 *True Relation of the Hardships Suffered by Governor Fernando de Soto and Certain Portuguese Gentlemen During the Discovery of the Province of Florida*. Edited and translated by J. A. Robertson. DeLand, Fla.: State Historical Society.

Gero, Joan M.
1991 "Genderlithics: Women's Roles in Stone Tool Production." In *Engendering Archaeology: Women and Prehistory*, edited by Joan Gero and Margaret Conkey, 163–193. Oxford: Blackwell.

Gifford, Edward Winslow
1931 "The Kamia of Imperial Valley." *Bureau of American Ethnology Bulletin 97*. Washington, D.C.
1932 "The Northfork Mono." *University of California Publications in American Archaeology and Ethnology* 31(2):15–65.

Gillespie, Susan D.
1994 "Ancestral Altars and Heirloomed Headdresses: A 'House' Interaction Model for Mesoamerica." Invited lecture presented at the University of Kentucky, Lexington.

Gilman, Patricia A.
1987 "Architecture as Artifact: Pit Structures and Pueblos in the American Southwest." *American Antiquity* 52:538–564.

Given, Brian
1994 *A Most Pernicious Thing: Gun Trading and Native Warfare in the Early Contact Period*. Ottawa: Carleton University Press.

Gordon, John L.
1980 "The Marriage Nexus Among the Manggarai of West Flores." In *The Flow of Life: Essays on Eastern Indonesia*. Edited by James Fox, 48–67. Cambridge, Mass.: Harvard University Press.

Gossen, Gary H.
1972 "Temporal and Spatial Equivalents in Chamula Ritual Symbolism." In *Reader in Comparative Religion: An Anthropological Approach*, 3rd ed., edited by William Lessa and Evon Vogt, 135–149. New York: Harper and Row.
1974 *Chamulas in the World of the Sun: Time and Space in a Maya Oral Tradition*. Cambridge, Mass.: Harvard University Press.

Gottlieb, Alma
1988 "Menstrual Cosmology among the Beng of Ivory Coast." In *Blood Magic*, edited by Thomas Buckley and Alma Gottlieb, 55–74. Berkeley: University of California Press.

Green, Dell F., and Gareth W. Lowe
1967   *Altamira and Padre Piedra, Early Preclassic Sites in Chiapas, Mexico*. Papers of the New World Archaeological Foundation No. 20. Provo, Utah, Brigham Young University.
Greenberg, David F.
1986   "Why Was the Berdache Ridiculed?" In *The Many Faces of Homosexuality*, edited by Evelyn Blackwood, 179–189. New York: Harrington Park.
Greenhill, Eleanor
1976   "Eleanor, Abbot Suger, and Saint-Denis." In *Eleanor of Aquitaine: Patron and Politician*, edited by William Kilber, 81–113. Austin: University of Texas Press.
Grieder, Terence
1982   *Origins of Precolumbian Art*. Austin: University of Texas Press.
Guenther, Todd R.
1991   "The Horse Creek Site: Some Evidence for Gender Roles in a Transitional Early to Middle Plains Archaic Base Camp." In *Approaches to Gender Processes on the Great Plains*, edited by marcel Kornfeld, 9–24. Memoir 26, Plains Anthropological Society.
Guillén, Ann Cyphers
1993   "Women, Rituals, and Social Dynamics at Ancient Chalcatzingo." *Latin American Antiquity* 4:209–224.
Gutierrez, Ramon A.
1991   *When Jesus Came, the Corn Mothers Went Away: Marriage, Sexuality, and Power in New Mexico, 1500–1848*. Stanford, Calif.: Stanford University Press.
Gwyne, Gretchen A.
1982   "The Late Archaic Archaeology of Mt. Sinai Harbor, New York: Human Ecology, Economy, and Residence Patterns of the Southern New England Coast." PhD diss., Anthropology, State University of New York at Stony Brook.
Hakluyt, Richard
1904   *The Principal Navigations, Voyages, Traffiques, and Discoveries of the English Nation*, vol. 9, 279–318. Glasgow: James MacLehose and Sons.
Hamilton, Margaret E.
1982   "Sexual Dimorphism in Skeletal Samples." In *Sexual Dimorphism in Homo sapiens*, edited by R. Hall, 107–163. New York: Praeger.
Handsman, Russel
1989   "Native Women and the Susquehannock 'Kings': An Archaeological Story about Colonialism." Paper presented in First Archaeological Conference, Baltimore.
Hanna, Margaret
1989   "Woman as Mediator and Facilitator: A Prehistoric Example from Western Manitoba." Paper presented at the Chacmool conference, Calgary.
Harlan, Mark
1987   "Chalcatzingo's Formative Figurines." In *Ancient Chalcatzingo*, edited by David Grove, 252–263. Austin: University of Texas Press.

Harrington, John P.
1942   *Culture Element Distributions: XIX, Central California Coast.* University of California Anthropological Records 7(1):1–46.
Harris, Marvin
1988   *Culture, People, Nature: An Introduction to General Anthropology.* 5th ed. New York: Harper and Row.
Hasenstab, Robert
1990   "Agriculture, Warfare, and Tribalization in the Iroquois Homeland of New York: A G.I.S. Analysis of Late Woodland Settlement." Unpublished PhD diss., Anthropology, University of Massachusetts, Amherst.
Hassan, Fekri A.
1981   *Demographic Archaeology.* New York: Academic Press.
Hastorf, Christine A.
1991   "Gender, Space, and Food in Prehistory." In *Engendering Archaeology: Women and Prehistory,* edited by Joan Gero and Margaret Conkey, 132–159. Oxford: Blackwell.
Hauser, Raymond E.
1990   "The *Berdache* and the Illinois Indian Tribe During the Last Half of the Seventeenth Century." *Ethnohistory* 37:45–65.
Hawkes, Kristen
1993   "Why Hunter-Gatherers Work: An Ancient Version of the Problem of Public Goods." *Current Anthropology* 34:341–369.
Hayden, Brian
1992   "Observing Prehistoric Women." In *Exploring Gender Through Archaeology,* edited by Cheryl Claassen, 33–47. Madison, Wis.: Prehistory Press.
Hays-Gilpin, Kelley
1991   "Anasazi Iconography: Medium and Motif." Paper presented at the third annual Southwest Symposium, Tucson, Ariz.
1994   "Gender Constructs in the Material Culture of Seventh Century Anasazi Farmers in Northeastern Arizona." Paper presented at the Material Culture and Gender Conference, Exeter, England.
Heizer, Robert F.
1955   "The Mission Indian Vocabularies of H. W. Henshaw." *University of California Anthropological Records* 15(2):85–202.
Heizer, Robert F., and M. A. Whipple
1971   "The Chumash Indians of Santa Barbara, by Pedro Fages." In *The California Indians: A Source Book,* edited by Robert Heizer and M. Whipple, 255–261. Berkeley: University of California Press.
Hemert-Engert, Adolph van, and Frederick J. Teggart (editors)
1910   "The Narrative of the Portola Expedition of 1769–1770, by Miguel Costanso." *Publication of the Academy of Pacific Coast History* 1(4):91–159.
Hendon, Julia A.
1987   "The Uses of Maya Structures: A Study of Architecture and Artifact Distribution at Sepulturas, Copan, Honduras." PhD diss., Anthropology, Harvard University. Ann Arbor, Mich.: University Microfilms.
1988   "Discusión preliminar del estudio de areas de actividad en Las Sepulturas,

Copan: Forma, función y distribución de las vasijas de barro." *Yaxkin* 11:47–82.

1989   "Elite Household Organization at Copan, Honduras: Analysis of Activity Distribution in the Sepulturas Zone." In *Household and Communities*, edited by S. MacEachern, D. Archer, and R. Garvin, 371–380. Proceedings of the 21st annual Chacmool conference. Calgary: Archaeological Association of the University of Calgary.

1991   "Status and Power in Classic Maya Society: An Archaeological Study." *American Anthropologist* 93:894–918.

1992a   "Architectural Symbols of the Maya Social Order: Residential Construction and Decoration in the Copan Valley, Honduras." In *Ancient Images, Ancient Thought: The Archaeology of Ideology*, edited by A. Goldsmith et al., 481–495. Proceedings of the twenty-third annual Chacmool conference. Calgary: Archaeological Association of the University of Calgary.

1992b   "Hilado y tejido en la epoca prehispanica: Tecnología y relaciones sociales de la producción textil." In *La indumentaria y el tejido mayas a través del tiempo*, edited by Linda Asturias de Barrios and Dina García, 7–16. Monografía 8. Guatemala City: Museo Ixchel del Traje Indígena.

1992c   "Variation in Classic Maya Sociopolitical Organization." *American Anthropologist* 94:940–941.

1994   "Gender Ideology and Social Evolution in Mesoamerica: A Critical Perspective on Modern Theories and Colonial Sources." Paper presented at the ninety-third annual meeting of the American Anthropological Association, Atlanta.

Hennepin, L.

1698a   *A New Discovery of a Vast Country in America, Extending above Four Thousand Miles, between New France and New Mexico.* For M. Bentley, J. Tonson, H. Bonwick, T. Goodwin, and S. Manship, London.

1698b   *A Continuation of a New Discovery of a Vast Country in America, Extending above Four Thousand Miles, between New France and New Mexico.* For M. Bentley, J. Tonson, H. Bonwick, T. Goodwin, and S. Manship, London.

Herrera, Antonio de

1945   *Historia general de los hechas de los Castellanos, en las islas, y terra-firme de el mar oceano.* Vol. 4. Buenos Aires: Editorial Guarania.

Hewitt, John N.

1932   "Status of Women in Iroquoian Polity Before 1784." *Annual Report of the Board of Regents: 1932*, 475–488. Washington, D.C.: Smithsonian Institution.

Hill, James

1966   "A Prehistoric Community in Eastern Arizona." *Southwestern Journal of Anthropology* 22:9–30.

Hodder, Ian

1984   "Burials, Houses, Women, and Men in the European Neolithic." In *Ideology, Power, and Prehistory*, edited by Daniel Miller and Christopher Tilley, 51–68. Cambridge: Cambridge University Press.

1991   "Gender Representation and Social Reality." In *The Archaeology of Gender*, edited by Dale Walde and Noreen Willows, 11–16. Calgary: University of Calgary Archaeological Association.

Hollimon, Sandra E.

1988   "Age and Sex Related Incidence of Degenerative Joint Disease in Skeletal Remains from Santa Cruz Island, California." In *Human Skeletal Biology: Contributions to the Understanding of California's Prehistoric Populations*, edited by G. Richards, 69–90. Archives of California Prehistory No. 24. Salinas, Calif.: Coyote Press.

1990   "Division of Labor and Gender Roles in Santa Barbara Channel Area Prehistory." PhD diss., Anthropology, University of California, Santa Barbara.

1991   "Health Consequences of Divisions of Labor Among the Chumash Indians of Southern California." In *The Archaeology of Gender*, edited by Dale Walde and Noreen Willows, 462–469. Calgary: Archaeological Association of the University of Calgary.

1996   "Gender in the Archaeological Record of the Santa Barbara Channel Area." In *Proceedings of the Society for California Archaeology*, edited by Judyth Reed, 9 : 205–208.

n.d.   "The Journey to Similaqsa: Chumash Cosmology and Mortuary Practices and Their Implications for Archaeology." In *Proceedings of the 27th Chacmool Conference*. Calgary: University of Calgary Press, in press.

Holmes, William H.

1883   "Art in Shell of the Ancient Americans." *Second Annual Report of the Bureau of American Ethnology*, 185–305. Washington, D.C.

1903   "Aboriginal Pottery of the Eastern United States." *Twentieth Annual Report of the Bureau of American Ethnology*, 1–237. Washington, D.C.

Hoskins, Janet

1987   "Complementarity in This World and the Next: Gender and Agency in Kodi Mortuary Ceremonies." In *Dealing with Inequality: Analysing Gender Relations in Melanesia and Beyond*, edited by Marilyn Strathern, 174–206. Cambridge: Cambridge University Press.

1989   "Why Do Ladies Sing the Blues? Indigo Dyeing, Cloth Production, and Gender Symbolism in Kodi." In *Cloth and Human Experience*, edited by Annette Weiner and Jane Schneider, 141–173. Washington, D.C.: Smithsonian Institution Press.

1990   "Doubling Dieties, Descent, and Personhood: An Exploration of Kodi Gender Categories." In *Power and Difference: Gender in Island Southeast Asia*, edited by Jane Atkinson and Shelly Errington, 273–306. Stanford, Calif.: Stanford University Press.

Houston, Stephen D.

1993   *Hieroglyphs and History at Dos Pilas: Dynastic Politics of the Classic Maya*. Austin: University of Texas Press.

Howard, James Henry

1968   *The Southeastern Ceremonial Complex and Its Interpretation*. Springfield, Mo.: Missouri Archaeological Society, Memoirs 6.

Hudecek-Cuffe, Caroline R.

1994   "Gender Relations and Plains Paleoindian Subsistence/Settlement Patterns: An Alternative Reconstruction." Paper presented at the third Archaeology and Gender Conference, Boone, N.C.

Hudson, Charles

1976   *The Southeastern Indians.* Knoxville: University of Tennessee Press.

Hudson, Travis, and Thomas C. Blackburn

1986   *The Material Culture of the Chumash Interaction Sphere.* Vol. 4 of *Ceremonial Paraphernalia, Games, and Amusements.* Ballena Press Anthropological Papers No. 30. Socorro, N.Mex.: Ballena Press.

Hudson's Bay Company Archives

1838   "Ile a La Crosse District Indian Census, 1838." B.239/a/10:fols.52a–57a. Winnipeg: Provincial Archives of Manitoba.

Hughes, Susan S.

1991   "Division of Labor at a Besant Hunting Camp in Eastern Montana." In *Approaches to Gender Processes on the Great Plains,* edited by Marcel Kornfeld, 24–49. Memoir 26, Plains Anthropological Society.

Hunt, George

1940   *The Wars of the Iroquois: A Study of Intertribal Trade Relations.* Madison: University of Wisconsin Press.

Jackson, Douglas K., Andrew C. Fortier, and Joyce A. Williams

1992   *The Sponemann Site 2: The Mississippian Oneota Occupations (11-Ms-517).* American Bottom Archaeology, FAI-270 Site Reports, No. 24. Urbana: University of Illinois Press.

Jackson, Tom

1991   "Pounding Acorn: Women's Production as Social and Economic Focus." In *Engendering Archaeology: Women and Prehistory,* edited by Joan Gero and Margaret Conkey, 301–326. Oxford: Blackwell.

Jacobs, Sue-Ellen, and Jason Cromwell

1992   "Visions and Revisions of Reality: Reflections on Sex, Sexuality, Gender, and Gender Variance." *Journal of Homosexuality* 23(4):43–69.

Jacobs, Sue-Ellen, and Wesley Thomas

1994   "Native American Two-Spirits." *Anthropology Newsletter* 35(8):7.

Jansen, Maarten

1982   "Viaje al otro mundo: La Tumba 1 de Zaachila." In *Coloquio internacional los indigenistas de México en la epoca precolombina y en la actualidid,* edited by Maarten Jansen and Ted Leyenaar, 87–118. Leiden: Rijksmuseum voor volkerkunde.

Jarvenpa, Robert

1979   "Recent Ethnographic Research: Upper Churchill River Drainage, Saskatchewan, Canada." *Arctic* 32:355–365.

1980   *The Trappers of Patuanak: Toward a Spatial Ecology of Modern Hunters.* Mercury Series, Canadian Ethnology Service Paper No. 67. Ottawa: National Museum of Man.

1987   "The Hudson's Bay Company, the Roman Catholic Church, and the

Chipewyan in the Late Fur Trade Period." In *Le Castor Fait Tout: Selected Papers of the Fifth North American Fur Trade Conference, 1985*, edited by B. Trigger, T. Morantz, and L. Dechene, 485–517. Montreal: St. Louis Historical Society.

Jarvenpa, Robert, and Hetty Jo Brumbach

1983   "Ethnoarchaeological Perspectives on an Athapaskan Moose Kill." *Arctic* 36:174–184.

1984   "The Microeconomics of Southern Chipewyan Fur Trade History." In *The Subarctic Fur Trade: Native Social and Economic Adaptations*, edited by S. Krech, 147–183. Vancouver: University of British Columbia Press.

1985   "Occupational Status, Ethnicity, and Ecology: Metis Cree Adaptations in a Canadian Trading Frontier." *Human Ecology* 13:309–329.

1988   "Sociospatial Organization and Decision Making Processes: Observations from the Chipewyan." *American Anthropologist* 90:598–618.

1993   "Ethnoarchaeology and Gender: Chipewyan Women as Hunters." Paper presented at the ninety-second annual meeting of the American Anthropological Association, Washington, D.C.

1995   "Ethnoarchaeology and Gender: Chipewyan Women as Hunters." In *Research in Economic Anthropology*, vol. 16, edited by Barry Isaac, 39–82. Greenwich, Conn.: JAI Press.

Jennings, Francis

1984   *The Ambiguous Iroquois Empire*. New York: Norton and Company.

Jennings, Jesse D.

1989   *Prehistory of North America*. 3rd ed. Mountain View, Calif.: Mayfield Publishing Co.

Jones, Christopher

1977   "Inauguration Dates of Three Late Classic Rulers of Tikal." *American Antiquity* 42:28–60.

Joutel, Henri

1962   [1714] *A Journal of La Salle's Last Voyage*. New York: Corinth Books.

Joyce, Rosemary A.

1990   "The Construction of Gender in Classic Maya Monuments." Paper presented at the annual meeting of the American Anthropological Association, New Orleans.

1991a   *Cerro Palenque: Power and Identity on the Maya Periphery*. Austin: University of Texas Press.

1991b   "The Construction of Gender in Classic Maya Monuments." Revised version of a paper presented at the annual meeting of the American Anthropological Association, New Orleans.

1992a   "Dimensiones simbólicas del traje en monumentos clasicos Mayas: Construcción del género a través del vestido." In *La indumentaria y el tejido mayas a través del tiempo*, edited by Linda Asturias de Barrios and Dina García, 29–38. Monografía 8. Museo Ixchel del Traje Indígena, Guatemala City.

1992b   "Images of Gender and Labor Organization in Classic Maya Society." In

Exploring Gender through Archaeology, edited by Cheryl Claassen, 63–70. Madison, Wis.: Prehistory Press.

1993   "Women's Work: Images of Production and Reproduction in Pre-Hispanic Southern Central America." *Current Anthropology* 34:255–274.

1994   "The Women of Tlatilco." Paper presented at the third Archaeology and Gender Conference, Boone, N.C.

Kalm, Peter

1966   *Travels in North America*. 2 vols. New York: Dover.

Kann, Veronica

1989   "Late Classic Politics, Cloth Production, and Women's Labor: An Interpretation of Female Figurines from Matacapán, Veracruz." Paper presented at the annual meeting of the Society for American Archaeology, Atlanta, Ga.

Kapches, Mima

1990   "The Spatial Dynamics of Ontario Iroquoian Longhouses." *American Antiquity* 55:49–67.

Katz, Jonathan

1976   *Gay American History*. New York: Thomas Y. Crowell.

Katzenburg, M. Anne

1989   "Stable Isotope Analysis of Archaeological Faunal Remains from Southern Ontario." *Journal of Archaeological Science* 16:319–329.

Kelley, Jane H.

1984   *The Archaeology of the Sierra Blanca Region of Southeastern New Mexico*. Anthropological Papers No. 74. Museum of Anthropology, University of Michigan, Ann Arbor.

Kelly, Robert L.

1992   "Mobility/Sedentism: Concepts, Archaeological Measures, and Effects." *Annual Review of Anthropology* 21:43–66.

King, Linda B.

1969   "The Medea Creek Cemetery (LAN-243): An Investigation of Social Organization from Mortuary Practices." *UCLA Archaeological Survey Annual Report* 11:23–68.

1982   "Medea Creek Cemetery: Late Inland Patterns of Social Organization, Exchange and Warfare." PhD diss., Anthropology, University of California, Los Angeles.

King, Mark

1990   "Poetics and Metaphor in Mixtec Writing." *Ancient Mesoamerica* 1:141–151.

Klippel, Walter E., and Darcy F. Morey

1986   "Contextual and Nutritional Analysis of Freshwater Gastropods from Middle Archaic Deposits at the Hays Site, Middle Tennessee." *American Antiquity* 51:799–813.

Knapp, Michael L.

1973   "Archaic Seasonal Patterning and Shellfish Use in Southeastern New England." Master's thesis, Hunter College, CUNY.

Knight, Chris
  1988   "Menstrual Synchrony and the Australian Rainbow Snake." In *Blood Magic*, edited by Thomas Buckley and Alma Gottlieb, 232–255. Berkeley: University of California Press.
  1991   *Blood Relations: Menstruation and the Origins of Culture.* New Haven, Conn.: Yale University Press.
Knight, Vernon James
  1990   "Social Organization and the Evolution of Hierarchy in Southeastern Chiefdoms." *Journal of Anthropological Research* 46 : 1–23.
Koehler, Lyle
  1980   *A Search for Power: The "Weaker Sex" in Seventeenth Century New England.* Champaign-Urbana: Illinois University Press.
Kowalewski, Stephen
  1983   "The Archaeological Evidence for Sa'a Yucu." In *The Cloud People: Divergent Evolution of the Zapotec and Mixtec Civilizations*, edited by Kent Flannery and Joyce Marcus, 289. New York: Academic Press.
Kroeber, Alfred L.
  1908   *A Mission Record of the California Indians.* University of California Publications in American Archaeology and Ethnology 37 : 1–70.
  1925   *Handbook of the Indians of California.* Bureau of American Ethnology Bulletin 78. Washington, D.C.: Smithsonian Institution.
Krueger, Harold W., and Charles H. Sullivan
  1984   "Models for Carbon Isotope Fractionation between Diet and Bone." In *Stable Isotopes in Nutrition*, edited by J. Turnlund and P. Johnson, 205–222. American Chemical Society, Symposium Series No. 258. Washington, D.C.
Lafitau, Joseph
  1974–1977   [1724] *Customs of the American Indians Compared with the Customs of Primitive Times.* 2 vols. Edited and translated by William Fenton and Elizabeth Moore. Toronto: The Champlain Society.
Lambert, Joseph B., Carol B. Szpunar, and Jane E. Buikstra
  1977   "Chemical Analysis of Excavated Human Bone from Middle and Late Woodland Sites." *Archaeometry* 21 : 115–129.
Landa, Fray Diego de
  1982   *Relación de los cosas de Yucatán.* Mexico City: Editorial Porrúa.
Lankford, George
  1987   *Native American Legends.* Little Rock: August House.
Larsen, Clark Spencer
  1984   "Health and Disease in Prehistoric Georgia: The Transition to Agriculture." In *Paleopathology at the Origins of Agriculture*, edited by Mark Cohen and George Armelagos, 367–392. Orlando, Fla.: Academic Press.
Latta, Martha A.
  1991   "The Captive Bride Syndrome: Iroquoian Behavior or Archaeological Myth?" In *The Archaeology of Gender*, edited by Dale Walde and Noreen Willows, 375–383. Calgary: Archaeological Association of the University of Calgary.

Laughlin, Robert M.
   1975   *The Great Tzotzil Dictionary of San Lorenzo Zinacantán.* Washington, D.C.: Smithsonian Institution Press.
   1988   *The Great Tzotzil Dictionary of Santo Domingo Zinacantán.* 3 vols. Smithsonian Contributions to Anthropology No. 31. Washington, D.C.: Smithsonian Institution Press.
Lavin, Lucianne
   1980   "Analysis of Ceramic Vessels from the Ben Hollister Site, Glastonbury, Connecticut." *Bulletin of the Archaeological Society of Connecticut* 43: 3–46.
   1984   "Connecticut Prehistory: A Synthesis of Current Archaeological Investigations." *Bulletin of the Archaeological Society of Connecticut* 47:5–40.
   1988   "The Morgan Site, Rocky Hill, Connecticut: A Late Woodland Farming Community in the Connecticut River Valley." *Bulletin of the Archaeological Society of Connecticut* 51:7–21.
Leach, Edmund R.
   1965   *Political Systems of Highland Burma: A Study of Kachin Social Structure.* Boston: Beacon Press.
   1971   *Rethinking Anthropology.* London School of Economics Monographs on Social Anthropology No. 22. London: The Athlone Press.
Leacock, Eleanor B.
   1981   *Myths of Male Dominance.* New York: Monthly Review Press.
   1986   "Women, Power, and Authority." In *Visibility and Power: Essays on Women in Society and Development,* edited by Leela Dube, Eleanor Leacock, and Shirley Ardener, 107–135. Delhi: Oxford University Press.
Lee, Carla, and Rebecca Storey
   1992   "Bioarchaeology and Human Adaptation at an Elite Compound, Copán." Paper presented at the fifty-seventh annual meeting of the Society for American Archaeology, Pittsburgh.
Lee, Richard B., and Irven DeVore (editors)
   1968   *Man the Hunter.* Chicago: Aldine.
Lee, Thomas A., Jr.
   1969   *The Artifacts of Chiapa de Corzo, Chiapas, Mexico.* Papers of the New World Archaeological Foundation, No. 26. Provo, Utah: Brigham Young University.
Lenig, Donald
   1965   *The Oak Hill Horizon and Its Relation to the Development of the Five Nations Iroquois Culture. Researches and Transactions* 15(1). Buffalo: New York State Archaeological Association.
León, Nicolás
   1901   *Lyobaa ó Mictlan.* Mexico City: N.p.
Le Page du Pratz, A.
   1976   *The History of Louisiana,* edited by J. Tregle, Jr. Baton Rouge: Louisiana State University Press.

Lévi-Strauss, Claude
1982   *The Way of the Masks.* Translated by Sylvia Modelski. Seattle: University of Washington Press.
1987   *Anthropology and Myth: Lectures, 1951 –1982.* Oxford: Basil Blackwell.
Lightfoot, Kent G.
1984   *Prehistoric Political Dynamics: A Case Study from the American Southwest.* DeKalb: Northern Illinois University Press.
Loeb, Edwin M.
1933   "The Eastern Kuksu Cult." *University of California Publications in American Archaeology and Ethnology* 33(2): 139–232.
Longacre, William A.
1964   "Archaeology as Anthropology: A Case Study." *Science* 144: 1454–1455.
1970   *Archaeology as Anthropology: A Case Study.* Anthropology Papers of the University of Arizona, No. 17.
Longpre, Robert
1977   *Ile a la Crosse.* Ile a la Crosse, Saskatchewan: Ile a la Crosse Local Community Authority and Bi-Centennial Committee.
Longyear, John M., III
1952   "Copan Ceramics: A Study of Southeastern Maya Pottery." Carnegia Institution of Washington, Publication No. 597. Washington, D.C.
Lorant, Stefan (editor)
1946   *The New World: The First Pictures of America Made by John White and Engraved by Theodore DeBry, with Contemporary Narratives of the Huguenot Settlement in Florida 1562 –1565 and the Virginia Colony 1585 –1590.* New York: Duell, Sloan and Pearce.
Lounsbury, Floyd
1961   "Iroquois-Cherokee Linguistic Relations." *Symposium on Cherokee and Iroquois Culture,* edited by William Fenton and John Gulick, 9–18. Bureau of American Ethnology Bulletin No. 180. Smithsonian Institution, Washington D.C.
1978   "Iroquoian Languages." In *Northeast,* edited by Bruce G. Trigger, 334–343, *Handbook of North American Indians,* vol. 15, William G. Sturtevant, general editor. Smithsonian Institution, Washington D.C.
Lowe, Gareth W.
1975   *The Early Preclassic Barra Phase of Altamira, Chiapas.* Papers of the New World Archaeological Foundation, No. 38. Provo, Utah: Brigham Young University.
1977   "The Mixe-Zoque as Competing Neighbors of the Lowland Maya." In *The Origins of Maya Civilization,* edited by R. E. W. Adams, 197–248. School of American Research Advanced Seminar Series, University of New Mexico, Albuquerque.
Lumb, Lisa
1992   "Recovering the Feminine in Indigenous Southeastern Beliefs: Women and Warfare." Manuscript in possession of Lyle Koehler.

MacCormack, Carol

1980   "Nature, Culture, and Gender: A Critique." In *Nature, Culture, and Gender*, edited by Carol MacCormack and Marilyn Strathern, 1–24. Cambridge: Cambridge University Press.

MacNeish, Richard S.

1952   *Iroquois Pottery Types: A Technique for the Study of Iroquois Prehistory.* Bulletin 124. Ottawa: National Museums of Canada.

Mallory, John K., III

1984   "Late Classic Maya Economic Specialization: Evidence from the Copan Obsidian Assemblage." PhD diss., Anthropology, Pennsylvania State University. Ann Arbor, Mich.: University Microfilms.

Marcus, Joyce

1983   "Monte Albán's Tomb 7." In *The Cloud People: Divergent Evolution of the Zapotec and Mixtec Civilizations*, edited by Kent Flannery and Joyce Marcus, 282–285. New York: Academic Press.

1989   "Zapotec Chiefdoms and the Nature of Formative Religions." In *Regional Perspectives on the Olmec*, edited by Robert Sharer and David Grove, 148–197. Cambridge: Cambridge University Press.

1993   "Men's and Women's Ritual in Formative Oaxaca." A paper presented in the Dumbarton Oaks symposium "Ritual, Social Organization, and Sacred Geography in Preclassic Mesoamerica," organized by David Grove and Rosemary Joyce.

Marcus, Joyce, and Kent Flannery

1983   "An Introduction to the Late Postclassic." In *The Cloud People: Divergent Evolution of the Zapotec and Mixtec Civilizations*, edited by Kent Flannery and Joyce Marcus, 217–226. New York: Academic Press.

Margry, Pierre (editor)

1875–1886   *Decouvertes et Etablissements des Francais dans l'Ouest et dans le Sud de l'Amerique Septentrionale (1614–1754). Memoires et Documents Originaux Recuirlis et Publies*, 6v. Paris: Maisonneuve et Cie, Libraires-editeurs.

Marquette, Jacques

1698   "A Discovery from Some New Countries and Nations in the Northern America." In L. Hennepin, *A Continuation of a New Discovery of a Vast Country in America, Extending above Four Thousand Miles, between New France and New Mexico*, 196–223. From M. Bentley, J. Tonson, H. Bonwick, T. Goodwin, and S. Manship, London.

Martin, Debra, and Nancy Akins

1994   "Patterns of Violence Against Women in the Prehistoric Southwest." Paper presented at the Southwest Symposium, Tempe, Ariz.

Martin, Emily

1992   *The Woman in the Body: A Cultural Analysis of Reproduction.* 2nd ed.: Boston: Beacon Press.

Mathews, Holly F.

1985   " 'We are Mayordomo': A Reinterpretation of Women's Roles in the Mexican Cargo System." *American Ethnologist* 12 : 285–301.

Maxwell, Diane
    1994   "Unearthing Long Forgotten Clues: Representations of Women in the Honduras Collection at the Royal Ontario Museum." Paper presented at the third Archaeology and Gender Conference, Women in Ancient America, Boone, N.C.

Mayfield, Thomas J.
    1993   *Indian Summer: Traditional Life Among the Choinumne Indians of California's San Joaquin Valley.* Berkeley: Heyday Books/California Historical Society.

McBride, Kevin
    1984   "The Archaeology of the Lower Connecticut River Valley." PhD diss., Anthropology, University of Connecticut, Storrs.
    1992   "Prehistoric and Historic Patterns of Wetland Use in Eastern Connecticut." *Man in the Northeast* 43:1–23.

McBride, Kevin, and N. Bellantoni
    1982   "The Utility of Ethnohistoric Models for Understanding Late Woodland–Contact Change in Southern New England." *Bulletin of the Archaeological Society of Connecticut* 45:51–64.

McBride, Kevin, and B. Dewar
    1987   "Agriculture and Cultural Evolution: Causes and Effects in the Lower Connecticut River Valley." In *Emergent Horticultural Economies of the Eastern Woodland,* edited by W. Keegan, 305–328. Carbondale, Ill.: Carbondale Center for Archaeological Investigation.

McCafferty, Geoffrey G., and Sharisse D. McCafferty
    1994a   "The Metamorphosis of Xochiquetzal: The Good, the Bad, and the Ugly." Paper presented at the third Archaeology and Gender Conference, Women in Ancient America, Boone, N.C.

McCafferty, Sharisse D., and Geoffrey G. McCafferty
    1989   "Weapons of Resistance: Material Metaphors of Gender Identity in Post-Classic Mexico." Paper presented at the annual meeting of the American Anthropological Association, Washington, D.C.
    1991   "Spinning and Weaving as Female Gender Identity in Postclassic Mexico." In *Textile Traditions of Mesoamerica and the Andes: An Anthology,* edited by Margot Schevill, Janet Berlo, and E. Dwyer, 19–44. New York: Garland.
    1994b   "Engendering Tomb 7 at Monte Alban: Respinning an Old Yarn." *Current Anthropology* 35:143–166.

McClintock, Martha K.
    1971   "Menstrual Syndrome and Suppression." *Nature* 229 (5282):244–245.

McElrath, Dale L.
    1986   *The McLean Site (11-5-640).* Urbana: Illinois Department of Transportation.

McKern, William C., P. F. Titterington, and James B. Griffin
    1945   "Painted Pottery Figures from Illinois." *American Antiquity* 3:297–302.

McKinnon, Susan
    1991   *From a Shattered Sun: Hierarchy, Gender, and Alliance in the Tanimbar Islands.* Madison: University of Wisconsin Press.

McManamon, Francis P.
  1983   "Prehistoric Cultural Adaptations on Cape Cod: Ecological Niches, Adaptive States and Temporal Variation." PhD diss., Anthropology, State University of New York at Binghamton.
McMeekin, Dorothy
  1992   "Representations on Pre-Columbian Spindle Whorls of the Floral and Fruit Structure of Economic Plants." *Economic Botany* 46:171–180.
Mead, Margaret
  1939   *From the South Seas: Studies of Adolescence and Sex in Primitive Societies.* New York: William Morrow and Company.
Meehan, Betty
  1982   *Shell Bed to Shell Midden.* Canberra: Australian Institute of Aboriginal Studies.
Meillassoux, Claude
  1981   *Maidens, Meal, and Money: Capitalism and the Domestic Community.* Cambridge: Cambridge University Press.
Merbs, Charles
  1983   *Patterns of Activity-Induced Pathology in a Canadian Inuit Population.* National Museum of Man Mercury Series, No. 119.
Milanich, Jerald, William C. Sturtevant, and Emilio Moran (editors and translators)
  1972   *Francisco Pareja's 1613 Confessionario: A Documentary Source for Timucuan Ethnography.* Tallahassee: Florida Division of Archives, History, and Records Management.
Miller, Daniel
  1985   *Artefacts as Categories.* Cambridge: Cambridge University Press.
Monaghan, John
  1990   "Performance and the Structure of Mixtec Codices." *Ancient Mesoamerica* 1:133–140.
Moore, Heidi
  1990   "Macrobotanical Remains." In *The Environmental Context of Decision Making: Coping Strategies Among Prehistoric Cultivators in Central New Mexico,* by A. Rautman, PhD Diss., Anthropology, University of Michigan, Ann Arbor.
Morgan, Lewis H.
  1901   *League of the Iroquois.* Edited by H. M. Lloyd. 2 vols. New York: Dodd, Mead. Reprinted. New Haven, Conn.: Human Relations Area Files.
Moss, Madonna
  1993   "Shellfish, Gender, and Status on the Northwest Coast: Reconciling Archeological, Ethnographic, and Ethnohistorical Records of the Tlingit." *American Anthropologist* 95:631–652.
Mourt, G.
  1866   [1622] *Mourt's Relation, or Journal of the Plantation at Plymouth.* Boston: John Kimball Wiggin.
Murdock, George P.
  1934   *Our Primitive Contemporaries.* New York: Macmillan.
  1967   "The Ethnographic Atlas: A Summary." *Ethnology* 6(2).

Needham, Rodney
   1980   "Principles and Variations in the Structure of Sumbanese Society." In *The Flow of Life: Essays on Eastern Indonesia*, edited by James Fox, 21–47. Cambridge, Mass.: Harvard University Press.
Neitzel, Jill
   1989   "Regional Exchange Networks in the American Southwest: A Comparative Analysis of Long-Distance Trade." In *The Sociopolitical Structure of Prehistoric Southwestern Societies*, edited by S. Upham, K. Lightfoot, and R. Jewett, 149–195. Boulder, Colo.: Westview Press.
Nelson, Richard K.
   1980   "Athapaskan Subsistence Adaptations in Alaska." In *Alaska Native Culture and History*, edited by Y. Kotani and W. Workman, 205–232. Senri Ethnological Studies No. 4, National Museum of Ethnology, Senri Expo Park, Suita, Osaka, Japan.
Niemczycki, Mary Ann
   1980   "Matrilocality and Iroquois Archaeology: Myth and Reality." Paper presented at the annual meeting of the Society for American Archaeology, Philadelphia.
O'Brien, Patricia
   1991   "Evidence for the Antiquity of Women's Roles in Pawnee Society." In *Approaches to Gender Processes on the Great Plains*, edited by Marcel Kornfeld, 51–64. Memoir 26, Plains Anthropological Society.
Oliveros, José Arturo
   1974   "Nuevas exploraciones en el Opeño, Michoacán." In *The Archaeology of West Mexico*, edited by Betty Bell, 182–201. Sociedad de Estudios Avanzados del Occidente de México, Ajijie, Jalisco, México.
Ortiz, Alfonzo
   1969   *The Tewa World: Space, Time, Being, and Becoming in a Pueblo Society.* Chicago: University of Chicago Press.
Paddock, John
   1983   *Lord Five Flower's Family.* Nashville: Vanderbilt University Publications in Anthropology No. 29.
Paige, Karen Ericksen
   1973   "Women Learn to Sing the Menstrual Blues." *Psychology Today* 7:41–46.
Paige, Karen Ericksen, and Jeffrey M. Paige
   1981   *The Politics of Reproductive Ritual,* Berkeley: University of California Press.
Parker, Arthur C.
   1916   "The Origins of the Iroquois as Suggested by Their Archaeology." *American Anthropologist* 18:479–507.
Parsons, Elsie C.
   1916   "The Zuni La'mana." *American Anthropologist* 18:521–528.
Parsons, Mary H.
   1972   "Spindle Whorls from the Teotihuacan Valley, Mexico." In *Miscellaneous Studies in Mexican Prehistory*, 45–79, 127–137. Anthropological Papers No. 45. Ann Arbor, Museum of Anthropology, University of Michigan.

Pauketat, Timothy R., and Thomas E. Emerson
1991   "The Ideology of Authority and the Power of the Pot." *American Anthropologist* 93:919–941.
Paul, Lois
1974   "The Mastery of Work and the Mystery of Sex in a Guatemalan Village." In *Woman, Culture, and Society,* edited by Michelle Rosaldo and Louise Lamphere, 281–299. Stanford, Calif.: Stanford University Press.
Perlman, Steven M.
1980   "An Optimum Diet Model, Coastal Variability, and Hunter-Gatherer Behavior." In *Advances in Archaeological Method and Theory,* vol. 2, edited by Michael Schiffer, 257–310. New York: Academic Press.
Pernet, Henry
1992   *Ritual Masks: Deceptions and Revelations.* Translated by Laura Grillo. Columbia: University of South Carolina Press.
Perrelli, Douglas
1994   "Gender, Mobility, and Subsistence in Iroquois Prehistory: An Ethnohistorical Approach to Archaeological Interpretation." Master's thesis, Anthropology, University of Buffalo.
Phillips, Philip, and James A. Brown
1978   *Pre-Columbian Shell Engravings from the Craig Mound at Spiro, Oklahoma, Part I.* Cambridge, Mass.: Peabody Museum of Archaeology and Ethnology, Harvard University.
Pickering, Robert B.
1984   "An Examination of Patterns of Arthritis in Middle Woodland, Late Woodland, and Mississippian Skeletal Series from the Lower Illinois Valley." PhD diss., Anthropology, Northwestern University.
Plog, Stephen, and Shirley Powell
1984   "Patterns of Culture Change: Alternative Interpretations." In *Papers on the Archaeology of Black Mesa, Arizona,* vol. 2, edited by Stephen Plog and Shirley Powell, 209–216. Carbondale: Southern Illinois University Press.
Pohl, John, M.D.
1994a   "Mexican Codices, Maps, and Lienzos as Social Contracts." In *Writing Without Words,* edited by Elizabeth Boone and Walter Mignolo, 137–160. Durham, N.C.: Duke University Press.
1994b   *Politics and Symbolism in the Mixtec Codices.* Nashville, Tenn.: Vanderbilt Publications in Anthropology No. 46.
1994c   "Weaving and Gift Exchange in the Mixtec Codices." In *Cloth and Curing: Community and Change in Oaxaca,* edited by Grace Johnson and Douglas Sharon, 3–13. San Diego Museum Papers No. 32.
n.d.   "The Wall Paintings of Mitla." In *Mesoamerican Architecture as a Cultural Symbol,* edited by Jeffrey Kowalewski. Oxford: Oxford University Press, in press.
Pool, Christopher A.
1992   "Integrating Ceramic Production and Distribution." In *Ceramic Production and Distribution: An Integrated Approach,* edited by G. Bey III and C. Pool, 275–314. Boulder, Colo.: Westview Press.

Powell, Mary Lucas
    1986   "Late Prehistoric Community Health in the Central Deep South: Biological and Social Dimensions of the Mississippian Chiefdom at Moundville, Alabama." In *Skeletal Analysis in Southeastern Archaeology*, edited by Janet Levy, 127–150. North Carolina Archaeological Council Publication No. 24, Raleigh.
    1992   "In the Best of Health? Disease and Trauma Among the Mississippian Elite." In *Lords of the Southeast: Social Inequality and the Native Elites of Southeastern North America*, edited by Alex Barker and Timothy Pauketat, 81–98. Archaeological Papers of the American Anthropological Association, Washington, D.C.
Powers, Stephen M.
    1976   *Tribes of California*. Berkeley: University of California Press.
Prentice, Guy
    1986   "An Analysis of the Symbolism Expressed by the Birger Figurine." *American Antiquity* 51 : 239–266.
Prezzano, Susan
    1986   "Physical Properties of Ceramic Sherds From Five Middle and Late Woodland Stage Components in the Susquehanna Drainage." Master's thesis, Anthropology, State University of New York, Binghamton.
    1993   "Longhouse, Village, and Palisade: Community Patterns at the Iroquois Southern Door." PhD diss., Anthropology, State University of New York, Binghamton.
Price, James E.
    1969   *Analysis of Middle Mississippian House*. Museum Briefs No. 1. Museum of Anthropology, University of Missouri, Columbia.
Price, James E., and James B. Griffin
    1979   *The Snodgrass Site of the Powers Phase of Southeast Missouri*. Anthropological Papers No. 66. Museum of Anthropology, University of Michigan, Ann Arbor.
Randle, Martha
    1951   "Iroquois Women Then and Now." In *Symposium on Local Diversity in Iroquois Culture*, edited by W. Fenton, 167–180. Bureau of American Ethnology Bulletin 149(8). Washington, D.C.
Rau, Charles
    1872   "Artificial Shell-Deposits in New Jersey." *Smithsonian Institution, Annual Report for 1864* : 370–374.
Rautman, Alison E.
    1993   "Resource Variability, Risk, and the Structure of Social Networks: An Example from the Prehistoric Southwest." *American Antiquity* 58 : 403–424.
Redfield, Robert, and Alfonso Villa Rojas
    1962   *Chan Kom: A Maya Village*. Abridged. Chicago: University of Chicago Press.
Renouf, M. A. P.
    1984   "Northern Coastal Hunter-Fishers: An Archaeological Model." *World Archaeology* 16 : 18–27.

Rice, Patricia C.
  1981 "Prehistoric Venuses: Symbols of Motherhood or Womanhood?" *Journal of Anthropological Research* 37:402–414.
Richards, Cara
  1957 "Matriarch or Mistake: The Role of Iroquois Women Through Time." In *Cultural Stability and Change*, edited by V. Ray, 36–45. Washington, D.C.: American Ethnological Society.
Richter, Daniel
  1992 *The Ordeal of the Longhouse*. Chapel Hill: University of North Carolina Press.
Ritchie, William
  1934 *An Algonkin-Iroquois Contact Site on Castle Creek, Broome County, New York*. Research Records of the Rochester Municipal Museum No. 2, Rochester, New York.
  1980 *The Archaeology of New York State*. 2nd rev. ed. Harrison, N.Y.: Harbor Hills Books.
Ritchie, William A., and Robert E. Funk
  1973 *Aboriginal Settlement Patterns in the Northeast*. Memoir 20, New York State Museum and Science Service, State Education Deparment, Albany.
Robertson, Merle Greene
  1985 *The Sculpture of Palenque*, vol. 3, *The Late Buildings of the Palace*. Princeton, N.J.: Princeton University Press.
Robinson, Paul A.
  1990 "The Struggle Within: The Indian Debate in Seventeenth Century Narrangansett Country." PhD Diss., Anthropology, State University of New York at Binghamton.
Rodgers, Susan
  1990 "The Symbolic Representation of Women in a Changing Batak Culture." In *Power and Difference: Gender in Island Southeast Asia*, edited by Jane Atkinson and Shelly Errington, 307–344. Stanford, Calif.: Stanford University Press.
Roscoe, Will
  1987 "Bibliography of Berdache and Alternative Gender Roles Among North American Indians." *Journal of Homosexuality* 14(3/4):81–171.
  1988 *Living the Spirit: A Gay American Indian Anthology*. New York: St. Martin's Press.
  1990 "The Life and Times of a Crow Berdache." *Montana: The Magazine of Western History* 40(1):46–55.
  1991 *The Zuni Man-Woman*. Albuquerque: University of New Mexico Press.
  1994 "How to Become a Berdache: Toward a Unified Analysis of Gender Diversity." In *Third Sex, Third Gender: Beyond Sexual Dimorphism in Culture and History*, edited by Gilbert Herdt, 329–372. Cambridge, Mass.: MIT Press.
  1995 "Was We'wha a Homosexual?: Native American Survivance and the Two-Spirit Tradition." *GLO* 2:193–235.

Rothenberg, Diane
1978   "Erosion of Power: An Economic Basis for the Selective Conservatism of Seneca Women in the Nineteenth Century." *Western Canadian Journal of Anthropology* 6(3): 106–122.
1980   "The Mothers of the Nation: Seneca Resistance to Quaker Intervention." In *Women and Colonization*, edited by M. Etienne and E. Leacock, 63–87. New York: Praeger.
Roys, Ralph L., France V. Scholes, and Eleanor B. Adams
1940   *Report and Census of the Indians of Cozumel, 1570.* Carnegie Institution of Washington Publication No. 523. Contributions to American Anthropology and History, vol. 6, no. 30. Washington, D.C.
Sahagún, Fray Bernardino de
1969   *Florentine Codex, Book 6, Rhetoric and Moral Philosophy.* Translated by Charles Dibble and Arthur Anderson. Santa Fe, N. Mex.: School of American Research and University of Utah.
Sahlins, Marshall D.
1972   *Stone Age Economics.* Chicago: Aldine.
Salwen, Bert
1962   "Sea Level and Archaeology in the Long Island Sound." *American Antiquity* 28: 46–55.
Sanders, William T.
1986   "Introduccíon." In *Proyecto arqueológico de Copán segunda fase: Excavaciones en el area urbana de Copán*, tomo 1, edited by William Sanders, 9–25. Tegucigalpa: Secretaría de Cultura y Turismo, Instituto Hondureño de Antropología e Historia.
1989   "Household, Lineage, and State in Eighth-Century Copán, Honduras." In *The House of the Bacabs, Copan Honduras*, edited by David Webster, 89–105. Studies in Pre-Columbian Art and Archaeology No. 29. Washington, D.C.: Dumbarton Oaks.
Sassaman, Kenneth E.
1992   "Lithic Technology and the Hunter-Gatherer Sexual Division of Labor." *North American Archaeologist* 13: 249–262.
1993   *Early Pottery in the Southeast: Tradition and Innovation in Cooking Technology.* Tuscaloosa: University of Alabama Press.
Saunders, Joe
1986   "The Economy of Hinds Cave." PhD diss., Anthropology, Southern Methodist University, Dallas, Tex.
Schele, Linda, and David Friedel
1990   *A Forest of Kings: The Untold Story of the Ancient Maya.* New York: William Morrow & Co.
Schlegal, Alice
1972   *Male Dominance and Female Autonomy.* New Haven, Conn.: HRAF Press.
Schwartz, Theodore
1978   "The Size and Shape of a Culture." In *Scale and Social Organization*, edited by Fredrik Barth, 215–252. New York: Columbia University Press.

Scull, Gideon (editor)

1885   *Voyages of Peter Esprit Radisson: Being an Account of His Travels and Experiences Among the North American Indians from 1652 to 1684*. Boston: The Prince Society.

Seler, Eduard

1993   [1904] "The Ruins of Mitla." In *Collected Works in Mesoamerican Linguistics and Archaeology*, vol. 4, edited by Frank Compato, 246–265. Culver City, Calif.: Labyrinthos.

Shapiro, Judith

1981   "Anthropology and the Study of Gender." *Soundings: An Interdisciplinary Journal* 64:446–465.

Shea, John G. (editor)

1861   *Early Voyages Up and Down the Mississippi, by Cavelier, St. Cosme, Le Sueur, Gravier, and Guignas*. Albany, N.Y.: Joel Munsell.

Sherman, D. George

1987   "Men Who Are Called 'Women' in Toba-Batak: Marriage, Fundamental Sex-Role Differences, and the Suitability of the Gloss 'Wife-Receiver.'" *American Anthropologist* 89:867–878.

Sherman, George, and Hedy Bruyns Sherman

1990   *Rice, Rupees, and Ritual: Economy and Society Among the Samosir Batak of Indonesia*. Stanford, Calif.: Stanford University Press.

Shermis, Steward

1982–84   "Domestic Violence in Two Skeletal Populations." *Ossa* 9–11:143–151.

Shore, Bradd

1981   "Sexuality and Gender in Samoa: Conceptions and Missed Conceptions." In *Sexual Meanings: The Cultural Construction of Gender and Sexuality*, edited by Sherry Ortner and Harriet Whitehead, 192–215. Cambridge: Cambridge University Press.

Shuttle, Penelope, and Peter Redgrove

1978   *The Wise Wound: Eve's Curse and Everywoman*. New York: Richard Marek.

Simon, Arleyn, and John Ravesloot

1995   "Saládo Ceramic Burial Offerings: A Consideration of Gender and Social Organization." *Journal of Anthropological Research* 51(2):103–124.

Smith, Bruce D.

1973   "Middle Mississippian Exploitation of Animal Populations." PhD diss., Anthropology, University of Michigan, Ann Arbor. Ann Arbor: University Microfilms.

1985   "Mississippian Patterns of Subsistence and Settlement." In *The Alabama Borderlands*, edited by R. Badger and L. Clayton, 64–79. Tuscaloosa: University of Alabama Press.

1987   "The Independent Domestication of Indigenous Seed Bearing Plants in Eastern North America." In *Emergent Horticultural Economies of the Eastern Woodland*, edited by W. Keegan, 305–328. Carbondale, Ill.: Carbondale Center for Archaeological Investigation.

Smith, Eric
   1983   "Anthropological Applications of Optimal Foraging Theory: A Critical Review." *Current Anthropology* 24:625–651.
Smith, Maria O.
   1996   "Bioarchaeological Inquiry into Archaic Period Populations of the Southeast: Trauma and Occupational Stress." In *Archaeology of the Mid-Holocene Southeast*, edited by Kenneth Sassaman and David Anderson, 137–157. Gainesville: University of Florida Press.
Snow, Dean
   1980   *The Archaeology of New England.* New York: Academic Press.
   1994a   "Paleoecology and the Prehistoric Incursion of Northern Iroquoians into the Lower Great Lakes Region." In *Great Lakes Archaeology and Paleoecology: Exploring Interdisciplinary Initiatives for the Nineties*, edited by B. Warner and R. MacDonald, 283–293. Waterloo, Ontario: Quarterly Science Institute, University of Waterloo.
   1994b   "Recent Archaeological Research in the Northeastern United States and Eastern Canada." *Journal of Archaeological Research* 2(3):199–220.
   1995   "Migration in Prehistory: The Northern Iroquoian Case." *American Antiquity* 60:59–79.
Sørensen, Marie Louise Stig
   1991   "The Construction of Gender Through Appearance." In *The Archaeology of Gender*, edited by Dale Walde and Noreen Willows, 121–129. Calgary: University of Calgary Archaeological Association.
Spain, Daphne
   1992   *Gendered Spaces.* Chapel Hill: University of North Carolina Press.
Speck, Frank G.
   1909   "Ethnology of the Yuchi Indians." *Anthropological Publications, University Museum, University of Pennsylvania* 1:102–112. Philadelphia.
Spector, Janet
   1983   "Male/Female Task Differentiation Among the Hidatsa: Toward the Development of an Archeological Approach to the Study of Gender." In *The Hidden Half*, edited by P. Albers and B. Medicine, 77–99. Washington, D.C.: University Press of America.
   1991   "What This Awl Means." In *Engendering Archaeology: Women and Prehistory*, edited by Joan Gero and Margaret Conkey, 388–406. Oxford: Blackwell.
   1993   *What This Awl Means: Feminist Archaeology at a Wahpeton Dakota Village.* St. Paul, Minnesota Historical Society Press.
Sperlich, Norbert, and Elizabeth Katz Sperlich
   1980   *Guatemalan Backstrap Weaving.* Norman: University of Oklahoma Press.
Speth, John D.
   1990   "Seasonality, Resource Stress, and Food Sharing in So-Called 'Egalitarian' Foraging Societies." *Journal of Anthropological Archaeology* 9:148–188.
Spielmann, Katherine A.
   1994   "Clustered Confederacies: Sociopolitical Organization in the Protohis-

toric Rio Grande." In *The Ancient Southwestern Community: Models and Methods for the Study of Prehistoric Social Organization*, edited by W. Wills and R. Leonard, 45–54. Albuquerque: University of New Mexico Press.

1995   "Glimpses of Gender in the Prehistoric Southwest." *Journal of Anthropological Research* 51(2):91–102.

Spink, Mary L.

1984   "Metates as Socioeconomic Indicators during the Classic Period at Copán, Honduras." PhD diss., Anthropology, Pennsylvania State University.

Spores, Ronald

1967   *The Mixtec Kings and Their People*. Norman: University of Oklahoma Press.

Stark, Miriam T.

1992   "From Sibling to Suki: Social Relations and Spatial Proximity in Kalinga Pottery Exchange." *Journal of Anthropological Archaeology* 11:137–151.

Stocker, Terry

1991   "Discussion: Empire Foundation, Figurine Function, and Figurine Distribution." In *The New World Figurine Project*, vol. 1, edited by Terry Stocker, 145–165. Provo, Utah: Research Press.

Storey, Rebecca

1985   "La paleodemografía de Copán." *Yaxkin* 8:151–160.

1986   "Entierros y clase social en Copán, Honduras: Aspectos biológicos." *Yaxkin* 9:55–61.

1992   "The Children of Copan: Issues in Paleopathology and Paleodemography." *Ancient Mesoamerica* 3:161–167.

Strathern, Marilyn

1984   "Domesticity and the Denigration of Women." In *Rethinking Women's Roles: Perspectives from the Pacific*, edited by Denise O'Brien and Sharon Tiffany, 13–31. Berkeley: University of California Press.

Sullivan, Thelma D.

1982   "Tlazolteotl-Ixcuina: The Great Spinner and Weaver." In *The Art and Iconography of Late Postclassic Central Mexico*, edited by Elizabeth Boone, 7–35. Washington, D.C.: Dumbarton Oaks.

Swanton, John R.

1911   *Indians of the Lower Mississippi Valley and Adjacent Coast of the Gulf of Mexico*. Bureau of American Ethnology Bulletin 43. Washington, D.C.

1928a   "Social Organization and Social Usages of the Indians of the Creek Confederacy." Bureau of American Ethnology 42nd annual report (1925), 43–472. Washington, D.C.

1928b   "Sun Worship in the Southeast." *American Anthropologist* 30:206–213.

1929   *Myths and Tales of the Southeastern Indians*. Bureau of American Ethnology Bulletin 88. Washington, D.C.

1931   *Source Material for the Social Ceremonial Life of the Choctaw Indians*. Bureau of American Ethnology Bulletin 103. Washington, D.C.

1946   *Indians of the Southeastern United States*. Bureau of American Ethnology Bulletin 137. Washington, D.C.

Szuter, Christine R.
    1989   "Women as Hunters: Gender and Hunting in the Prehistoric American Southwest by Horticulturalists." Paper presented at the Chacmool conference, Calgary.
Tafoya, Terry
    1981   "Dancing with Dash-Kayah: The Mask of the Cannibal Woman." *Parabola* 6(3):6–11.
Talalay, Lauren E.
    1993   *Deities, Dolls, and Devices: Neolithic Figurines from Franchti Cave, Greece.* Bloomington: Indiana University Press.
Tedlock, Dennis (translator)
    1985   *Popol Vuh: The Mayan Book of the Dawn of Life.* New York: Simon and Schuster.
Thomas, Cyrus
    1985   [1894] "Report on the Mound Explorations of the Bureau of American Ethnology." Washington, D.C.: Smithsonian Institution Press.
Thompson, J. Eric S.
    1938   "Sixteenth and Seventeenth Century Reports on the Chol Maya." *American Anthropologist* 40:584–604.
    1956   *Notes on the Use of Cacao in Middle America.* Notes on Middle American Archaeology and Ethnology No. 128. Cambridge: Carnegie Institution of Washington.
Thwaites, Reuben G. (editor)
    1959   *Jesuit Relations and Allied Documents: Travels and Explorations of the Jesuit Missionaries in New France, 1610–1791.* 73 vols. Reprinted. New York: Pageant.
Tooker, Elisabeth
    1978   "The League of the Iroquois: Its History, Politics, and Ritual." In *Northeast,* edited by Bruce Trigger, 418–441. *Handbook of North American Indians,* vol. 15, William Sturtevant, general editor. Washington, D.C.: Smithsonian Institution.
    1984   "Women in Iroquoian Society." In *Extending the Rafters: Interdisciplinary Approaches to Iroquoian Studies,* edited by M. Foster, J. Campisi, and M. Mithun, 109–123. Albany: State University of New York Press.
    1991   *An Ethnography of the Huron Indians, 1615–1649.* Syracuse, N.Y.: Syracuse University Press.
Traube, Elizabeth
    1986   *Cosmology and Social Life: Ritual Exchange Among the Mambai of Timor.* Chicago: University of Chicago Press.
Trigg, Heather B.
    1994   "Archaeobotanical Analysis of LA2091." Unpublished manuscript.
Trigger, Bruce
    1978   "Iroquoian Matriliny." *Pennsylvania Archaeologist* 48:55–65.
Tringham, Ruth
    1991   "Households with Faces: The Challenge of Gender in Prehistoric Architectural Remains." In *Engendering Archaeology: Women and Pre-*

history, edited by Joan Gero and Margaret Conkey, 93–131. Oxford: Blackwell.

Tuck, James
1971 *Onondaga Iroquois Prehistory: A Study in Settlement Archaeology.* Syracuse, N.Y.: Syracuse University Press.

Turnbull, Colin M.
1981 "Mbuti Womanhood." In *Woman the Gatherer*, edited by Frances Dahlberg, 205–219. New Haven, Conn.: Yale University Press.

Turner, Victor
1974 *Dramas, Fields, and Metaphors: Symbolic Action in Human Society.* Ithaca, N.Y.: Cornell University Press.

Underhill, Ruth
1936 *The Autobiography of a Papago Woman.* Memoir 46, American Anthropological Association.

Upham, Stedman
1982 *Politics and Power: An Economic and Political History of the Western Pueblo.* New York: Academic Press.

Valeri, Valerio
1980 "Notes on the Meaning of Marriage Prestations Among the Huaulu of Seram." In *The Flow of Life: Essays on Eastern Indonesia*, edited by James Fox, 178–192. Cambridge, Mass.: Harvard University Press.

van der Merwe, Nicholas, and Joseph C. Vogel
1978 "13C Content of Human Collagen as a Measure of Prehistoric Diet in Woodland North America." *Nature* 276:815–816.

Varney, Milton H.
1990 "Petroglyphs—Lost Forever." *Missouri Archaeological Society Quarterly* 7(1):17–18.

Verazzano, Geovanni
1970 [1524–1528] *The Voyages of Geovanni da Verazzano.* Edited by L. Wroth. New Haven, Conn.: Yale University Press.

Voegelin, Erminie W.
1938 "Tubatulabal Ethnography." *University of California Anthropological Records* 2(1):1–84.

Vogt, Evon Z.
1969 *Zinacantán: A Maya Community in the Highlands of Chiapas.* Cambridge, Mass.: Harvard University Press.
1976 *Tortillas for the Gods: A Symbolic Analysis of Zinacanteco Rituals.* Cambridge, Mass.: Harvard University Press.

Walde, Dale, and Noreen Willows (editors)
1991 *The Archaeology of Gender.* Proceedings of the twenty-second Chacmool conference. Calgary: Archaeological Association of the University of Calgary.

Walker, Phillip L., and Sandra E. Hollimon
1989 "Changes in Osteoarthritis Associated with the Development of a Maritime Economy among Southern California Indians." *International Journal of Physical Anthropology* 4(3):171–183.

Walthall, John A., F. Terry Norris, and Barbara D. Stafford
  1992   "Woman Chief's Village: An Illini Winter Hunting Camp." In *Calumet and Fleur-de-Lys: Archaeology of Indian and French Contact in the Midcontinent*, edited by James Walthall and Thomas Emerson, 129–153. Washington, D.C.: Smithsonian Institution Press.
Ward, Trawick, and Steve Davis
  1988   "Archaeology of the Historic Occaneechi Indians." *Southern Indian Studies* 36–37.
Waselkov, Gregory
  1987   "Shellfish Gathering and Shell Midden Archaeology." In *Advances in Archaeological Method and Theory*, vol. 10, edited by Michael Schiffer, 93–210. New York: Academic Press.
Washburn, Sherwood L., and C. S. Lancaster
  1968   "The Evolution of Hunting." In *Man the Hunter*, edited by R. Lee and I. DeVore, 293–303. Chicago: Aldine.
Watanabe, Hitoshi
  1968   "Subsistence and Ecology of Northern Food Gatherers with Special Reference to the Ainu." In *Man the Hunter*, edited by R. Lee and I. DeVore, 68–77. Chicago: Aldine.
Watson, Patty Jo, and Mary Kennedy
  1991   "The Development of Horticulture in the Eastern Woodlands of North America: Women's Role." In *Engendering Archaeology: Women and Prehistory*, edited by Joan Gero and Margaret Conkey, 255–275. Oxford: Blackwell.
Webster, David, and Nancy Gonlin
  1988   "Household Remains of the Humblest Maya." *Journal of Field Archaeology* 15:169–190.
Weideger, Paula
  1976   *Menstruation and Menopause: The Physiology and Psychology, the Myth and Reality*. New York: Knopf.
Weiner, Annette B.
  1989   "Why Cloth? Wealth, Gender, and Power in Oceania." In *Cloth and Human Experience*, edited by Annette Weiner and Jane Schneider, 33–72. Washington, D.C.: Smithsonian Institution Press.
  1992   *Inalienable Possessions: The Paradox of Keeping-While-Giving*. Berkeley: University of California Press.
Whallon, Robert, Jr.
  1968   "Investigations of Late Prehistoric Social Organization in New York State." In *New Perspectives in Archeology*, edited by Sally Binford and Lewis Binford, 223–244. Chicago: Aldine.
Whitehead, Harriet
  1981   "The Bow and the Burden Strap: A New Look at Institutionalized Homosexuality in Native North America." In *Sexual Meanings: The Cultural Construction of Gender and Sexuality*, edited by Sherry Ortner and Harriet Whitehead, 80–115. Cambridge: Cambridge University Press.

Whitthoft, John
  1959   "Ancestry of the Susquehannocks." In *Susquehannock Miscellany*, edited
          by John Whitthoft and Fred Kinsey, 19–60. Harrisburg, Penn.: Pennsyl-
          vania Historical and Museum Commission.
Widmer, Randolph
  1988   *The Evolution of the Calusa: A Nonagricultural Chiefdom on the Southwest
          Florida Coast.* Tuscaloosa: University of Alabama Press.
Wiessner, Polly
  1986   "!Kung San Networks in a Generational Perspective." In *The Past and
          Future of !Kung Ethnography: Critical Reflections and Symbolic Perspec-
          tives,* edited by M. Biesele with R. Gordon and R. Lee, 103–135. Hamburg:
          Helmut Buske Verlag.
Wilbur, Marguerite Eyer (editor)
  1937   *Duflot de Mofras' Travels on the Pacific Coast.* Vol. 2. Santa Ana, Calif.:
          Fine Arts Press.
Wilcox, David R.
  1984   "Multi-Ethnic Division of Labor in the Protohistoric Southwest." *Papers
          of the Archaeological Society of New Mexico* 9:141–156.
Wilk, Richard R.
  1988   "Maya Household Organization: Evidence and Analogies." In *Household
          and Community in the Mesoamerican Past,* edited by Richard Wilk and
          Wendy Ashmore, 135–169. Albuquerque: University of New Mexico Press.
Williams, Roger
  1973   [1643] *A Key into the Language of America [1636–38].* Edited by J. Teunis-
          sen and E. Hinz. Detroit, Mich.: Wayne State University Press.
Williams, Walter L.
  1986   *The Spirit and the Flesh: Sexual Diversity in American Indian Culture.*
          Boston: Beacon Press.
Willoughby, Charles Clark
  1932   "Notes on the History and Symbolism of the Muskhogeans and the People
          of Etowah." In *Etowah Papers: Exploration of the Etowah Site in Georgia,*
          edited by W. Moorehead, 7–62. New Haven, Conn.: Yale University Press.
Wills, Wirt H.
  1988   *Early Prehistoric Agriculture in the American Southwest.* Santa Fe,
          N. Mex.: SAR Press.
Wilson, Diane E.
  1993   "Gender, Diet, Health, and Social Status in the Mississippian Powers
          Phase Turner Cemetery Population." Master's thesis, Anthropology, Uni-
          versity of Texas at Austin.
  1994   "Division of Labor and Stress Loads at the Sanders Site (41Lr2), Lamar
          County, Texas." *Bulletin of the Texas Archeological Society* 65:129–160.
Winterhalder, Bruce, and E. A. Smith (editors)
  1981   *Hunter-Gatherer Foraging Strategies: Ethnographic and Archaeological
          Analyses.* Chicago: University of Chicago Press.
Wisdom, Charles
  1940   *The Chorti Indians of Guatemala.* Chicago: University of Chicago Press.

Wiseman, Regge
1986   *An Initial Study of the Origins of Chupadero Black-on-White.* Technical Note 2. Albuquerque, N.Mex.: Albuquerque Archaeological Society.

Wouden, F. A. E. van
1968   *Types of Social Structure in Eastern Indonesia.* Edited and translated by Rodney Needham. The Hague: Martinus Nijhoff.

Wylie, Alison
1991   "Gender Theory and the Archaeological Record: Why Is There No Archaeology of Gender?" In *Engendering Archaeology: Women and Prehistory,* edited by Joan Gero and Margaret Conkey, 31–54. Oxford: Blackwell.
1992   "The Interplay of Evidential Constraints and Political Interests: Recent Archaeological Research on Gender." *American Antiquity* 57 : 15–35.

Yates, Lorenzo G.
1957   "Fragments of the History of a Lost Tribe." *University of California Archaeological Survey Report* 38 : 36–39.

Yesner, David R.
1980   "Maritime Hunter-Gatherers: Ecology and Prehistory." *Current Anthropology* 21 : 727–50.

Contributors

Jeffrey Bendremer, Anthropology, University of Connecticut, Storrs, Connecticut, 06269.

Hetty Jo Brumbach, Anthropology, State University of New York, Albany, New York, 12222.

Cheryl Claassen, Anthropology, Appalachian State University, Boone, North Carolina, 28608.

Patricia Galloway, Mississippi Department Archives and History, PO Box 571, Jackson, Mississippi, 39205.

Susan D. Gillespie, Anthropology, University of Illinois, Champagne-Urbana, Illinois, 61801.

Byron Hamann, Anthropology, Vanderbilt University, Nashville, Tennessee, 37235.

Julia A. Hendon, Associate, Peabody Museum; Human Resources Data Administrator, Arts and Sciences Personnel Office, Harvard University, 21 Divinity Avenue, Cambridge, Massachusetts, 02138.

Sandra E. Hollimon, 25050 Coast Highway 1, Jenner, California, 95450.

Robert Jarvenpa, Anthropology, State University of New York, Albany, New York, 12222.

Rosemary A. Joyce, Director, Phoebe Hearst Museum, University of California, Berkeley, California, 94720.

Lyle Koehler, R.R. 4 Box 327, Sparta, Wisconsin, 54656.

Richard G. Lesure, Anthropology, University of California, Los Angeles, California, 90024.

Susan C. Prezzano, Anthropology-Geography-Earth Science, Clarion University of Pennsylvania, Clarion, Pennsylvania, 16214.

Alison E. Rautman, Anthropology, Michigan State University, East Lansing, Michigan, 48823.

Mary Beth Williams, Anthropology, University of Massachusetts, Amherst, Massachusetts, 01003.

Diane Wilson, Anthropology, University of Texas, Austin, Texas, 78712.

Index